D1601143

Unreal Cities

William Blake, "London," *Songs of Innocence and of Experience*, 1794. Rosenwald Collection, Library of Congress.

Unreal Cities

Urban Figuration in
Wordsworth, Baudelaire, Whitman, Eliot,
and Williams

William Chapman Sharpe

The Johns Hopkins University Press
Baltimore and London

This book has been brought to publication
with the generous assistance of a subvention
from Barnard College.

The Johns Hopkins University Press, 701 West 40th Street
Baltimore, Maryland 21211
The Johns Hopkins Press Ltd., London

Library of Congress Cataloging-in-Publication Data
Sharpe, William Chapman, 1951–
Unreal cities : urban figuration in Wordsworth, Baudelaire,
Whitman, Eliot, and Williams / William Chapman Sharpe.
p.   cm.
Includes bibliographical references.
ISBN 0-8018-3972-6 (alk. paper)
1. American poetry—History and criticism.   2. Cities and towns in
literature.   3. Wordsworth, William, 1770–1850—Criticism and
interpretation.   4. Baudelaire, Charles, 1821–1867—Criticism and
interpretation.   I. Title.
PS310.C5S85   1990
809.1'9321732—dc20   89-24616
CIP

To my mother,
Marie Chapman Sharpe,
and in memory of my father,
George Ezbon Sharpe

Contents

. . . the city must never be confused with the words that describe it. And yet between the one and the other there is a connection.

—Italo Calvino, Invisible Cities

Preface and
Acknowledgments

A writer's country is a territory within his own brain; and we run the risk of disillusionment if we try to turn such phantom cities into tangible brick and mortar.

— Virginia Woolf, "Literary Geography"

This is a book not about cities of brick and mortar, but about the "unreal cities"—cities of mind, cities of words—into which the metropolis has been transformed by the power of art. For the city dwells as much in us as we in it. It lives as fully in the imagination as in the material world, a circumstance that challenges the critic who would invade the "phantom cities" constructed by poets. We cannot pretend to know, from the study of literary texts, the actual Paris of Baudelaire or the London of Blake, Wordsworth, or Eliot. But through our reading we can begin to understand how these cities were perceived by the poets who lived in them, and also how the literary representation of that perception has been shaped by earlier texts about the city. This second point must be stressed, for there is no unmediated artistic response to the city. "City poetry" is a compound of contemporary impressions on the one hand and, on the other, of poetic structures already in place. My intention in this book is to demonstrate how such preexisting forms and figures have influenced the poetic art of the modern city.

I have concentrated on the textual rather than the political pressures that shape urban poetic vision because I believe that the obviously social nature of the topic has caused the more purely literary—although equally "urban"—qualities of city poetry to be slighted. There are valuable studies that treat these poems in relation to history and politics, and throughout the book my notes indicate the contextual analyses I have found helpful. But since many of the readers of these works have not lived in London or Paris, New York or Paterson, even when the poems were first published, it is also clear that poems like "Les Sept Vieillards" and "Crossing Brooklyn Ferry" speak to their audiences through widely shared presuppositions about the representation of the city, an understanding of urban myth and textual conventions that each reader must possess. Thus a vital part of what Baudelaire and Whitman communicate about urban consciousness of the 1850s is lost if we fail to recognize the extent to which they rely upon a process of literary figuration, a process whereby figures of thought and word actively metamorphose the human figures passing on the street.

Despite critical debates between formalists and historicists, the study of the city and its art is not a matter of "either/or," of embracing one approach to the exclusion of others. Rather, as the postmodern architect Robert Venturi has said, we must try to accept the challenging complexity of "both/and." In the spirit of complementarity, then, this book seeks to do the kind of close reading that has been most neglected, to show how the major poems of the city interact with one another, with certain principal themes, and with a common, omnipresent intertext.

While the concept of the city in Western culture owes much to the classical tradition of Greece and Rome, here I have chosen to focus instead on the Judeo-Christian Bible as the privileged reference point of the urban poet. The biblical accounts of Cain and Babel, New Jerusalem and Babylon, have played a central role in structuring the representation of the "unreal city" of modern poetry from Blake to Williams. Not only have the otherworldly cities of Babylon and New Jerusalem provided a visionary context for viewing all earthly cities as ultimately insubstantial or unreal, but the sexualization of these cities as Whore and Virgin has given a transcendent significance to a quintessentially urban incident—the male poet's sudden encounter with an unknown woman on the street. The stories of Cain and Babel have proven equally durable images for alienation, exile, and the failure to communicate—what might be called the sensory and psychological unreality of city life. Taken together, these biblical prototypes have exerted a profound influence upon the poetic conception of imaginative cities that continues to shape our outlook today.

In treating the city as the predominant image of modern life, the poetry of Wordsworth, Baudelaire, Whitman, Eliot, and Williams dramatically highlights the dynamic relations between poet and tradition, self and Other, male and female, sexual desire and textual distance. Only Baudelaire stands outside the Anglo-American poetic tradition that I am tracing, but his achievement and influence have placed him in many ways at the heart of it.

This book explores the revelatory meeting with a stranger in the crowd, identified by Walter Benjamin as the focal point of Baudelaire's vision of the city. For Baudelaire's definitive poem on the subject, "A une passante," provides more than an evocative name for the figure of the passing stranger; it exemplifies a key feature of all the textual cities examined here. In them, the *passant(e)*, whether male or female, functions as an emotional and symbolic center, compressing in a single image the sexual and linguistic forces that engender the urban text. The passing stranger serves as the point at which other concerns of city poetry—a sense of unreality, the mobility of desire, the fluid interplay between the sexual nature of urban experience and the textuality of the city itself—all converge.

Using Blake's "London" as a framework, the introductory chapter presents these elements of city poetry in relation to their biblical heritage and the story of the first urban man, Cain. Examining the idea of the city as a text, the second chapter concentrates on Wordsworth's most troubling stranger, the Blind Beggar in Book VII of *The Prelude*. The chapter on Baudelaire's "holy prostitution" analyzes the encounter in the *Tableaux parisiens* between poet and passersby, particularly the unknown woman who embodies the elusiveness of urban desire. With Whitman I take up, in contrast, the poet's identification with passing strangers, and his readers as versions of them, in "Crossing Brooklyn Ferry." My chapter on *The Waste Land* then considers how Eliot transforms the unexpected meeting with the stranger into an image of regenerative reading that can make the unreal city real once more. Finally, a chapter on Williams' *Paterson* explores how the poet's open "marriage" to the feminine Other revises the gender-based metaphors of urban figuration, even amid the persistence of biblical archetypes. While in the postmodern era the city has not ceased to signify, the poet now rejoices in its indeterminacy as previous *topoi* of city poetry are continually deconstructed and reinscribed.

Like city poets, critics must confront the unending task of finding words to describe the unreal cities of modern life. And like all cities and texts, this book has at times seemed a part of what

Williams calls "that complex / atom, always breaking down." It could not have reached its present state without the help of the following institutions and individuals.

Grateful acknowledgment is made to the New Directions Publishing Corporation for permission to quote from the works of William Carlos Williams, including *Paterson*, copyright 1946, 1948, 1949, 1951, 1958, by William Carlos Williams; *Selected Letters*, copyright 1957, by William Carlos Williams; and *Collected Poems*, reprinted by permission of New Directions Publishing Corp.

I thank the editors of the journals in which some material from the Wordsworth, Whitman, and Williams chapters appeared: "Urban Theory and Critical Blight: Accommodating the Unreal City," *New Orleans Review* 10.1 (1983): 79–88; "City / Body / Text: Walt Whitman's Urban Incarnation," *Cycnos: Politique et Poétique de la Ville* (Nice, 1984), 39–48; and "'That Complex Atom': The City and Form in William Carlos Williams' *Paterson*," *Poesis* 6.2 (1985): 65–93.

The project was begun with the assistance of a Mellon Fellowship at the Society of Fellows in the Humanities at Columbia University. I want to express my deep appreciation to the Society of Fellows and its director, Loretta Nassar, for providing intellectual stimulation, financial assistance, and moral support. The Society's benefits are both cumulative and continuing; I cannot imagine a better place to work and learn.

I also want to thank the School of Criticism and Theory for a fellowship and a valuable education; my ideas took shape as a result of the methods and friends it introduced me to one summer in Evanston.

My understanding of urban culture has been greatly enhanced by teaching abroad. In France, the Fulbright Commission, the University of Nice, and particularly Jacqueline Ollier and her Interspace group provided me with opportunities to lecture and exchange ideas in memorable surroundings. In Italy, Rosa Maria Colombo, Agostino Lombardo, and the English Department of the University of Rome welcomed me warmly, and I thank them for the invitation to give a series of lectures on the poetry of the city in May, 1986.

My teachers and subsequently colleagues at Columbia University have shown me over the years the value of an urbane education in an urban environment. I am particularly indebted to Carl Woodring, Karl Kroeber, Steven Marcus, and Michael Riffaterre for their wisdom and example. Michael Wood, now at the University of Exeter, saw me through early drafts by keeping an eye on the

larger picture. A passing remark from John D. Rosenberg stimu-
lated me to begin the distant ancestor of this project many years
ago, and his understanding and insight have guided me ever since.

In later stages of writing, Emily Elliot Gould and Stephanie
Coen provided expert research assistance. At the Johns Hopkins
University Press, I have benefited from the advice of George F.
Thompson and of the outside reviewers who carefully read and
commented on the manuscript for the Press: Joseph Riddel, Marcel
Smith, and Arnold Weinstein.

Many friends have contributed to this project, and I hope they
will find in these pages the imprint of their interest and enthusiasm. I owe much to discussions with my colleagues in the Barnard
English Department, and with Pete de Bolla, William Germano,
Bruce Henricksen, Deborah Epstein Nord, and Steven Winspur;
they had good ideas when I needed them. Leonard Wallock and
Richard Janko provided invaluable encouragement. Christopher
Baswell, Christopher Benfey, Michele Hannoosh, Kathryn Hum-
phreys, and Gregory Jay all read large portions of the manuscript,
and improved it with their suggestions. Each was instrumental in
helping me see what I wanted to say, and how best to say it. The
late Marian Gerber Greenberg believed in this book, and her example inspires me still.

Finally, I want to thank Heather Henderson, who, beyond all
saying, urged and edited the book into being. She made *Unreal
Cities* a reality.

A debt that cannot be expressed is acknowledged in the dedication.

Unreal Cities

Chapter One

Unreal Cities
An Introduction

The archetypal city-dweller desires rest but is always on the move. In the Bible, humanity's effort to make a place for itself in the world begins with a forced march: the exiled founder of the first city, Cain, seeks a place of refuge for his wife, his son Enoch, and succeeding generations.[1] In punishment for killing his brother Abel, Cain must wander: "a fugitive and a vagabond shalt thou be in the earth" (Gen. 4:12).[2] And so that his suffering may not be abated, he becomes literally a "marked man": "the Lord set a mark upon Cain, lest any finding him should kill him" (Gen. 4:15). Singled out by the earliest "writing," Cain founds a city, one whose distance from Eden ironically becomes a reminder of his exiled state, a repetition and reification of God's initial mark of displeasure. But from the very beginning this urban marking is ambiguous—a divided sign—for it also carries with it a protective function, the promise of salvation. In response to Cain's fear of being killed (Gen. 4:14), God sets his mark upon Cain not only to punish but also to preserve him.

Thus, from its biblical origin, the city, sign of human estrangement from God, also raises the hope of an ultimate if distant reconciliation. That an originary urban man should carry the signs of a double destiny is truly prophetic. For like Cain, the mythic, metaphoric cities of Western literature have also come to bear this double mark of loss and potential redemption, of punishment deserved and salvation deferred:

> I wander thro' each charter'd street,
> Near where the charter'd Thames does flow,
> And mark in every face I meet
> Marks of weakness, marks of woe.[3]

The words of Blake's "London" (1793) illustrate how the alienation of modern urban life continues to be viewed through biblical arche-

1

types. The poem's evocation of three preeminent biblical cities—
Babel, Babylon, and New Jerusalem—points toward three principal visions of the city: the city as a text, as a sexual entity, and as
unreal. Moreover, Blake gives special emphasis to the figure that
contains them all, the city as symbolized by the passing stranger,
the Other who still carries Cain's divided sign.[4]

MOBILITY AND MARKING

Like the story of Cain, Blake's poem shows that mobility and
marking are interdependent features of both cities and texts.[5] Men
strive to control their world through mapping, street building, and
sign writing, but these avatars of Cain's mark instead produce only
further signs, further wandering and marking. City building is
therefore contradictory: an effort to define space and arrest motion, it also partakes inevitably of the ceaseless activity of differing
inherent in all forms of sign making. Founded by the first "written" individual, the postlapsarian city embodies the divided and
perplexed sign of its founder. The city is like a text, a site whose
existence signals both loss and promise, and whose ambiguity requires interpretation.

Blake's "London" begins with the mobile and unspecified capital "I," the wandering poet who is a stranger to us, and whose own
marks indicate only the path he has taken.[6] The identity of the
wandering "I" depends in part upon what it sees—streets, a river,
a crowd of unknown others. For the city poet is himself a passing
stranger who comes to know or to reveal himself in the poem
through his reflection in the faces of other strangers. This interaction of seer and seen accounts for the instability of urban writing,
the re-marking of something in a face that flits by in the crowd.
While streets and river can be controlled legally by the writing of
charters, Blake's "I" seeks to order what he observes by marking
down what is already marked and remarkable, universal suffering.
In order to give direction to his motion, to define his landscape, the
writer imposes and preserves these signs of urban disaffection: "I
mark in every face I meet. . . ."

But just as Cain's mark preserves him for further wandering, so
Blake's lines reveal a deep psychological and spiritual homelessness, for his efforts to master his environment serve only to remind him of his alienation from it. The chartering of streets and
river represents society's attempt to define its world, to bring
under one law parts of the city and parts of nature, and to ensure

uniformity.[7] Yet, as the metonymy of the poem insists, the process only produces more signs of estrangement, more weakness and woe, qualities that are as crucial to heavenly marking as they are to earthly differentiation.[8]

In the book of Ezekiel, the prophet has a vision of how the Lord will purge his city of "the great abominations that the house of Israel committeth here" (Ezek. 8:6). In a gesture later echoed in Revelation, an angel with an inkhorn marks those to be saved during the purifying of Jerusalem:

> And [the Lord] called to the man clothed with linen, which had the writer's inkhorn by his side;
> And the Lord said unto him, Go through the midst of the city, through the midst of Jerusalem, and set a mark upon the foreheads of the men that sigh and that cry for all the abominations that be done in the midst thereof.
> And to the [executioners of the city] he said in mine hearing, Go ye after him through the city, and smite: let not your eye spare, neither have ye pity:
> Slay utterly old and young, both maids, and little children, and women: but come not near any man upon whom is the mark.
>
> (Ezek. 9:3–6)[9]

Ezekiel's mark singles out those who are to be spared rather than punished, but like the marks borne by Blake's Londoners it is also a Cain-like sign of woe (and implicitly of weakness or helplessness) over the condition of the city. The angel prefigures the poet: he notes, first in perception and then in the flesh, those who sigh and cry, in order that others who come after may read them (the double "them" of person and mark). Ezekiel's vision thus suggests that Blake's speaker is not merely an outraged or estranged citizen in a city of economic and psychological servitude, but an instrument of judgment who actually puts the marks of weakness and woe upon the people he sees. By writing their misery he may save them from it. An active mark-maker as well as a passive re-marker, the poet both metaphorically (in his text) and actually (in the citizens' faces) sets down the signs of a profound discontent, divine as well as human.[10]

But the signs that the city poet makes, as well as those he takes note of, may proliferate in such a way that singling out and preserving the good of the city becomes a difficult if not impossible task. In Ezekiel, only a few citizens reveal their worth by sighing over Israel's abominations, but in "London," "every face" and later "every voice" compel the poet's notice. If every person carries the sign of a universal condition that the poet perceives, the mark becomes invisible; it no longer communicates. The poet must rely on some difference between the city and himself, between its signs and his, in order to "make his mark" as poet and prophet. He must practice a kind of divine or angelic writing in order to gain critical distance, in order to notice, note, and intervene. Yet as a human writer, a man of the streets himself, he inherits the limitations of speaking in a fallen tongue: the problem not of achieving difference, but of overcoming the barriers that it places between all the citizens of the earth.

The divisions of man, city, and sign that begin with Cain are exacerbated in the story of the first major city, Babel. After the fall of Babel, men and women become divided not only from God but from themselves through God's sundering of their language. Yet it is not only pride, as is usually said, that motivates their daring construction.[11] The people of Babel raise their tower in order to "make us a name, lest we be scattered abroad upon the face of the whole earth" (Gen. 11:4). The building of the tower is a kind of proto-writing, the mark or "name" by which they hope to preserve their unity and identity. But their effort to avoid the fate of their ancestor Cain—dispersal—ironically provokes the same result: Cain's already exilic home is further shattered by the breaking of Babel's unified language. This inhibits the cooperation necessary to create a community; indeed "they left off to build the city" (Gen. 11:8).

Longing to make a name, the people of Babel exemplify the intransigence of language and the impossibility of ever adequately naming anything: "Therefore is the name of it called Babel [Confusion], because the Lord did there confound the language of all the earth" (Gen. 11:9). They receive not one name, but many. Their confounded language becomes the auditory symbol of human limitation. In his poem, Blake presents the inarticulate cries of the post-Babel city as the anguished expression of a self-imposed slavery and restriction:

> In every cry of every Man,
> In every Infant's cry of fear,
> In every voice, in every ban,
> The mind-forg'd manacles I hear.

Like the misguided people of Babel, Blake's Londoners have accomplished something together: their own estrangement and imprisonment. The reiterated "every" and the capitalized, representative nouns emphasize the universality of this urban condition; the many voices of the city unite only in their common despair. Speaking their divided language, the people of the city cannot say anything positively; they can only express fear or make prohibitions.

Yet the listening poet refuses to take the vengeful stance of the Lord in Ezekiel's account: "Therefore will I also deal in fury: . . . though they cry in mine ears with a loud voice, yet will I not hear them" (Ezek. 8:18). For standing on the edge of this crowd, possessing at least the minimal distance necessary to perceive that the manacles are the product of interior consciousness rather than exterior coercion, the poet seems to be an exception to his own rule. As he shifts from recording sights to sounds, the poet's own voice seems to defy the self-imprisoning cries of men and infants. For unless this poem too is an unselfconscious lament, there exists some position outside of "London" to which poet and reader can refer. Traces of it appear in the allusions to Ezekiel's city, where God intervenes to restore Jerusalem to Himself.

However, the manacles of Blake's poem suggest that Ezekiel's Jerusalem has become not the New Jerusalem of Christian hope but the Babylon of Hebrew captivity. It is under the sign of this fallen city, as we shall see, that the Harlot appears and that the poet wanders directionless in the first stanza. He may mark like Ezekiel's angel (though without the same authority or effect, since he marks everyone), but he is also a latter-day Cain reenacting his peripatetic punishment in labyrinthine London. That Blake's poem recounts a Babylonian captivity is corroborated by his own illustration for "London" and the text that describes it: "I see London, blind & age-bent, begging thro' the Streets / Of Babylon, led by a child; his tears run down his beard." Although these lines come from *Jerusalem* (Plate 84: 11–12), they describe what Blake's readers see when they read "London" as it was originally printed in *Songs of Experience:* a child leading a hunched and bearded old man with a crutch along a wall to a closed door. Once again the poet adopts a position both inside and outside the earthly city: Blake the Londoner visualizes the blind wanderings of his anthropomorphized fallen city through the streets of its metaphorical ancestor. Therefore, although the "mind-forg'd" quality of their enslavement suggests that these prisoners may one day be able to free themselves, Blake's London—and the poem of that name—is presently entrapped in the larger symbolic urban construct of Babylon, where wandering is a mark of exile and loss.

In Babylon/London, marks are necessarily different and double, like Cain's; the marks of woe which should save also condemn because this misery is self-induced, the product of "mind-forg'd manacles." What should liberate enslaves. The poet has the prophetic, even God-like, power to mark Londoners as self-murderers who also have divine protection. But at the same time he himself is one of these enchained wanderers, and as long as the manacles of earthly Babylon exist, he can expect no swift or resounding judgment—only proliferating signs of that deferred judgment upon which he can meditate:

> How the Chimney-sweeper's cry
> Every black'ning Church appalls;
> And the hapless Soldier's sigh
> Runs in blood down Palace walls.

Like the vocal signs of stanza two, these complex images of social collusion show how individuals create a social order that enslaves them. With increasing specificity the poet returns to the social relations originally suggested by the "charter'd" nature of the city. He moves beyond the universal misery of the earlier stanzas in order to condemn Church and State for their part in the oppression of children (sweeps) and men (soldiers). Often cited as an instance of how Blake reveals the suppressed and exploitative connections between different layers of society and between institutions and individuals, this stanza compels attention because it implicates paternal palace and maternal church in the wretchedness of those for whom they should care. The poet's hearing transforms and translates the weak vocal protests of Sweeper and Soldier into powerful graphic signs written in soot and blood on the walls of those whom they denounce. These new signs suggest additional, perhaps more precise, ways of reading the generalized woeful marks of stanza one.

In fact, not only the maintenance and preservation of the city, symbolized by Sweeper and Soldier, but also its foundation depend on woe and weakness—that of the exile, the murderer. For on a social level, too, the double function of Cain's mark is significant: civilization bears its discontents from the start, the urban man always a metaphoric fratricide trying to live in harmony with others. From an original failure of brotherhood stems the enduring paradox of the city as a fraternal community founded upon division and rivalry. In the classical tradition, the story of Romulus and Remus reaffirms this: brother kills brother during the process of marking out the city's boundaries, indicating how collectivity is perilously based on separation, exclusion, and violence. The sacrifices of Sweeper and Soldier in the interests of Church and State, imaged by their position outside the walls of those institutions, play out the contradictions of urban settlement and city life.

The increased particularization in this stanza does not, however, reduce the complexity of urban marking, but rather compounds it. The sweep's marks are black on black; the bloody sighs and signs on the palace *run:* like the auditory signs of the city, the written ones are also inarticulate or indecipherable. By implying but never naming the source of London's ills, Blake recalls the ancient failure of society to make a name for itself. Thus the poem closes with an inversion of God's Word, the reverberating curse of an urban language that cannot explain itself or the city:

> But most thro' midnight streets I hear
> How the youthful Harlot's curse
> Blasts the new born Infant's tear,
> And blights with plagues the Marriage hearse.

Darkness upon darkness, the curse interjects the promiscuous harlotry of signs into the marriage bed of divine linguistic fidelity, and never minds the child. Blake's final stanza shifts from the ways in which the cries of children and men (sweepers and soldiers) reveal their oppression to how a woman's curse even more insistently ("most . . . I hear") announces something worse: her exploitation infects the next generation and "blights" the institution of marriage. The Harlot's nocturnal perambulations counterpoint the poet's wandering throughout the poem, as do the marks of diseased weakness and accursed woe that she leaves upon the newly married and the newly born. Her position as the final figure in this drama emphasizes her importance as victim and agent, as the culminating symbol of urban life. With her body turned into a commodity that can be "charter'd" like the streets or river, the streetwalker becomes the living embodiment of the city and its appalling condition.[12]

The outcast Harlot's curse repeats and intensifies the original curse of Cain (Gen. 4:11) as well as that of his (and her original) parents, Adam and Eve. Her curse is the mark God sets upon her for being a daughter of Eve (menstruation) and the mark of her occupation (venereal disease), but it is also a blighted and blighting speech that perverts God's originally fecund Logos. Directly or indirectly, she condemns herself, her customers, and the nameless

Infant who may belong to any of them. Despite his curse, Cain founded and named a city for his descendants; the story suggests that the origin of cities and their continuity depends on families, succession, legitimacy. The Harlot's curse upsets this patriarchal pattern: the unknown infant's dubious lineage and inherited disease threaten the health of the city while blinding society to the nature of its most intimate relations.

Paralleling the movement from Sweeper and Soldier to Harlot is a strong shift from the visualized graphic evidence of economic and military enslavement (blackened and bloody walls) to the Harlot's unseen withering of language, marital love, and infant tears. Many commentators have suggested that the blasted tear represents a child born blind, a common result of parental syphilis.[13] The venereal disease carried by the Harlot would thus physically infect the marriage bed, whose sanctity her profession has already broken. In this context, the "ban" of stanza two that provided one more example of "mind-forg'd manacles" here takes on added importance as an extension of the Harlot's cry. For its root meaning is "curse"; "banns" of marriage are read in order to permit public interdiction of an approaching wedding if either party is unfit. The Harlot effectively bans true marriage by cursing it. As Revelation announces, "the voice of the bridegroom and of the bride shall be heard no more" in the fornicating, worldly city of Babylon (Rev. 18:23). The marital vows are mocked by the infidelity that ironically "contracted" the disease, turning the marriage procession, with its promise of procreative harmony, into a funeral cortège that mourns the loss of love, sight, trust, and familial joy. The happy family that Blake illustrates on the title page to *Songs of Innocence* has been replaced by the dead parents round whose bier the children weep on the title page of *Songs of Experience*.[14]

The unseen but audible figure of the Harlot reminds poet and reader that this sexually fallen city is only an unreal counter-image, like Babylon itself, of the true and eternal heavenly city of God. For the very title of Blake's poem, a poem that emphasizes the Harlot's curse as its most important voice, leads the reader to associate city and Harlot, evoking one of the most powerful of all biblical texts: "And upon her forehead was a name written, MYSTERY, BABYLON THE GREAT, THE MOTHER OF HARLOTS AND ABOMINATIONS OF THE EARTH" (Rev. 17:5). Even as he reinforces the connection between biblical and urban marking, Blake simultaneously points to Revelation's metaphor of the earthly city as fallen woman, and recalls the city's status as a mere shadow of the virginal city that will replace it, the New Jerusalem. As St. Augustine writes in *The City of God*, this is the inescapable condition of human existence; paralleling Adam's fall from God into history and consciousness, the earthly city is "a fall into falsehood, unreality."[15]

THE CITY AND SEXUALITY

Those who faithfully possess virginal brides reap the rewards of an undivided, unviolated truth, while those who lie with the many-pleasured harlot fall into the multiplicity of error and self-division; they gain the world but lose their souls. The most striking aspect of Revelation is that both cities should be personified as female, and their sexual purity made equivalent to their spiritual value.[16] The city as representative woman forms an integral part of the contrast between heavenly and earthly states, and reveals much about Western male views of the city as a female space to be mastered or seduced by, a space in which actual women are often rigorously controlled.[17]

Yet the towered city can lose its potency, can fall, as Babel did, into a dissemination and dispersal that produce no certifiable progeny, no unified name. Along with Babel, Babylon and the New Jerusalem are the metaphoric cities most central not only to Blake's vision of London, but to that of subsequent poets as well. The persistent tension in Western literature between harlot and bride, whore and virgin, reflects a post-Babel effort to control the possible meanings of cities, women, and words. It is a masculine quest to stabilize the mobility of a sexually imaged reality. With her promiscuous violation of the marriage bed, Blake's Harlot both invokes and challenges the womanly cities of the New Jerusalem and Babylon upon which her symbolic power is built. For "London" invites comparison to the New Jerusalem, even as it denies earthly access to that city.

In Revelation, the New Jerusalem is first seen "prepared as a bride adorned for her husband" (Rev. 21:2); later, when the angel says to John, "Come hither, I will shew thee the bride, the Lamb's wife" (Rev. 21:9), the possession and marriage appear complete. As the subsequent description of the crystalline metropolis indicates, the city *is* the bride, pure in every way: "And there shall in no wise enter into it any thing that defileth, neither whatsoever worketh abomination, or maketh a lie: but they which are written in the Lamb's book of life" (Rev. 21:27). In contrast to the "fornicating" city of Babylon, used familiarly by all the merchants and kings of the earth (Rev. 18:3), the holy city is a virgin who shall not be violated or entered by any except those "husbands" or deputies of the Lamb who have textual authority that they are pure like her. In fact, the saved are doubly inscribed as belonging to the Lamb, for a redemptive mark of possession distinguishes them: "His name shall be in their foreheads" (Rev. 22:4). The crystal clarity of the New Jerusalem's walls, streets, and river, of the Lamb's light and His book of Life (Rev. 21:11–22:5), elucidates the opacity of meaning in the fallen world and in its language after Babel. The Holy City repeats Creation without a division of the Word.

Although all earthly cities may aspire to the heavenly order of New Jerusalem,[18] in a sense they are all suburbs of another legendary but earthly city, Babylon. The double sense of Blake's "Marriage hearse" implies this, combining the aspiration to divine marriage with the worldly fate that befalls it. The belated cities of guilt and loss, sin and death have been built to duplicate divine archetypes, but they can express only a fallen world and a fallen mankind. For if, in William Cowper's famous phrase, "God made the country, and man made the town" (*The Task* [1785] I, 749), then man is unable to inscribe a life-giving Word there. The earthly city remains only a wilderness of streets, a maze or labyrinth that imitates the wilderness of difference he built the city to escape.

And so the virgin's opposite, the Whore of Babylon, wears her own sign written "upon her forehead," one that links her to Cain, sinful and exiled founder of the first city: "MYSTERY, BABYLON THE GREAT . . ." (Rev. 17:5). With the allusive power of the text with which she is written and the Name she cannot have, Blake's Harlot recapitulates the textuality of the city inherent in the Western tradition since Cain's mark. Furthermore, she testifies to the way that divine writing adjusts itself to compensate for mundane markings, or the lack thereof. The physical mark of harlotry would be an absent one, the missing hymen that the virgin would preserve as the positive sign of her purity. But to read it would be to violate it, and so the harlot is clearly written with the legend of her shame, while the virgin remains unwritten or inviolate in the midst of her heavily inscribed city.

The New Jerusalem recreates Eden by erasing Cain's mark ("And there shall be no more curse" [Rev. 22:3]) and reinscribing the name of God in the foreheads of the 144,000 saved (Rev. 22:4). Blake's marks, however, generate a less conclusive dynamic, maintaining both the loss and the deferred salvation of Cain's mark. Through the pressure of the biblical intertext, the Harlot suggests the Virgin, wandering promises rest, marking recalls an originary Logos, and "mind-forg'd manacles" imply at least the possibility of a new consciousness that will bring release.

It is not, however, the word of God and a divine marriage removing the curse to which Blake's Harlot bears witness, but rather a broken worldly marriage causing the constant *repetition* of that curse: "But most . . . I hear." In "London" the curse is maintained, and a marriage hearse rather than a marriage is the final image. A nameless infant replaces the hope Cain had for Enoch, his son and city, and the sins of the fathers, original and committed, visit themselves upon the children and the city. In contrast to the perpetual light of the New Jerusalem, the midnight city of the Harlot is, like the candleless Babylon, forever sightless (Rev. 18:23). Finally, the Harlot's curse blasts language itself, and through words that the poem never utters, condemns its urban sighs and signs to labyrinthine repetitions of its inability to voice the missing, saving Word. What aspired to be a Name, a Word, is only the City of God's inverted face, an unreal Babylon, an untranslatable Babel. The harlotized metropolis represents religious, social, and personal estrangement through the deepest image of insecurity, a fundamental sexual uncertainty undermining male possession of wife, mother, child, and compliant, monogamous city. Only the self-written and therefore self-recognizing quality of the poet's urban marking, with its condemning mark that also saves, offers hope of "knowing" and redeeming the unreal city.

THE PASSING STRANGER

Given the precarious sexual economy of urban conceptualization and settlement, city building may be seen from one point of view as an attempt to undo the effects of sex and history. For some, the city strives to create in its enclosure a mothering womb, a final refuge that will obliterate the dangers of the world and the birth-trauma of Eden's loss.[19] Yet the city as protective enclosure quickly becomes vulnerable to the male penetrator of its fold, the writer who seeks to know it.[20] The passing stranger or Baudelairean "*passante*," the woman "known" momentarily by the male poet, brings this male-female dynamic to the fore, since she images a feminized city that "only they who are written" in God's book may enter. The building of a city, in space or in poetry, thereby becomes a sexual act dependent on textual authority. It represents an attempt at protective procreation, a striving to overcome differences—even through domination—by locating a place of consummation and union, where male and female can perhaps be one.

Blake's "London" describes a double confrontation with the passing stranger, first in the visual contact between marking poet and woeful faces, and then in the culminating auditory encounter with the Harlot. The former meeting introduces the idea of city as text and poet as maker and reader of it, and the latter emphasizes the individual stranger, whose implicit name and biblical associations underscore the sexuality, unreality, and textuality of the city. Since Blake, the great poetry of the city has in a similar fashion concentrated on the momentary confrontation with the Other, the emergence of the stranger from the crowd and his or her immediate disappearance back into it.[21] The complex of literary forces that helps shape this *topos* makes it impossible to speak solely of the stranger, for to describe how this image condenses and galvanizes the overall city vision of a poet means considering in turn the unreal city, the city of words, and the sexually defined city, describing how they all relate to and are contained in the meeting with the *passante*.

This meeting with the passing stranger is possible only in the vast modern city, where people are unknown to one another, where people cannot be relocated once lost, where the first sight of someone may be the last. The shared glance between poet and passer-by is like a lightning flash illuminating the dilemma of possession and loss, of literary presence and personal absence. The *passante* poem thus brings to the fore the oppositions that urban life and writing render most intense: self and Other, male and female, the known and the unknown, order and chaos, individual and crowd. While the poet may picture himself as violator and victim, a person who loses what he gains because his private desire has too hazardously chanced itself in a public space, the poem also makes clear the metaphoric and physical weapons that the city poet uses to assail such polarities: the image of the city as a woman and the use of the gaze as the readiest means of annihilating her distance and penetrating her reserve.[22]

As an examination of Wordsworth's experiences in London will show, the classic trajectory of modern city poetry involves a movement from initial disorientation to a feeling of the city's impenetrability or mystery, followed in turn by alienation from city, self, and Other, and then finally a sense of hallucination, of being adrift in the unreal city. Like the mythic king Oedipus, who sought to know the secret of his own city, the poet moves from a position capable of detached judgment to one of moral ambiguity, self-implication, and guilt. His confidence in language, in his ability to "place" and to "name," gives way to a radical questioning of his own authority and of the power of language to control the relation between self and Other. In similar fashion the poet rediscovers in his poem the responsibilities and rootlessness of Cain, the frustration of building and naming that are the heritage of Babel.

It has been said that the problem of the city novel is "how to experience, order, recognize and represent the stranger."[23] One might say the same for the poetry of the city. How can strangers and their texts be "written" without compromising their otherness and mystery? Unlike the detective, who seeks to construct a complete and plausible narrative out of unintegrated experience, the true urban writer requires "a deeper training" that "would practice toleration of disintegrated parts";[24] like the best city poetry, it would keep the stranger strange.

But to do this successfully, the poet must try as hard as possible to comprehend and apprehend the city he writes. The elusive nature of *passante* and text ensures that the poet who fails to keep his distance will, paradoxically, be rewarded by the vitality of an urban marking that will make possession impossible. In the fleeting figure of the *passante*, the known and unknown city temporarily meet. For by definition the *passante* poem is about the mobility of desire and the quest of the poet to "fix" momentarily—if only in the poem—the name and outline of the object he longs for. The poet who, like Blake, becomes a *passante* is another Cain, an incarnation of that desire, marked by his own sense of loss and determined to exploit the special protection that the poem and his status as wanderer accord him. He builds a written city to control the urban wilderness around him.

With the advent of Romantic subjectivity and the unprecedented growth of the city, the detached, comprehensive, topographical poem of place popular in the eighteenth century is increasingly supplanted by the idea of the poem as a place of its own.[25] These categories, of course, should not be considered rigid or mutually exclusive. Some poems may explicitly encompass two or even three levels of place; *Paterson,* for example, builds itself upon the identification of poem, city, and protagonist, all having the same name. But while the poetry of the modern city may still name or describe recognizable aspects of real cities, psychological and textual landscapes often overshadow the mimetically presented city of earlier times. If Blake's "London" has a River Thames

and chimney sweeps, the delocalized, symbol-saturated streets
have antecedents in Genesis, Ezekiel, and Revelation that confirm
the unreal metaphoricity of this modern metropolis.[26] When city
experience is perceived as becoming more and more fractured,
when neither the whole of the city nor its social order seems ame-
nable to a single discourse, the poem of private response creates its
own public space from the inside out.

But the place that the city text creates is itself in motion, a literary image of the ever-unfulfilled linguistic desire to thwart the mu-
tability of life and meaning. With the demise of the topographical
view and the stable point of view it represents, the *genius loci*, or
spirit of place, has been sent packing—becoming now the *flâneur*
or *passante* who wanders the boulevards of modern life and poetry.
The only place they come to rest, momentarily, is the poem, a temporary home in language apart from but reproducing the disruptive forces of city life.

Amid the transitory, jumbled, and arbitrary organization of the
newspaper, which Walter Benjamin saw as the symbol of modern
urban consciousness,[27] the quest to rewrite the passing stranger
into a permanent friend spills over from art into life. In *The Art of
the City*, Peter Conrad cites the "Personals" columns in the *Village
Voice* as evidence of New York's being "an aleatory island." More
persistent than Baudelaire, these urban adventurers attempt to
track down their own particular *passante*:

> Woman eating at 2nd Ave Deli (E 10th St) Fri aft at 4. You had
> small Barnes & Noble bag w/ you. I'm the man you saw get-
> ting his check when you turned around. Call 777-5291 any-
> time after 2 pm.

> 11/11/80, 8:45 PM, Times Sq RR. You were boarding train,
> we smiled, you seemed interested. Wearing blue jacket, tan
> pants, brown hair, beard. Tel: 201-648-2306. Mark.[28]

The very existence of these ads points to a special quality of modern urban experience—its ephemerality—that is emphasized in
the literature written about it. These searchers write their own
poems of urban desire and temporary mastery. For, Conrad notes,
"They can identify their prospective partners only by attaching
them to places as speedily forgetful as the fast food deli or the RR
subway";[29] the written notation of the encounter and the *passante*'s
description is the only possession available to them. The poem is
the place where, as in the city itself, one can momentarily name

and "know" the object of desire before the relentless forces of dispersal take over. As Walter Benjamin observes, "The veil [that the city] has covertly woven out of our lives shows the images of people less than those of the sites of our encounters with others or ourselves."[30] Faced with ceaseless motion and ever-shifting tableaux, the questing poet tries to still the city momentarily in his poetry, to make the poem itself a place of meeting. He metaphorizes the city as a feminine Other in order to define and possess it. If only for an instant, the poet arrests the image of the *passante* before she disappears into the crowd.

From Blake's encounter with the midnight voices of the Babelish and Babylonian modern city one can piece together the components of a new and major urban *topos*, the encounter with the Other. It encompasses in microcosm certain distinctive and interlocking features of city poetry: the representation of the city as a feminized figure of mobile desire, as a shifting, unstable text, as an entity unreal to the soul and the senses. The sexually charged meeting with the stranger takes place in an arena built upon the double unreality of the city—on the one hand, the persistent awareness of the otherworldly unreal cities of Revelation, New Jerusalem, and Babylon, that frame this world, and on the other hand, the hallucinatory unreality of contemporary urban life. The figures for each of these conditions, the bride of the New Jerusalem, the Whore of Babylon, and the passers-by of poets from Blake to Williams, turn back toward the material world by using the terms of its most intense reality, that of sexual possession and loss. Confronting in the city streets the Other whom Williams incisively calls "the virgin and the whore, / an identity," the masculine poet undergoes his own revelation as he attempts to control and define the elusive object of urban desire. Only by writing the city can he momentarily make the unreal real and still its motion, possessing in the poem what eludes him in the flesh—until the forces of dissemination and difference, the double mark of Cain and Babel, indicate that even the textual city is ever elsewhere, and that the site of the poem marks its loss. In city poetry the stranger is always passing.

Chapter Two

The Other as Text
Wordsworth's Blind Beggar

. . . as she enters these causeways where poverty eats away at the tarmac like a drought, where people lead their invisible lives . . . something new begins to assail her. Under the pressure of these streets, which are growing narrower by the minute, more crowded by the inch, she has lost her "city eyes." When you have city eyes you cannot see the invisible people, the men with elephantiasis of the balls and the beggars in boxcars don't impinge on you. . . . My mother lost her city eyes and the newness of what she was seeing made her flush, newness like a hailstorm pricking her cheeks. Look, my God . . .

—Salman Rushdie, *Midnight's Children*

The city assaults every sense, but in literature the shock is primarily visual. Sight is not only the chief sense enabling us to function in the city, but also the one most likely to upset our self-possession and equilibrium. Thus while Max Weber notes that with the increasing "complexity of social structure . . . a premium is placed in the urban world on visual recognition,"[1] Walter Benjamin points out the corollary, the deliberate blindness one must cultivate to maintain equanimity or even identity in the city. "The eye of the city dweller," he says, "is overburdened with protective functions."[2]

In Book VII of *The Prelude*, Wordsworth's account of his residence in London reveals him to be a vulnerable observer, lacking what Salman Rushdie calls "city eyes." Although Wordsworth struggles to shield himself from the frightening immediacy of his experience, it is the great achievement of his urban descriptions that they record an unresolved contest between the poetic consciousness and the city.[3] The ability to create compelling literature about the city depends on the writer's willingness to risk the impact of the tortured lives and disconcerting events that proliferate around him. Puncturing habitual defenses, what Wordsworth terms "the danger of the crowd" liberates a new and distressing receptivity of vision. In the suspension of customary modes of perception and response, writer and reader regard the faces around them as if for the first time, with the paradoxical sense of distance and proximity that the compression of a city street produces.

Wordsworth did not deliberately seek out the shocks that London furnished him; his poetic dismissal of the metropolis is well known, from "the dissolute city" of "Michael" to the opening of *The Prelude:*

> A captive greets thee, coming from a house
> Of bondage, from yon city's walls set free,
> A prison where he hath been long immured.
>
> (I, 6–8)[4]

But in Book VII of *The Prelude* and in the sonnet "Westminster Bridge," Wordsworth makes an exemplary effort to comprehend the babel and beauty of London, to give it lasting form by reference to the underlying spiritual and moral values that nature has previously taught him. In doing so he articulates many of the now-classic *topoi* of modern poetry: the disorienting crowd, the hallucinatory sense of its unreality, and its dangerously unsettling effect on personal identity and purpose.

Strikingly, what he glimpses on the streets is less instructive than his frustrated attempts not to see so much, to control his vision. Abroad in London, he takes little note of the more singular passers-by:

> Such candidates for regard,
> Although well pleased to be where they were found,
> I did not hunt after or greatly prize,
> Nor made unto myself a secret boast
> Of reading them with quick and curious eye.
>
> (VII, 577–81)

In the textual city, seeing is reading, but Wordsworth is an unwilling *flâneur.* Unlike the strolling detectives who will succeed him—such as the narrators of Poe's "The Man of the Crowd" or Baudelaire's *Le Spleen de Paris*—he finds no pleasure in deciphering the barely legible mysteries written in the gait, dress, and faces of strangers. A Bartleby of the teeming throng, he prefers not to. In his eagerness to overlook many sights, in his reluctant fascination with others, the author of *The Prelude* anticipates and confirms Georg Simmel's thesis that to survive psychologically in the city is to see selectively.[5] Even among the most intelligent and inquisitive,

Simmel says, "self-preservation in the face of the large city" demands such reserve and denial. If one were to react to the constant, abrasive contact with strangers in the open way common to the small town, "one would be completely atomized internally and come to an unimaginable psychic state."[6]

Yet precisely because of his rural values, untrained defenses, and poetic integrity, Wordsworth does eventually suffer that extreme mental stress. Initially, he pines for the village while practicing the guarded glances of the alert urbanite, striving to maintain a distance from the overly visible secrets of his fellow citizens. But the poet in search of himself must unsparingly register the unexpected tremors that shake his deepest convictions. Chance and the crowd thrust upon his notice a figure that does indeed present the "unimaginable" aspect of urban identity, the Other who cannot be overlooked. The threatening nature of Wordsworth's London becomes most apparent when his unhardened, untutored eyes meet no eyes at all—or perhaps the ultimate city eyes—in the gaze of a blind beggar.

LOST AMID THE MOVING PAGEANT

In *The Prelude*, Wordsworth's passage from city-eyed blindness to sudden illumination by a blind beggar begins amid mystery and uncertainty. It pits the desire for knowledge of self and Other against the incomprehensible enormity of the city:

> O friend, one feeling was there which belonged
> To this great city by exclusive right:
> How often in the overflowing streets
> Have I gone forwards with the crowd, and said
> Unto myself, 'The face of every one
> That passes by me is a mystery.'
> Thus have I looked, nor ceased to look, oppressed
> By thoughts of what, and whither, when and how,
> Until the shapes before my eyes became
> A second-sight procession, such as glides
> Over still mountains, or appears in dreams,
> And all the ballast of familiar life—
> The present, and the past, hope, fear, all stays,
> All laws of acting, thinking, speaking man—
> Went from me, neither knowing me, nor known.
>
> (VII, 593–607)

The invocation to the well-known friend, Coleridge, leads quickly to an unparticularized, hallucinatory excursion into the surging crowd that not only is composed of strangers but also renders the poet unknowing himself.

Wordsworth's lines imply the unreality of the city in several ways, anticipating passages of alienation and estrangement in city literature from Baudelaire's spectral "fourmillante cité" to Eliot's crowd of automatons flowing over London Bridge. The oppression of unanswered questions about the city, "thoughts of what, and whither, when and how," threatens to dissolve the very materiality of the city. Distraught by the quintessential enigma of the city and his fellow citizens, the poet senses his own identity unraveling as "all stays" depart from him. Unlike the complete legibility of the inhabitants of the New Jerusalem (Rev. 22:4), these worldly faces conceal rather than reveal, aligning themselves with the mystery of another city, Babylon (Rev. 17:5). The insubstantiality of London/Babylon undermines the poet's quest, for no solid understanding can be founded upon a chimera. Because it is a search for knowledge only of Babylon, his search will merit the subsequent rebuke "from another world."

For Wordsworth, to enter the crowd is to suspend ordinary sensory contact with the world, as the consciousness loses "all the ballast of familiar life" and moves into a dreamlike state, in the crowd but lost to it. The reiterated emphasis on the poet's effort to see intensifies the distance between the ordinary (and quite acute) perception to which he is accustomed, and the trancelike "second sight" that, rather than summoning up scenes of visionary power, induces a kind of blankness, a negative condition of sensory lawlessness. Wordsworth's frustrated scrutiny prepares the reader for the imminent encounter with the blind man, where second sight gives way to no sight at all:

> And once, far travelled in such mood, beyond
> The reach of common indications, lost
> Amid the moving pageant, 'twas my chance
> Abruptly to be smitten with the view
> Of a blind beggar, who, with upright face,
> Stood propped against a wall, upon his chest
> Wearing a written paper, to explain
> The story of the man, and who he was.
> My mind did at this spectacle turn round
> As with the might of waters, and it seemed

To me that in this label was a type
Or emblem of the utmost that we know
Both of ourselves and of the universe,
And on the shape of this unmoving man,
His fixèd face and sightless eyes, I looked,
As if admonished from another world.

(VII, 608–23)

As in Blake's "London," sight and blindness, marking and reading, contend with one another. But if the voice of Babylon forces the sense of hearing to take priority in Blake's midnight streets, it is the essential opacity of earthly vision that humbles the spectator in Wordsworth's crowd. The unspeaking beggar is like Tiresias or a seer, for the self-knowledge he teaches, the vision he imparts, is indeed blinding.

THE SHOCK OF THE OTHER

All religions have honored the beggar. For he proves that in a matter at the same time as prosaic and holy, banal and regenerating as the giving of alms, intellect and morality, consistency and principles are miserably inadequate.
—Walter Benjamin

Like the Cumberland beggar whom Wordsworth describes earlier in *The Prelude* (IV, 400–504), the blind beggar ought to elicit from passers-by an acknowledgment of their membership in a larger human community, calling from them an exercise of charity and compassion.[7] "My trust is in the God of Heaven, / And in the eye of him that passes me," declares the rural mendicant (IV, 494–95). But though the urban beggar too must depend upon the eye of the passing stranger, he creates the opposite effect. He seems to deny human fellowship rather than promote it, and to censure rather than encourage efforts at human understanding. Seeing him against the ever-present background of the crowd that surges throughout Book VII—"Here, there, and everywhere, a weary throng" (171)—Wordsworth describes his meeting with the beggar as a sudden, traumatic shock. "Smitten with the view," the poet records the first close encounter with the Other in modern city poetry. Equally important, he is an Other already written yet unreadable: his sign or label marks him as victim and "emblem," and forewarns Wordsworth of the impossiblity of knowledge of the city. He seems a figure as old as Babel, connecting the ancient *topos* of urban indecipherability to the more modern image of the unknown face in the street.[8]

Walter Benjamin's meditations on how the artist reacts to the sensory overload of urban existence seem particularly relevant to Wordsworth's situation in London.[9] Benjamin distinguishes between two modes of experience: *Erlebnis*, in which the shocks characteristic of city life are "cushioned, parried by consciousness," thereby becoming "a moment that has been lived"; and *Erfahrung*, wherein receptivity to traumatic experience becomes an enduring knowledge that one lives with.[10] The more efficiently city dwellers screen out the adverse stimuli that buffet them—what Wordsworth himself alludes to as the city's "shock / For eyes and ears" (1850: VII, 685–86)—the less open they are to the abiding impressions necessary to artistic creation. They can successfully avoid emotional damage by "assigning to an incident a precise point in time in consciousness" but only "at the cost of the integrity of its contents."[11] This turning of potentially vital experience into ephemeral information, Benjamin finds, is the typical result of modern urban life. Though many of Wordsworth's best poems about nature would seem to spring from a Proustian *mémoire involuntaire*, in London Wordsworth finds the shocks too numerous, and he strives, like most city dwellers, to maintain conscious control.

In the blind beggar episode, however, he finds himself forced back into the painful but poetically rewarding state of *Erfahrung*. The experience cannot be dismissed: both physically and psychologically, the impression is too immediate, too close to home. The poet cannot penetrate to any deeper meaning to accommodate the shock the beggar has given him, for there is no getting behind the beggar's eyes, or the characters of his label. Where one expects to find the soul of the man, there is only more surface.[12] The opacity of his eyes suggests the illegibility of the label whose text Wordsworth never supplies. The impassivity of both man and text deflects the reader's attention—that of Wordsworth as well as his audience—back upon the interpreter.

And yet the beggar's eyes do give "light," as they reflect the poet's own would-be mastery of the Other, and how little knowledge that truly involves. "Neither knowing me nor known"—in the arresting encounter with the beggar it is now the baffled self to whom these lines apply, not merely the crowd of strangers. The stranger helps define the self by virtue of the self-image and desires he reflects, and the self turns out to be Other, known only through what is unknown, identified by difference and strangeness.[13] The force of the beggar's representation of the limits of human knowledge reveals the self as stranger, undercutting the usual opposition of self and Other so intensely felt elsewhere in Wordsworth's poetry. Although Wordsworth argues in his "Prospectus" how "exquisitely the individual Mind / . . . / . . . to the external World / Is fitted," the poet's urban experience prompts him to question the nature of individual identity and its relation to the "external World." What is not separate cannot be joined. London thus frustrates the "natural supernaturalism" that would for Wordsworth transfer Revelation's divine marriage to the coupling of imagination and world.[14] Throughout Book VII of *The Prelude*, the disruptive forces of the city repeatedly prevent the possibility of such a union.[15]

Whatever self-definition the beggar's mirroring eyes may offer, his text, like an epitaph, speaks "from another world," refusing reciprocity and silencing interlocution.[16] The label shatters the totality of the mirror's contents by providing an impoverished but indisputable textual supplement that dramatically deflates the value of specular knowledge: "The story of the man, and who he was."

Jacques Lacan's work on specularity helps us to understand the visual short-circuit that the beggar's sudden appearance engineers. For Lacan, the breaking of the "phallic" gaze that represents the onlooker's desire to penetrate the object initiates a symbolic castration that renders the poet's glance or stylus impotent. Thwarting the sexual domination of the masculine gaze, the blind man's look becomes a *fascinum*, or evil eye, "which has the effect of arresting movement"—as is the case in this poem—"and, literally, of killing life"—or preventing insemination.[17] The poet's frustrated quest to "know" in an epistemological or metaphysical sense veils a concern for his potency as man or writer. Certainly his aversion to the harlotry and "babel din" of the city—which threaten the author with the promiscuity of bodies and signs—figures strongly in the dynamic that seeks to convert London/Babylon into a pure, harmonious New Jerusalem. The beggar's unmanning stare devastatingly reminds the poet of his bondage to the fallen towers of Babylon and Babel, and his exclusion from the "other world" of unmediated, legitimate paternity and authorship. The beggar's impenetrable blindness becomes in itself a dominating gaze that catches the looker looking and turns the initially confident subject into self-conscious object. In this respect it is the beggar who possesses the ideal "city eyes": they deflect all glances, give off shock but cannot be shocked, and protect the beggar by returning to the poet his own look, drained of all content and certainty.[18]

A major source of the beggar's power is that he is unmoving, unlike the peripatetic poet; his fixed face and his body propped against a wall, a further suggestion of the boundaries of insight, contrast with the poet's physical mobility as he is carried forward in the crowd, and with the internal motion instigated by the sight: "My mind did at this spectacle turn round / As with the might of waters." Paralleling the shift from private to public (Coleridge to crowd) and then to private once again (poet, beggar, and label), the movement from physical mobility to shocked stasis and then inner turmoil highlights the volatility and instability of boundaries in the city, the fluid nature of its emotional impressions. The beggar is a marginal figure, without occupation, yet by transforming his private life into public business he reintroduces the central problem first posed by Cain: "Am I my brother's keeper?" Do we invade the beggar's privacy, or does *he* invade the "privacy" of persons in public places by making his own publicly private appeal to each of us? And how are we, cast in the position of the poet, to read him?

Wordsworth offers no definitive answer. Because he cannot complacently read this face, unlike the faces of his rural neighbors which speak "volumes" to him (IV, 59), he is unable to establish the brotherly communal bond that would prompt his immediate and willing almsgiving. Does he ever drop a coin into the beggar's cup? Imaging the break between man and man, eye and eye, written paper and poetic paragraph, Wordsworth's text breaks here, with the admonishment "from another world." The poet's offering falls into that gap—waiting for a sharp-eyed reader, willing his own interpretive blindness, to pick it up.

TRUTH IN LABELING? THE TEXTUALITY OF THE CITY

The beggar's label is one more urban mark or sign in a long tradition: from the imprint of Cain to the signed foreheads of harlots and saints in Revelation, and the marked passers-by of Blake, Baudelaire, Whitman, Eliot, and Williams, city people are inscribed by the hand of God and man. Like Cain's mark, the beggar's sign neither saves nor condemns; it indicates a condition beyond comprehension or judgment.

The most disturbing thing of all about the beggar is unnamed, though it is there for all to read. The "written paper" that he wears "to explain / The story of the man, and who he was" is, of course, his autobiography. In confronting the beggar, then, Wordsworth is not only meeting with the shortcomings of his social conscience, a condemnation of his reifying tendencies as a poet,[19] not only confronting the boundaries of human understanding, but also facing an unfaceable image of himself and of the failure of autobiographical writing. The blind man wearing words that he cannot see or read becomes a type for the poet attempting, at this very moment, to write his own life. As a failed reader of the blind man and his text, the poet must turn his own "sightless eyes" upon his own enterprise—thereby calling into question the whole project of *The Prelude*. In the city, Wordsworth's usually illuminating "spots of time" become blind spots, which disclose not what he has learned about himself and the universe, but rather that they can never be known.

The original version of lines 617–20 made the devastating equation between human knowledge, literature, and the label even clearer:

> and I thought
> That even the very most of what we know
> Both of ourselves and of the universe,
> *The whole of what is written to our view*,
> Is but a label on a blind man's chest.
>
> (my emphasis)[20]

The poet is forced to repress this "knowledge" if he wants to continue. He opposes the underlying unity he finds in nature to the disorienting surface triviality of London, attempting to ground his insights in an experience outside the city. He shores up and frames the indecipherability of the city with the legible rural text of God's creation, just as Book VII is framed by other largely rural episodes. But at the "center" of his life's book is a blind man and his story. In questioning the power of writing to establish or communicate knowledge of self and Other, Wordsworth is responding not just to the immediate situation of the beggar, or even to his own preoccupation with the limits of autobiography, but also to the larger issue of Book VII—the question of whether, in the city, one can read, write, or speak at all.

In *The Prelude*, Wordsworth gives one of the first and most intense views of the modern written city, whose multiple texts, taking the form of shop signs, advertisements, and other communications, indicate the complex networks of urban interaction. In fact, as the metaphor introducing Wordsworth's actual experience in London suggests, the city is a vast text that he must learn to read: "And now I looked upon the real scene, / Familiarly perused it day by day" (139–40).[21]

But how "real" is the textual scene that the poet finds himself perusing and that he, a few lines later, will call "a frequent day-dream"? His confidence in the power of words to shape or define reality meets a stiff challenge during the course of his London experience, but at the outset of Book VII, when he feels in control of his language and memories, Wordsworth exclaims, "Oh wondrous power of words, how sweet they are / According to the meaning which they bring" (121–22). The proviso is significant, given the subsequent eruption of a wayward textuality into his description of the city. For in Wordsworth's London two crowds constantly jostle each other, competing for attention and definition:

> The comers and the goers face to face—
> Face after face—the string of dazzling wares,
> Shop after shop, with symbols, blazoned names,
> And all the tradesmen's honours overhead:
> Here, fronts of houses, like a title-page
> With letters huge inscribed from top to toe.
>
> (VII, 172–77)

People and signs furnish the texture of the city, demanding to be deciphered.[22] But while the city and its very houses are like open books, waiting to be read, the citizens remain closed to each other:

> Above all, one thought
> Baffled my understanding, how men lived
> Even next-door neighbours, as we say, yet still
> Strangers, and knowing not each other's names.
>
> (VII, 117–20)

Wordsworth's city is composed of strangers who cannot be named. By virtue of his written paper, the blind beggar seems, at first, to bridge the gap between textualized objects and unreadable men. He, at least, is nameable, legible, displaying signs whose referent is securely attached. The blind beggar ought not to be a mystery, for unlike those blank thousands that puzzle the poet at the start of the passage, he has a name and a history that can be read by anyone. Yet, like Jack the Giant Killer, the other labeled character in Book VII (310), he is in a certain sense INVISIBLE—both to himself, and to those who have city eyes. In the theater, the word INVISIBLE worn by the actor playing Jack represents the power of language. It perpetrates a "delusion bold" (308) to make what is not into what is, to sustain the illusion by letting an audience read what they should not be able to see.

But with the beggar one sees what one cannot read; he is proposed as a mimetic inscription of the limitations of writing and knowledge. For the beggar reveals to the poet, far more strongly than even the theater does, that the entire city, or rather one's knowledge of it, is illusory: the "delusion bold" of linguistic stability calls for a willing suspension of disbelief in order to arrest the play of interpretation. Just as the beggar's sightless eyes cast the poet's gaze back upon himself, the "written paper" of the poem mirrors the unfathomable surface of the city.

BABEL AND THE DANGER OF THE CROWD

Later in *The Prelude*, Wordsworth uses the simile, "Exposed, and lifeless as a written book" (VIII, 727) to describe how one's sight acclimates to darkness, eventually reducing shifting shadows to a static clarity. His vision of London reverses the process: the city, like the beggar's apocalyptic label, is a potentially dead text that quickens into life almost spontaneously; what the poet perhaps wishes were inert signs become animated by the play of language and his own imagination. Throughout his stay in London he finds himself facing a familiar and troubling archetype of urban existence:

> And first, the look and aspect of the place—
> The broad highway appearance, as it strikes
> On strangers of all ages, the quick dance
> Of colours, lights and forms, the Babel din . . .
>
> (VII, 154–57)

Amid this "endless stream of men and moving things" (158) there is an interaction that can be expressed only in terms of its incomprehensibility. The Babel story equates the city with its language, and in the absence of a common speech the city builders cannot continue or complete their task. When language and communication fail, the tower falls, the city is ruined.

Writers often try to explain the failures of the city in terms that Augustine would have understood: the city is unmistakably hu-

man, rather than divine, the epitome of the manmade, the artificial. As such, it is culture's greatest and worst achievement, a con-
cretization of human history, a fixed and yet ever-changing form of
human energy. The emphasis on the city as a representation of the
human moral condition potentially enables the poet to speak in
praise of a *civitas dei*. But in actuality writers most often concentrate on the deterioration of community and personality that the
modern city seems to enforce. In the Preface to *Lyrical Ballads*
(1802) Wordsworth complains of the "almost savage torpor" of the
modern mind, which has blunted its "discriminating powers." As
a primary cause he singles out

> the increasing accumulation of men in cities, where the uni-
> formity of their occupations produces a craving for extraordi-
> nary incident, which the rapid communication of intelligence
> hourly gratifies. To this tendency of life and manners the
> literature and theatrical exhibitions of the country have con-
> formed themselves.[23]

The sensational stimulations that city residents demand remind
us that, historically and etymologically, Babel is also, of course,
Babylon. Thus the linguistic alienation of human cities coincides
with their spiritual estrangement.[24] As archetypal universal cities,
Babel and Babylon, both of which mean "Gate of God," reiterate
their post-Edenic status; urbanites find themselves at the threshold, but never in the midst, of the *civitas dei*.

And so the modern city is often depicted as a Babel or a "blank
confusion," as Wordsworth later says of Bartholomew Fair. Yet the
breaking up of man's common language by God does not actually
generate an undifferentiated chaos, as Wordsworth's phrase would
at first seem to imply; rather it repeats God's creation through differentiation, light from dark, water from earth, Eve from Adam.
The problem is not the lack of difference, but rather an excess of it.
And this is precisely Wordsworth's point. The passage describing
Bartholomew Fair puts this in perspective: one must be able to
work with "forms distinct" (VIII, 598), as the poet later remarks, if
one wants to see, let alone create. But the city's surplus of activity
continually blurs these distinctions:

> O, blank confusion, and a type not false
> Of what the mighty city is itself
> To all, except a straggler here and there—
> To the whole swarm of its inhabitants—

An undistinguishable world to men,
The slaves unrespited of low pursuits,
Living amid the same perpetual flow
Of trivial objects, melted and reduced
To one identity by differences
That have no law, no meaning, and no end—
Oppression under which even highest minds
Must labour, whence the strongest are not free.

(VII, 696–707)

More severe even than the mind-forged manacles of Blake, the fetters of infinite urban and linguistic "differences / That have no law" are inescapable.[25] In their unruliness, these differences recall the hallucinatory conditions of the "second-sight procession," but having no meaning and end they promise no compensatory final vision. As an arche-"type not false" of the entire city, the Babel of Bartholomew Fair thus represents the ultimate paralysis of the worldly urban imagination. Like the other "type" in Book VII, the beggar's label, the Fair in its overplenitude exposes the boundaries of human understanding rather than the values of human inter- course. For Wordsworth, total difference has the effect of produc- ing an undifferentiated totality ("melted and reduced / To one identity"). It thus prohibits the establishing of particular identities, either of persons or things, upon which Wordsworth's poetry de- pends. Worse still, the expression of these identities depends upon words that bear the Babel-inflicted taint of differences that can never be unified into a fully coherent language.

For Wordsworth prefers to perceive and create through *distance*, not difference. Filtered through the lenses of memory and the physi- cal space necessary to view awe-inspiring mountains or sleeping cities from afar, his poetic imagination customarily works best under conditions of removal and retrospection. Safely escaped from London in Book VIII, he thanks his Genius for the detachment and country education that have enabled him to keep his mental bearings in the metropolis:

blessèd be the God
Of Nature and of man that this was so,
That men did at the first present themselves
Before my untaught eyes thus purified,
Removed, and at a distance that was fit.

(VIII, 436–40)

It is precisely this "fit distance" between subject and object that makes the rest of *The Prelude* possible, and it is a prerequisite for all his poetry. He emphasizes a purity of vision that cannot, unlike its claustrophobic urban counterpart, damage "untaught eyes." Wordsworth seeks a vantage point of clear perspective from which to gain control of those moments that threaten his moral equilibrium or identity. Thus he speaks in the 1850 *Prelude* of "city smoke, by distance ruralised" (I, 89). And thus he artificially, almost desperately, tries to pull himself out of the crush at Bartholomew Fair:

> For once the Muse's help will we implore,
> And she shall lodge us—wafted on her wings
> Above the press and danger of the crowd—
> Upon some showman's platform.
>
> (VII, 656–59)

The "danger of the crowd" sums up in a phrase the poet's troubled relation to the city, and the rather rusty device of appealing to the Muse indicates how far he is willing to go to establish a commanding distance, even the inglorious one of a showman's platform.[26] Poet as huckster: again the theatrical and literary illusions of the unreal city stand revealed by this momentary panic.[27]

What makes Book VII of *The Prelude* so fascinating is Wordsworth's willingness to be explicit about his dismay in the tumult of London streets, and the transparent inadequacy of his efforts to regain control at the end of the section. Throughout "Residence in London" he repeatedly reaches for the underlying sense of unity he finds in nature, and he concludes by an appeal to its integrity and permanence:

> But though the picture weary out the eye,
> By nature an unmanageable sight,
> It is not wholly so to him who looks
> In steadiness, who hath among least things
> An under-sense of greatest, sees the parts
> As parts, but with a feeling of the whole.
> . . . .
> This did I feel in that vast receptacle.
> The spirit of Nature was upon me here,
> The soul of beauty and enduring life
> Was present as a habit, and diffused—
> Through meagre lines and colours, and the press

Of self-destroying, transitory things—
Composure and ennobling harmony.
(VII, 708–13; 735–41)

Once again a deeper vision proposes to assuage weary urban eyes.
Attempting to counteract his description of the "unmanageable
sight[s]" first of Bartholomew Fair and then of London itself, these
lines show the poet searching for a way to offset the "self-destroying" experience of the city by recourse to the "enduring life" of Nature.[28] Having anatomized the city's surface discontinuity, he must
descend to the inner whole; buffeted to distraction by ephemera,
he must find a poetic and personal "composure" in the concord of
art. But though he seeks to visualize an inner repose that can quiet
the auditory bedlam of the crowd, the final metaphor seems ill-
chosen. The carefully placed "harmony" that closes the book jars
too painfully with the discordant shocks of the blind beggar and
his city: "What a hell / For eyes and ears, what anarchy and din /
Barbarian and infernal" (659–61). As the force of such passages attests, the severity of the challenge to the poet's convictions exceeds
his ability to overcome it.

And he knows this. He must repress the lessons taught by the
blind beggar—lessons about the insufficiency of his understanding, the failure of writing to convey a life, the fundamental blankness of the city text—if he is to continue writing at all. Because
shock and proximity, mutiplicity and triviality are antithetical to
his poetic creed, Wordsworth has to demonstrate how inimical
they are to any creative life. Thus in Bartholomew Fair he finds "A
work . . . that lays, / If any spectacle on earth can do, / The whole
creative powers of man asleep" (653–55).[29] The surprise of the final
word is conditioned by an Augustan and modern expectation that
the city will stimulate the poet; but it is considerably lessened
when we reflect on Wordsworth's self-confessed need for distance
and unity.[30] Blurring before his eyes, the multiple impressions of
the whirling city become indistinguishable, unwritable, unthink-
able, as if the mysteries of the beggar's label had no end.

ADMONISHED FROM ANOTHER WORLD

The beggar *is* another world, and he admonishes both poet and
reader for presuming to read and write his text, for trying to diminish the impact of his strangeness. The passage provides an especially valuable example of urban revelation because it shows the

startled poet in the process of rejecting an appropriative vision of the city, one seeking to impose an imaginative order and confinement on those within it. In this rare Wordsworthian instance of unmastered shock, the blind beggar insists on the autonomy of the unknowable Other, the frightening independence of each member of the urban community.

But there is another Revelation here, and another world apart from that of the Other. In the midst of the Babel and Babylonian clamor of the earthly city, heaven speaks: "And I heard a voice from heaven, as the voice of many waters, and as the voice of a great thunder" (Rev. 14:2; see also 19:6). In addition to suggesting what might be meant by the image of the poet's mind turning round "as with the might of waters," these words describe the voice of apocalypse, speaking the words which only the Saved can understand, and truly "admonish[ing] from another world." As with Blake, the images of Babylon always imply and usually elicit reference to its opposite, the New Jerusalem. The image of waters itself harbors double and opposed meanings: the "peoples, and multitudes, and nations, and tongues," such as those Wordsworth contends with in the cacophony of London, constitute the "waters where the whore sitteth" (Rev. 17:15). The roaring of heavenly justice and the uproar of worldly confusion meet in Wordsworth's text. The one exposes his limited knowledge; the other prevents him from hearing a single, unified Word in the midst of overly differentiated, and ultimately blank, texts. Staring at the "fixèd face and sightless eyes" of the beggar, the poet does at least *see* something, but it is a vision that will not reveal itself, an inversion of the clarity of the original revelation upon which his later text is based: "And I John saw . . ." (Rev. 21:2).[31]

The blind beggar also stands at the threshold of another world—his paltry label mocks the poet's attempts to "know" him, invoking the Heavenly City which admonishes the writer for his presumption. Thus the beggar represents both the other world and the world of the Other, which also limits or defines each individual. In either case, he marks a boundary of knowledge that cannot be crossed.

In the rest of *The Prelude* Wordsworth strives to achieve a biblical comprehension of the majesty and divinity of the city, but he seems to be able to do so only from afar, filtering his impressions of London through the screen of memory. As a child, his earliest distant anticipations of the city are filled with wonder rather than

dread. He imagines that the envied schoolmate who journeys to
London will return transformed by his contact with the enchanted
realm, radiating "some beams of glory brought away / From that
new region" (VII, 103–4). Later, when he makes his own first visit
to the city, even his aversion to its physical meanness cannot destroy his deeper feelings of amazement at its sheer size and power:

> Never shall I forget the hour,
> The moment rather say, when, having thridded
> The labyrinth of suburban villages,
> At length I did unto myself first seem
> To enter the great city. On the roof
> Of an itinerant vehicle I sate,
> With vulgar men about me, vulgar forms
> Of houses, pavements, streets, of men and things,
> Mean shapes on every side; but, at the time,
> When to myself it fairly might be said
> (The very moment that I seemed to know)
> 'The threshhold now is overpast', great God!
> That aught *external* to the living mind
> Should have such mighty sway, yet so it was.
> . . . .
> All that took place within me came and went
> As in a moment, and I only now
> Remember that it was a thing divine.

(VIII, 689–702, 708–10)

The epithet ("great God!") repeated with slight variation from
"Westminster Bridge" (where the poet exclaims, "Dear God") and
his assessment of the moment as "a thing divine" suggest how persistently he seeks to make the motif of New Jerusalem structure his
apprehension of the city. Having missed the actual moment when
he crossed the Alps (VI, 491–524), the poet devotes his utmost attention to the liminal moment of reaching London, thereby award-
ing to the city the sublime, soul-stirring impact he had originally
expected to receive from nature.[32] What seems most to impress
Wordsworth—and suggests otherworldly powers—is not London's fame, achievements, or actual splendor, but rather its size.
For the poet who is concerned with the growth of the poetic mind
and who claims in the "Prospectus" to his major work that the
Mind of Man is more sublime than Jehovah and the heaven of
heavens (28–41), the idea that there can be anything "*external*" to
rival consciousness itself is truly staggering.

After the disappointing alpine experience, Wordsworth had celebrated the independence of the imagination from nature (VI, 525–48). Book VII of *The Prelude* is, in a sense, the place where the poet meets his match, coming into conflict with an entity so vast and multifarious that he cannot successfully recoil from the encounter and, with the aid of memory, shape a "spot of time" into evidence of the intellect's harmonious marriage to nature. Though it seems at first divine, by virtue of its "mighty sway" the contentious city will more often play the willful harlot than the compliant virgin. As the poet remarks later, love cannot thrive "In cities, where the human heart is sick, / And the eye feeds it not, and cannot feed" (XII, 202–3).

Wordsworth's inability to assimilate the experience of the city into his conceptual framework depends upon many factors—his definition of creativity, his bafflement by the city's polysemous textuality, its overloading of the senses, its mysterious Others, its overall confusion. In fact, the mind has already become a city when, earlier in the poem, Wordsworth discusses how the storms of urban distraction "Passed not beyond the suburbs of the mind" (VII, 507). The image implies the existence of an unviolated, stable center of consciousness. But if that center is itself a city, as he suggests, then what kind of a city can the mind be to resist the disorder of London?[33]

The sonnet "Composed upon Westminster Bridge, September 3, 1802" provides a vision of that ideal urban world. Although in *The Prelude* London generates "blank confusion," a manmade Babel, and only rarely seems a "thing divine," in "Westminster Bridge" the poet's early morning impressions of London suggest in almost biblical fashion the archetypal union of God, mind, and city.

> Earth has not anything to show more fair:
> Dull would he be of soul who could pass by
> A sight so touching in its majesty:
> This City now doth, like a garment, wear
> The beauty of the morning; silent, bare,
> Ships, towers, domes, theatres, and temples lie
> Open unto the fields, and to the sky;
> All bright and glittering in the smokeless air.
> Never did sun more beautifully steep
> In his first splendour, valley, rock, or hill;
> Ne'er saw I, never felt, a calm so deep!
> The river glideth at his own sweet will:

Dear God! the very houses seem asleep;
And all that mighty heart is lying still![34]

Here the poet strives to replicate in his own mind the clarity of vision belonging to the heavenly city rather than the turmoil of the
earthly one. Yet despite its laudatory tone, many readers find in
the poem a subtly adversarial view of the town, one which illumi-
nates—and is illuminated by—the ideal marriage of imagination
and city that Wordsworth fails to create in *The Prelude*.

Critics have long noted that Wordsworth, customarily appalled
by the city's noise, vice, and disorder, can enjoy the sight of London only when it appears innocently dormant or, in fact, dead: "all
that mighty heart is lying still."[35] Indeed, only because its characteristic bustle has ceased can the pure outlines of the city be seen at
all.[36] Almost literally turning the city out into the country ("Open
unto the fields, and to the sky"), Wordsworth pastoralizes the metropolis to regain the natural world with which he feels more comfortable. The poet delights in the view because he is physically removed from it, pausing on the far shore as he heads out of town.
The aesthetic is one based on the idea of "fit distance"—without
which the poet feels he can have no proper apprehension of any
scene.[37]

In such readings the deeper impulses of the writer are clearly at
odds with what, on the surface at least, is one of the most moving
tributes to urban beauty ever written. Is there a way to appreciate
Wordsworth's genuine admiration of the sight, while at the same
time comprehending the fear of urban chaos that appears to underlie it? The dynamic tension between the images of Babylon and
New Jerusalem that structure *The Prelude*'s urban vision in fact provides such a perspective. The semirepressed Babylonian aspects of
London, its smoke, commerce, and sin, mingle with emblems of
higher things: the ships, towers, and theaters of worldly pastimes
are interspersed with the domes (St. Paul's necessarily predominant) and temples dedicated to the world beyond. Recalling St.
John's vision of the heavenly city, Wordsworth's opening lines inform us that his subject is beyond earthly beauty, that it touches
sensitive souls rather than dull ones, and that the city is arrayed, if
not exactly as a bride, then in the pure garments of the morning.[38]
Married to the unsullied poetic imagination, it lies unselfconsciously "open" to a cleansed nature rather than to aggressive
men.

Moreover, the brightness and glitter of New Jerusalem appear in the aftermath of Babylon's smoking ruin, just as the new urban heaven replaces, with even greater radiance, the old, lost, pastoral paradise of Eden:

> Never did sun more beautifully steep
> In his first splendour, valley, rock, or hill;
> Ne'er saw I, never felt, a calm so deep!

Wordsworth's apparent tranquilizing of the teeming city, then, is not merely a perverse effort to praise it for seeming to be what it is not (the country). Rather, the poem adopts an apocalyptic point of view, exploring what it might be like to view the final metropolis which supersedes both garden and town. Hence the breathtaking wonder—"Dear God!"—and the intimate address to Him whose city it is. Here, Revelation's River of Life can glide, unlike Blake's "charter'd Thames," at "his own sweet will," the postlapsarian dangers of willfulness having come to an end. The anxieties over the wayward energies of contemporary London that underpin the sonnet may now be seen as intimating, not so much Wordsworth's awe at the repose of the sleeping giant, as the legitimate concerns of the visionary dreamer who fears he might wake up. The sleeping houses and the stilled heart that conclude the poem represent the poet's parting attempt to impose on the present city his vision of the celestial one. Pitting his desire for the static perfection of the New Jerusalem against the mobility of its earthly counterpart, he can say only what he wishes were true, and turn from London before its Babylonian day begins.

SOME UNHAPPY WOMAN:
WORDSWORTH'S HARLOT

"Westminster Bridge" provides a valuable reference point for Book VII of The Prelude because it is more explicit, not just about Wordsworth's desire to envision New Jerusalem on earth, but also about the poet's fascination with the deathliness of the city, and his aesthetic preference for stillness rather than activity. Moreover, it helps uncover a similar set of priorities in the nighttime scene immediately following the encounter with the blind beggar. From the hallucination and mystery at its start to the otherworldly admonishment at its end, the blind beggar passage raises troubling questions about the nature of urban perception and the poet's engagement with the city, questions the poet wishes to evade even as he strives to answer them:

Though reared upon the base of outward things,
These chiefly are such structures as the mind
Builds for itself. Scenes different there are—
Full-formed—which take, with small internal help,
Possession of the faculties: the peace
Of night, for instance, the solemnity
Of Nature's intermediate hours of rest
When the great tide of human life stands still,
The business of the day to come unborn,
Of that gone by locked up as in the grave;
The calmness, beauty, of the spectacle,
Sky, stillness, moonshine, empty streets, and sounds
Unfrequent as in desarts; at late hours
Of winter evenings when unwholesome rains
Are falling hard, with people yet astir,
The feeble salutation from the voice
Of some unhappy woman now and then
Heard as we pass, when no one looks about,
Nothing is listened to. But these I fear
Are falsely catalogued: things that are, are not,
Even as we give them welcome, or assist—
Are prompt, or are remiss.

                                        (VII, 624–45)

Experiences such as those with the blind beggar are "mind-forg'd,"
ones that "the mind / Builds for itself," and Wordsworth contrasts
them to his preferred scenes of solitude and quiet. These more attractive scenes—like the view of London sleeping in "Westminster
Bridge" or of the natural landscape in the rest of *The Prelude*—are
not merely "reared upon the base of outward things" but are sol-
idly connected to them. But even these scenes seem unreal, and
must be questioned—"things that are, are not." Thus the appealing nocturnal cityscape is itself "falsely catalogued" as being "full-
formed." The deserted, moonlit streets may be more reassuring
than the meeting with the beggar, but they are equally a product of
the imagination's interaction with the city, whether or not the mind
"assists."

    Amid the uncertainty of the poet's perception lies, once again,
the suggestion of an unreal city. The phrase "The blended calmness of the heavens and earth" (1850: 660), which Wordsworth later
inserted after "as in the grave," echoes Revelation, and verbal parallels between this passage and "Westminster Bridge" (especially

the reiterated emphasis on stillness, peace, and sleep) suggest how Wordsworth seeks to repress the textual and sexual crises of Babylonian London. For the night scene following the blind beggar passage does not stop where the sonnet does; rather, because it deals with night instead of morning, it exposes the metaphor of the city as harlot/Babylon that actuates both visions:

> The feeble salutation from the voice
> Of some unhappy woman now and then
> Heard as we pass, when no one looks about,
> Nothing is listened to.

The harlot whose Blakean midnight cry breaks the silence feebly but tellingly accosts the author of these lines. The city of Babylonian sexual mystery and misery intimated here reminds us of the "fallen" Maid of Buttermere's story, which Wordsworth rehearses earlier in Book VII (321–412). His recollection of the first time he heard "the voice of woman utter blasphemy" and of his first view of prostitutes then follows (413–35). The harlot's verbal salutation, "Heard as we pass," complements the voiceless text and other-worldly remonstrance of the blind beggar; yet the poet, bent on secrecy, is already trying to forget the lesson. Instead of Blake's insistent "but most I hear," Wordsworth admits that "when no one looks about, / Nothing is listened to." The poet becomes a passing customer, mentioning yet repressing his sexual interest in and imaging of the city, wishing (in both poems) Babylon into New Jerusalem and an actual woman into "things that . . . are not." Unlike Blake's "London," Wordsworth's handling of the same motifs represents an effort to avoid marking and re-marking, to suppress the sexual knowledge of these other worlds.

Wordsworth's carefully circumscribed fascination with sexual fall seeps almost imperceptibly into his poetry through the covert use of the Babylon/New Jerusalem polarity. But as this passage shows when taken in its entirety, even the effort to make the scene unreal cannot disguise how the virginal calm of the city inexorably shades into the prostitute's invitation. Wordsworth is unable to sustain the dichotomy (which Baudelaire and Williams will abandon altogether) because the harlot, like her idealized counterpart, participates as a human commodity in the reified economy of urban signification and exchange. As marks of unsatisfied desire (for flesh, for knowledge, for clear vision), the citizens and texts of Wordsworth's London circulate in a perpetual Bartholomew Fair that never sells identity, only difference and deferral. Attempting to stop the whirl of Babylon's unstable desires by appeal to the pristine stasis of the Heavenly City, the poet is inevitably foiled by the very texts and textuality of these reference points. "Mystery" cannot be read into "mastery," and the name autobiography inscribes is shown to be INVISIBLE, fraught with illusion and arbitrariness.

Thus the encounter with the blind beggar and the meditation on unreality that follows in reaction to it concentrate the predominant cross-tensions of city poetry—sexuality, unreality, textuality—into a single situation, that of passing poet meeting urban Other. In Book VII of *The Prelude* the eruption of these issues, prompted by the compression of the city, reveals them to be larger than the book that tries to lay their ghost with the final word of "harmony." Nonetheless, Wordsworth's strength as a poet of the city comes through most powerfully here, in his willingness to work without that "fit distance" which is, in the urban world, truly blind and beggarly.

Chapter Three

Poet as *Passant*

Baudelaire's "Holy Prostitution"

*In Chloe, a great city, the people who move through the streets are all strang-
ers. At each encounter, they imagine a thousand things about one another;
meetings which could take place between them, conversations, surprises, ca-
resses, bites. But no one greets anyone; eyes lock for a second, then dart
away, seeking other eyes, never stopping.*

—Italo Calvino, *Invisible Cities*

Although Blake and Wordsworth begin the poetic exploration
of the apocalyptic modern metropolis, the unreal city of the
nineteenth century finds its laureate in Baudelaire. Baudelaire's poetry is revolutionary because it insists on the motley
splendor of the entire city and all its inhabitants, no matter how
bizarre, perverse, or degraded. Baudelaire dedicates himself to
creating a new, comprehensive urban aesthetic that can take in
"tous les hôpitaux et . . . tous les palais." Previously, only Blake
had consistently seen the city as a vast, interlocking system of social forces that possessed both a moral and a symbolic dimension
burning luminously behind the details of mundane urban existence. Yet if Blake revealed how "mind-forg'd manacles" shackle
the lives of representative citizens (the Sweeper, the Soldier, the
Harlot), Baudelaire managed to particularize the archetypal urban
situation of the wandering poet into something more personal,
more intensely threatening, and at the same time more typical of
the city as we know it today. The element which he brought to the
fore—or which he could not repress—was the crowd. Combining
Wordsworth's sense of imperiled consciousness at Bartholomew
Fair with Blake's visionary understanding of the city as an imaginative structure, Baudelaire elevates the poet's disorienting encounter with the stranger in the crowd to a primal moment of modern
literature.

In 1846, as a young art critic, Baudelaire had declared that the

39

"heroism of modern life" consisted to a large degree in "the spectacle of elegant life and of the thousands of floating existences
which circulate in the underworld of a great city." If we would only
look about us, he insisted, we would discover that "Parisian life is
rich in poetic and wondrous subjects. The marvelous envelops us
and saturates us like the atmosphere, but we do not see it." [1] This
insight sparked Baudelaire's lifelong effort to transform the artistic
potential of the city into poetic reality, an effort which culminated
in his creation of the *Tableaux parisiens* section of the 1861 edition of
Les Fleurs du mal. The poems assembled there announced the poet's
determination to fling himself into urban experience, and to record
unflinchingly the sublime terrors and pleasures known only to the
man of the crowd.

With the exception of "Le Soleil" and "A une mendiante rousse,"
which had appeared in the 1857 edition, Baudelaire wrote an entirely new set of poems for the first half of *Tableaux parisiens*. From
"Paysage" to "Le Squelette laboureur," they are largely poems in
which the encounter of the poet with strangers in the street plays a
central role. [2] In particular, the series made up of "Les Sept Vieillards," "Les Petites Vieilles," "Les Aveugles," and "A une passante" constitutes the climax of Baudelaire's confrontation with the
disintegratory forces of urban life. In the ever-moving crowd, the
poet who would objectify others is himself made the object of attention; seeking to fix the passer-by or *passant(e)* with his gaze, he
becomes the *passant* whom they assail.

As the poet's sense of identity crumbles, the landscape of the
Tableaux parisiens inexorably enfolds him in the unreality of its hallucinatory scenes. Paris becomes a phantasmal site where city,
street, and text begin to merge, where in the sudden meeting with
the unknown Other, heaven and hell, sexuality and textuality combine in the figure of the passing woman. For Baudelaire "holy prostitution" becomes an image of his art and of the sexual ecstasy of
merging with the crowd. Attempting to embrace rather than flee
the charms of the Babylonian Harlot, the poet pursues, "across the
chaos of living cities," the mobile image of unfulfilled desire. He
seeks to possess in poetry that which the deafening street promises, frustrates, and snatches away.

CITY FULL OF DREAMS

The title *Tableaux parisiens* suggests that the poet aims to step
back and arrest the incessant motion of the city, to capture its spe-

cial qualities in a series of sketches which, like a painter's canvas or *tableaux vivants*, will artistically freeze the life of Paris.[3] Baudelaire does in fact begin *Tableaux parisiens* with an effort to take imaginative control of the urban tumult. By avoiding direct contact with the city streets where unsettling encounters take place, the ironically entitled "Paysage" asserts the poet's ability to depict the contours of the town with impunity. The poet, dreamily gazing from his attic window over the smoky roofs of Paris, paints an urban landscape whose remoteness from him is among its chief attractions:

> Les deux mains au menton, du haut de ma mansarde,
> Je verrai l'atelier qui chante et qui bavarde;
> Les tuyaux, les clochers, ces mâts de la cité,
> Et les grands ciels qui font rêver d'éternité.

> [Chin in hands, from the height of my mansard window I will see the workshop full of singing and chatter, the chimneys, the clock towers, those masts of the city, and the great skies that make one dream of eternity.]

Here, the poet says, he will be insulated from the riot ("L'Emeute") of the city below, which will vainly beat, like rain, at his window.

The future tense identifies this as a landscape of desire, born of the need to escape or remake the disorder of the actual city. But although the poet speaks of "composing eclogues" in his garret, "Paysage" rejects the Wordsworthian belief in the countryside as the source of true happiness, moving instead directly from the distant city to a psychologically induced pastoral vision. In the concluding lines, the poet closes himself in his room during winter and there creates "le Printemps avec ma volonté" ["Springtime with my willpower"]. As he converts his burning thoughts into balmy weather ("de faire / De mes pensers brûlants une tiède atmosphère"), he enjoys an inner life that mocks and transcends the outside world with its natural seasons. The imagined city is preferable to the "real" one. As Baudelaire remarks in the *Salon de 1846*, "The first business of an artist is to substitute man for nature, and to protest against her" (II: 473).[4]

In "Paysage" the poet can order urban experience through imaginative and physical detachment, but it is the strategy of an earlier era, belonging to the original *tableau de Paris* and useless at close quarters in the turbulence of the crowd. As the second poem of *Tableaux parisiens*, "Le Soleil," shows, creating the poetry of the modern city is a struggle to be fought in the streets, not with out-

moded eclogues, but with stones from the thoroughfares themselves. Blake's "London" turns on the metaphor of walking as
marking or writing; in "Le Soleil" Baudelaire makes the correspondence literal. When he passes through shabby neighborhoods, he
says,

> Je vais m'exercer seul à ma fantasque escrime,
> Flairant dans tous les coins les hasards de la rime,
> Trébuchant sur les mots comme sur les pavés,
> Heurtant parfois des vers depuis longtemps rêvés.[5]

[I go practicing my bizarre fencing alone, scenting chance
rhymes in every corner, stumbling over words like paving
stones, striking sometimes long-dreamt-of verses.]

To pace the city, "Le Soleil" shows, is to become an active—and
embattled—sign maker. As the semiologist Michel de Certeau observes, "The act of walking is to the urban system what the act of
speaking . . . is to language."[6] The poet's walking becomes a form
of writing, forcibly hewing text out of the raw materials of the city,
"Heurtant parfois des vers depuis longtemps rêvés." Tracing a
history and inscribing a self upon the streets, walls, and random
passers-by, the poet produces a discourse of desire, quest, and loss
which records only his passage, never his present position. Thus
Baudelaire depicts the writer as practicing a "fantasque escrime,"[7]
pugnaciously endeavoring to distill eloquence from uproar and
living words from silent stones. Here is the portrait of the artist as
street-fighting man, Baudelaire's revolutionary poetry recalling his
action on the barricades in 1848.[8]

With its vision of the city as a combat zone, "Le Soleil" under-
cuts the tranquillity of "Paysage." Yet the poem ends on a note of
harmony when the sun, "like a poet," descends on the city, ennobling even the vilest things and "s'introduit en roi, sans bruit et sans
valets, / Dans tous les hôpitaux et dans tous les palais" ["he enters
like a king, without commotion or attendants, all the hospitals and
all the palaces"]. "Sans bruit" suggests that a balance has momentarily been struck between artistic struggle and urban chaos, as sun
and poet reach into the utmost corners of the city, illuminating and
transforming it, transcending the uproar of the streets.

"Le Cygne" seems designed to unsettle this equilibrium, as the
poet's encounters in the city become progressively more disturbing.[9] If the poet was able to fence Paris to a draw in "Le Soleil," in
"Le Cygne" the city is too quick for him:

Le vieux Paris n'est plus (la forme d'une ville
Change plus vite, hélas! que le coeur d'un mortel).

[Old Paris is no more (the shape of a city changes faster, alas!
than the heart of mortal man).]

The primary image of this displacement is a swan that the poet
once saw bathing in the dust among the rubble and "bric-à-brac
confus" caused by Haussmann's massive reconstruction of Paris.
Like the swan who yearns in vain for "son beau lac natal" ["his
beautiful native lake"], the poet must learn to make the best of his
estrangement, not only from the city of his youth, but also from
the grand poetic themes of the past. Henceforth the jumble of the
city itself—"palais neufs, échafaudages, blocs, / Vieux faubourgs"
["new palaces, scaffoldings, blocks of stone, old neighborhoods"]—
will become his materials and his texts, the visible signs of his longing, since "tout pour moi devient allégorie" ["everything becomes
allegory for me"].

As in "Le Soleil," the physical city and the poetry about it have
become almost interchangeable. But here the Cain-like wandering
poet, oppressed by images of old Paris, the swan, and other exiles
ranging from Andromache to a homesick African woman, can
effect no miraculous transformation of his environment or his mel-
ancholic alienation from it. The "allégorie" remains one of original,
irrecoverable loss, and the poet can only roam vanished streets,
marking that loss through his own mixture of urban memory and
desire. In "Le Cygne" modern Paris seems less real than the emotion its barren streets represent; it becomes a textual referent which
defines by negation the more durable city hidden in "le coeur d'un
mortel."

In bringing to the fore the pervasive themes of urban exile and
poetic alienation, "Le Cygne" prepares the reader for the more
abrupt shocks of "Les Sept Vieillards." The sense of dislocation
that has been building gradually in the opening poems of *Tableaux
parisiens* culminates in "Les Sept Vieillards" near the point of death
or insanity. Struggling along between the tall banks of apartment
houses, in a river of fog surging with mystery, the weary poet finds
himself suddenly overwhelmed by the spectacle of a "cortège infernal": seven malicious, hideous old men parade past him, each the
double of the last. Unnerving the poet both in its hallucinatory
quality and in its apparently hellish origin, the experience calls into
question the substantiality of the urban world around him:

Fourmillante cité, cité pleine de rêves,
Où le spectre en plein jour raccroche le passant!
Les mystères partout coulent comme des sèves
Dans les canaux étroits du colosse puissant.

[Teeming city, city full of dreams, where in broad daylight the
specter accosts the passer-by! Mysteries flow everywhere like
sap in the narrow veins of the powerful colossus.]

Even before the old men appear, aesthetic detachment and
physical laws are suspended by the city of dreams. As ghosts grab
hold of flesh and blood in broad daylight, the boundary between
the real and the preternatural vanishes, and the poet who would
watch and objectify the passing spectacle as an uninvolved *flâneur*
becomes himself the "passant." By collapsing the distance between
bemused, remote observer and picturesque, depersonalized urban
"type," Baudelaire subverts a central tenet of the *tableau de Paris*:
"You must not confuse the *flâneur* [*l'homme qui se promène*] with the
passerby [*passant*]." [10] When, near the end of the poem, the speaker
asks that the (male) reader share a "frisson fraternel" with him
because of his frightening experience, one crucial function of the
poem becomes clear: it transforms the reader too into a *passant*,
spectrally accosting him as the specter does the poet. [11] This move,
which makes the poet and reader as vulnerable to the gaze of the
Other as the Other has been to them, animates Baudelaire's poetics
of encounter in the *Tableaux parisiens*.

The verb that Baudelaire uses to describe the action of the city's
specters, *raccrocher*, is the slang term for how the prostitute "hooks"
or solicits her customer. The wandering poet thus ensnared casts
us back to the Harlot and the midnight walks of Blake and Wordsworth. That the figure of the prostitute should be tinged with
ghostliness or death is already implicit in the fatal attractions of the
Whore of Babylon, though Baudelaire will deepen the connection
between woman and death in "A une passante." And elsewhere
in his work Baudelaire explicitly associates prostitution and art:
"Qu'est-ce que l'art? Prostitution" (1: 649). Thus "Les Sept Vieillards" not only replicates the experience undergone by the poet in
the city; it also acts as prostitute to the reader's *passant*, attempting
to seduce as it reveals itself to the eye. Instead of seeking to break
out of harlotry's bonds, as do Blake and Wordsworth, Baudelaire
interweaves them with the lines of his city poetry. Even here,
when the woman is not named, her spectral mark is present. Yet if
brushes with death in the guise of the feminine Other appear to

underlie such writing, they also, like Wordsworth's blind beggar, provide continual reminders of "another world" against which to evaluate the experiences of Parisian Babylon.

For like Wordsworth's London, the city of "Les Sept Vieillards" is unreal. As T. S. Eliot, who found in this poem the source of his phrase "unreal city," wrote of Baudelaire: "Either because he cannot adjust himself to the actual world he has to reject it in favour of Heaven and Hell, or because he has the perception of Heaven and Hell he rejects the present world: both ways of putting it are tenable." [12] In either case, the infernal city is so immediately apparent to Baudelaire that the ultimate unearthliness of his urban milieu never seems in doubt. Although like Wordsworth and Eliot he views the city in terms of an opposition between New Jerusalem and Babylon, Baudelaire's "cité pleine de rêves" appears most decisively configured around the negative pole of this antithesis. Far more than Wordsworth, Baudelaire contemplates the fallen sexuality of Babylon and the related images of the Infernal City, Satan, demons, and hellish torment. Both poets are stopped in their tracks by the vision of strangers, but the authority speaking through these apparitions differs radically: if Heaven admonishes Wordsworth through the person of the beggar, Hell seeks to ensnare Baudelaire, as multiplying demons seem to emerge from hell for the express purpose of humiliating him: "A quel complot infâme étais-je donc en butte?" ["Of what infamous plot was I the victim?"].

The power of sight both conveys this villainy and determines how the *vieillards* are first met by the poet—through their eyes:

> Tout à coup, un vieillard dont les guenilles jaunes
> Imitaient la couleur de ce ciel pluvieux,
> Et dont l'aspect aurait fait pleuvoir les aumônes,
> Sans la méchanceté qui luisait dans ses yeux,
>
> M'apparut.

[All at once, an old man whose yellow rags imitated the color of the rainy sky, and whose air would have provoked showers of alms, except for the wickedness which gleamed in his eyes, appeared to me.]

The beggarly old man possesses not only a wicked look but an eye "steeped in gall" and a gaze that "puts an edge on the frosty air." When his double appears, the nefarious eye recurs as well. Baudelaire emphasizes the most disturbing aspect of the entire incident:

the poet is being looked at rather than looking. Caught without the aggressive initiative that his own bold gaze would provide, the poet is defenseless before the piercing glance of the Other.

In "Droit dans les yeux" Roland Barthes comments that because the gaze always searches for something or someone, we are likely to forget just this possibility: "In the verb 'regarder,' the frontiers of the active and the passive are uncertain." [13] Thus the poet of "Les Sept Vieillards" learns that the scales can be tipped in another's favor. Even more directly than Wordsworth, he undergoes the near-fatal stare that Barthes, citing Lacan, calls the *fascinum*, or evil eye, which arrests movement, causes impotence, and even kills. [14] Lacan does posit the idea of a life-preserving "counter-eye," associated with the phallus, which provides its own "milk" and acts as a fertilizing agent. [15] But the poet's inability to deploy metaphorically any such weapon in "Les Sept Vieillards" indicates that the evil eye has already taken effect. His poetic potency has been dried up by the gaze of the *vieillard* who himself strangely bursts with fecundating power.

The unstoppable replication of the old man's image defeats the poet's desire to still the mobility of meaning in his life, city, and text; longing to control, he is controlled, victim of a castration complex prompted by the groundless motion of signification. For to look and to desire is to recognize a wholeness that has been sundered, a lack whose fulfillment is always elsewhere. Lacan writes that "it is in so far as all human desire is based on castration that the eye assumes its virulent, aggressive function," [16] and thus the penetrating, phallic gaze which seeks to dominate discovers its own unlucky "detachment" in the play of objects and emotions beyond its power. This desire to "know," to organize and comprehend the shattering, aleatory events of urban life, is precisely the ever-frustrated, ever-engaging quest of the *Tableaux parisiens*. What makes "Les Sept Vieillards" so remarkable is the degree to which Baudelaire's poetic "I" exposes itself to the chilling, unmanning eye of the Other.

As with Wordsworth, the poet's identity appears endangered by his specular experience. Buffeted by the apparition of proliferating strangers, he seems to lose control of who and where he is: "Vainement ma raison voulait prendre la barre" ["vainly my reason tried to take the helm"]. As phantoms multiply around him they seem to pull the poet deeper into the hallucinatory dreamworld of the metropolis. The reader unavoidably follows, equally unable to distinguish whether these sights are "real," whether he too is the victim of an "infamous plot." Those readers who do not voluntarily respond with a "fraternal shiver" near the end of the poem are threatened with the revelation that there is an "air éternel" to these apparitions; the phantasmal, the poet seems to be saying, may be the most real, the most inescapable. And these phantoms both signal and embody the omnipresence of the crowd.

"The crowd," writes Walter Benjamin, "of whose existence Baudelaire is always aware, has not served as the model for any of his works, but it is imprinted on his creativity as a hidden figure." [17] In "Les Sept Vieillards" the "hidden figure" quite literally emerges with a vengeance, for the maliciously reproducing old men constitute their own unruly crowd. They frighteningly externalize the poet's overpopulated consciousness, the masses that, Benjamin contends, have "become so much a part of Baudelaire." [18] They represent not merely the poet's alienation from his surroundings—the intense Otherness that shakes him until he is "Blessé par le mystère et par l'absurdité!"—but also, paradoxically, his inability to separate himself from them.

For the final terror that the poem unfolds is, like Wordsworth's confounding at Bartholomew Fair, the sense that everything will be reduced to a monstrous, all-engulfing sameness: "Et mon âme dansait, dansait, vieille gabarre / Sans mâts, sur une mer monstrueuse et sans bords!" ["And my soul was dancing, dancing, an old lighter without masts, on a monstrous and shoreless sea!"]. As the poem concludes, the poet can find no place to land, no solid ground. Reproducing at will, the seven old men inundate the city with their unnatural, obliterating genesis; they are as dirty yellow as the sea of fog from which they emerge and which has already engulfed the street. Their proliferation casts the poet adrift on a boundless, stormy sea, transforming him into a kind of despairing Noah, without cargo or covenant. Certain that these deranging visions have come from hell ("du même enfer venu"), the poet is indeed "admonished from another world." But for what reason? No explanation is offered, save that the poem's deluged ending has apparently been conditioned by its fluid and spectral opening: "Les mystères partout coulent comme des sèves / Dans les canaux étroits du colosse puissant."

Characteristic of the slippery, unstable nature of poetic experience in the *Tableaux parisiens*, the poem's lines brim with dreams and nightmares, threatening to wash away the "facts" about the "fourmillante cité," even as they present them. As an ordered description of these disorienting events, the poem would seem to represent the poet's attempt to escape the grotesque and deathly uniformity that the self-duplicating old men bring: "Aurais-je, sans mourir, contemplé le huitième?" ["Could I, without dying, have contemplated the eighth?"]. But it also functions like the flooded street in channeling these multiplying terrors to the reader. The endless wonders that Paris offers can undo the poet as well as make him, for to be unable to differentiate impressions, or to fall victim to a paranoia that finds evil design rather than artistic opportunity in random events, may well mean poetic death. In the tempestuous street that is the poem, finding the means to navigate the waves of urban mystery becomes the poet's most pressing task.[19]

In contrast, "Les Petites Vieilles," the companion piece to "Les Sept Vieillards," is often singled out as one of Baudelaire's supreme expressions of human sympathy, "suffused by that generous, self-forgetful identification with suffering that marks the most intense city poetry of *Les Fleurs du mal*."[20] For although "Les Petites Vieilles" opens upon a similarly dreamlike landscape, the speaker's active, inquisitive role differs radically from his passive victimization in the previous poem:

> Dans les plis sinueux des vieilles capitales,
> Où tout, même l'horreur, tourne aux enchantements,
> Je guette, obéissant à mes humeurs fatales,
> Des êtres singuliers, décrépits et charmants.

[In the sinuous folds of ancient capitals, where everything, even horror, turns into enchantment. Following my fatal whims, I look out for certain singular creatures, decrepit and charming.]

Lying in wait for these bent and bizarre little old women, the poet spies their fragile bodies quivering with the din of the traffic ("Frémissant au fracas roulant des omnibus"). They now absorb the physical tremors of the city that had rolled over the poet himself ("Le faubourg secoué par les lourds tombereaux") in "Les Sept Vieillards."

But the gender-specific quality of this unusual identification should be noted. Like Wordsworth, Baudelaire discovers that the penetration of the male gaze works both ways—when turned, or returned, male upon male, it stops the masculine poet in his tracks, like an evil eye; it plunges him into doubt, uncertainty, even madness. Yet in contrast to the "méchanceté" that gleams in the eyes of the infernal *vieillards*, he finds that the *petites vieilles* have "divine

eyes," which, though they "pierce like a gimlet," are as full of wonder as those of little girls. As he turns his gaze upon the female
Other, he recovers his senses and his tongue and throws himself
into their lives with abandon: [21] "Mon coeur multiplié jouit de tous
vos vices! / Mon âme resplendit de toutes vos vertus!" ["My multi-
plied heart thrills with all your vices! My spirit is resplendent with
all your virtues!"]. [22] The verb "jouir," with its dual meaning of "enjoy" and "have an orgasm," indicates how complete this inter-
mingling is.

The seven spectral old men threaten to overwhelm the poet and
his sense of identity by the voracious sameness of their otherness.
The old women, however, are only "feeble phantoms" who inspire
pity. They reveal to the poet's gaze the reassuring otherness of
their sameness, their "familiarity" to him in the root sense. "Ruines!
ma famille!" he salutes them. Many bonds of circumstance tie the
poet to the old women (they are "blessés," or wounded by urban
life, as he is in "Les Sept Vieillards") but the strongest link is
clearly genealogical. [23] While the unnerving *vieillards* reproduce like
a "disgusting Phoenix," each one "son and father of himself," the
petites vieilles restore to this cycle the missing figure of woman.
They give birth to an order that the poet can understand, one in
which all can take their places as father, mother, son, and daughter. Although Baudelaire alludes to the old women as widows and
mothers, he finally confesses that he regards them tenderly, paternally: "Tout comme si j'étais votre père, ô merveille!" ["As if I were
your father, O wonder!"]. This assures the poet an intimate yet
commanding relation to them, confirmed in the poem's last lines:

> Où serez-vous demain, Eves octogénaires,
> Sur qui pèse la griffe effroyable de Dieu?

[Where will you be tomorrow, octogenarian Eves, upon
whom weighs the terrifying claw of God?]

As he poetically creates and paternally watches over the lives of
these elderly Eves, the poet acts as God the Father, but in viewing
them as archetypal mothers and sharers in urban exile, he is also
Cain, their son. The "claw of God" that falls upon them evokes the
mark of Cain, even as it signifies the expulsion from Eden and the
entrance into mortality stressed by the poem's earlier references to
coffins and death. Moreover, the sexual nature of the Fall and the
unique circumstances of Eve's birth give the genealogical motif a
final twist. As both Edenic Innocent and knowing Temptress, Eve

is the mother of all kinds of women, a point Baudelaire reinforces
with an allusion to the recurrent duality of whoŕe and virgin:
"Mères au coeur saignant, courtisanes ou saintes" ["mothers with
a bleeding heart, courtesans or saints"]. But Eve was born of
Adam's rib, and is thus partner to her *own* "mother" or "father."[24]
In any case, the pervasive awareness of the sexuality of these
women implicitly interjects the poet as lover into the family circle
where he has already declared himself father and son. "Where will
you be tomorrow?" he asks the old women, a final question anticipating that addressed to the vanishing woman of "A une passante"
(When will I see you . . ?"). The marks of death, "éternité," and
widowhood weigh heavily upon them all, and into the place of the
absent father or husband, the poet insinuates or thrusts himself.

BATHING IN THE CROWD

In the prose poem "Les Foules," the poet claims as his special
domain precisely this ability to penetrate the lives of others and
blend with them ecstatically:

> Il n'est pas donné à chacun de prendre un bain de multi-
> tude. . . . Le poète jouit de cet incomparable privilège, qu'il
> peut à sa guise être lui-même et autrui. Comme ces âmes er-
> rantes qui cherchent un corps, il entre, quand il veut, dans le
> personnage de chacun. Pour lui seul, tout est vacant.
>
> (I: 291)

> [Not everyone has the ability to bathe in the multitude. . . .
> The poet enjoys that incomparable privilege, that he can as he
> pleases be himself and another. Like those wandering souls
> that seek a body, he enters, when he wishes, into the charac-
> ter of each one. For him alone, everything is vacant.]

The sexual quality of this casual plunge into the Other animates
Baudelaire's various descriptions of "bathing in the crowd," further illuminating the urban encounters of the *Tableaux parisiens*.[25]
For in "Les Foules" Baudelaire transforms the notion of art as prostitution into a passionate aesthetic of the city street. This poetic
practice revels in physical and emotional intimacy, usually established through eye contact with the Other, even as it questions the
stability of personal identity in the "fourmillant tableau" of Paris:

> Ce que les hommes nomment amour est bien petit, bien re-
> streint et bien faible, comparé à cette ineffable orgie, à cette

sainte prostitution de l'âme qui se donne tout entière, poésie
et charité, à l'imprévu qui se montre, à l'inconnu qui passe.

(1: 291)

[That which men call love is very small, very narrow, and very
weak, compared to that ineffable orgy, to that holy prostitution of the soul which gives itself entirely, poetry and charity,
to the unforeseen which shows itself, to the stranger who
passes by.]

Alert to the sexuality of transient urban experience, Baudelaire elevates the fleeting contact with strangers in the crowd to the level
not only of an art but also of a religion. It is a "holy prostitution"
that he practices, a mingling of Babylon and New Jerusalem that he
praises.

This giving of oneself (which anticipates Eliot's "awful daring of
a moment's surrender") is a moment both of artistry ("poésie") and
generosity ("charité"), as the poet fills with his spirit the empty
vessels of those beggarly souls around him. While "charité" might
also signify Christian brotherly love, Baudelaire insists that this
chance conjunction of encounter and art be consummated in the
flesh:

Le promeneur solitaire et pensif tire une singulière ivresse de
cette universelle communion. Celui-là qui épouse facilement
la foule connaît des jouissances fiévreuses.

(1: 291)

[The solitary and pensive stroller draws a special intoxication
from that universal communion. He who easily marries the
crowd knows feverish ecstasies.]

The skillful *flâneur* weds the crowd as freely and appropriately as
the Lamb marries the Holy City in Revelation, a communion sealed
by the sexually charged word "jouissance."[26] As Baudelaire observes in "Fusées," "The pleasure of being in the crowd is a mysterious expression of the bliss [*jouissance*] of multiplying numbers"
(1: 649). The suggestion of the biblical injunction to be fruitful and
multiply underlines the procreative aim of the poet's immersion in
the crowd: knowing others and producing poetry are part of the
same "mysterious" activity.

This poetic fecundation occurs primarily through the agency of
the glance. "Si de certaines places paraissent lui être fermées,"
Baudelaire writes of the poet in "Les Foules," "c'est qu'*à ses yeux*

elles ne valent pas la peine d'être visitées" ["If certain spots seem
closed to him, it is only that *to his eyes* they are not worth the
trouble of being visited"] (1: 291; my emphasis). What the poet
sees, he enters. In "Les Petites Vieilles" the eyes of the old women
and of the poet who regards them are mentioned repeatedly; the
poet spies on the women with his "oeil inquiet" fixed on their tot-
tering steps. In "Les Sept Vieillards" the poet's act of looking at the
old men—or rather their gaze at him—actually begets their monstrous regeneration.

Similarly, in other street poems such as "Les Aveugles," "A une
mendiante rousse," and "A une passante," the acts of looking and
being looked at precipitate the poet's psychological response that
forms the substance of the poem. Though the eye can aggressively
glance into the hearts of others, its receptive function, its role in
internalizing the complex interplay of emotions in the crowd, is
equally important. It can even shape the landscape. The Thames of
Wordsworth and Blake has been replaced in "Les Sept Vieillards"
by rivers of fog the same yellow color as the old men's gall-steeped
eyes, and in "Les Petites Vieilles" by rivers of tears (a motif repeated in "Le Cygne"). In this way Baudelaire creates a geography
mediated by the eye in order to investigate the city and the crowd
within. As he puts it simply in his notebooks, "Moi, c'est tous;
Tous, c'est moi. Tourbillon" ["Me, that's everyone; Everyone, that's
me. Vortex"] (1: 651).[27]

Assessing the effect of this interpenetration of poet and crowd,
Benjamin notes that in the *Tableaux parisiens* the poet deliberately
sacrifices his emotional stability in order to fling himself into the
path of this ever-renewing assault on the self. Baudelaire's vulner-
ability—and success—in writing about the city thus derives from
his refusal to separate the psychic damage of his encounters from
the self that must painfully reexperience them in the process of
composition. Benjamin concludes: "Of all the experiences which
made his life what it was, Baudelaire singled out his having been
jostled by the crowd as the decisive, unique experience."[28] Baudelaire's own metaphors allow us to be more precise about this
process: the poet enters the crowd as a prostitute does her marketplace, willingly surrendering himself to the stimulating but demanding shocks, penetrations, and gazes of this "ineffable orgy."
Like the prostitute, he himself is the commodity he offers, and it is
only by sacrificing his "integrity" and wholeness that he can turn it
to his advantage.[29] He sets up a precarious economy of the "I" and

eye whose profit depends on laying himself open and giving himself away.

The poet's empathetic efforts to comprehend the lives of others may be a mark of security and maturity, as he himself seems to claim at the end of "Les Fenêtres": "And I go to bed, proud of having lived and suffered in others than myself" (1: 339). But the extremity of his will-to-multiplicity, his eagerness to throw himself into the world of the Other, also suggests vacuity, loneliness, and the need to escape himself. Thwarted desire and a desperate quest for completeness provide the impetus for the immersion, yet the process, by the poet's own account, is blissfully fulfilling. Whatever the motivation, such excursions into the Other—and the recounting of them—function as devices for the assertion of the poet's own authenticity in the midst of multitudes that may otherwise overcome him with repeated shocks, or dissolve him in a sea of anonymity.[30] The fictiveness of this assertion makes no difference to him: as the narrator remarks of the woman whose life he imagines in "Les Fenêtres," "What does it matter what might be the reality existing outside of me, so long as she has helped me to live, to feel that I am and that which I am?"—"que je suis et ce que je suis" (1: 339).[31] To write the lives of others, then, or to tell the history of encounters with them, is to bring the self into sharper focus against the blurring continuum of the crowd.

The poem that follows "Les Sept Vieillards" and "Les Petites Vieilles" exemplifies just this struggle. "Les Aveugles" transforms the poet's adversarial relation to the crowd into one of profound self-identification, while still posing disturbing questions about his ability to comprehend and exercise poetic control over his apparently helpless subject. His use here of sexuality and the gaze indicate that such scrutiny of others may well be no defense against— and may even be a revelation of—poetic insecurity and lack of insight. For as in the case of Wordsworth and the beggar, the crucial, complicating factor is that of blindness.

BLINDNESS AND BABEL

"Les Aveugles" opens with the poet contemplating the "ridiculous" and "frightful" sight of blind men darting their eyes uselessly about. What particularly disturbs him is that

> Leurs yeux, d'où la divine étincelle est partie,
> Comme s'ils regardaient au loin, restent levés

Au ciel; on ne les voit jamais vers les pavés
Pencher rêveusement leur tête appesantie.

[Their eyes, from which the divine spark has departed, remain lifted to the sky, as if they were looking at it from afar;
one never sees them bend their heavy heads dreamily over
the pavement.]

Although the blind men's eyes have lost the celestial quality that
distinguishes those of the *petites vieilles*, they still look "rêveusement" toward heaven. The poem reaches its climax when the poet
exclaims in frustration:

Vois! je me traîne aussi! mais, plus qu'eux hébété,
Je dis: Que cherchent-ils au Ciel, tous ces aveugles?

[Look! I drag myself along too! but, even more dazed than
they are, I say: What are they looking for in the sky, all these
blind men?]

In his own desire to see (comprehend) and be seen (recognized),
he insists that someone look at him dragging through the city as if
he were blind, too. It is from this distraught condition of being
sighted, yet figuratively even more in the dark than they are, that
the poet demands, "Que cherchent-ils au Ciel, tous ces aveugles?"

If Baudelaire's usual sympathy for the exile seems to change to
scorn for the blind men, it is because they in their turn parody the
poet's own search for meaning. Certainly his difference from them
is ironically underscored when he shouts "Vois!" But the admis-
sion that he is "plus qu'eux hébété" by the city, although intended
to make the blind men appear even more foolish, indicates to the
reader the deeper affinity that binds them. The poet may mock
the blind for seeking explanations from on high rather than from
the reality of the stones beneath their feet, but can these hiero-
glyphs of the city be read, any more than the poet can fathom the
actions of the blind men? Thus Baudelaire, standing ironically behind his speaker, allows the blind searches of "Les Aveugles" to
mock the poet's ability as urban *flâneur*, voyeur, and seer. A major
difference between the encounters with blind men in Wordsworth
and Baudelaire lies in the unwillingness of the latter's narrator to
admit the resemblance between them.

The metaphoric blindness that refuses to acknowledge this bond
may be a function of the city's total dedication to pleasure. The
poet characterizes the metropolis as "Eprise du plaisir jusqu'à

l'atrocité" ["smitten with pleasure even to atrocity"] and in his original version of this phrase Baudelaire brought out its sexual implications even further: "Cherchant la jouissance avec férocité" ["Ferociously looking for (sexual) ecstasy"] (1: 1022). If the "globes ténébreux" of the *aveugles* baffle the power of the poet's gaze, this poetic impotence or symbolic castration may well be related to the city's cruel and unfulfilling quest for satisfaction. As he wanders the streets looking for his own delights, his own lives to share, the poet's "daze" betrays his bewilderment in an all-too-sensory world, one that blocks the eye's access to the heaven-directed vision of the blind men.

In a characteristic effort to comprehend what the blind men's disability might mean for them, the poet imagines them crossing the city as if traversing "le noir illimité, / Ce frère du silence éternel" ["limitless night, that brother of eternal silence"]. Jumping from blindness to deafness, he then immediately invokes the most deafening thing he knows: "O cité! / . . . autour de nous tu chantes, ris et beugles" ["O City! . . . around us you sing, laugh, and bellow"]. Not seeing the city would be like not hearing the urban uproar, and the poet who questions the efficacy of his sight by comparing himself to the blind men thereby also suggests that the city is too much for his ears. Both senses, he implies, are "hébété," stunned by it. Thus, when he prefaces his final question, "Que cherchent-ils . . . ?" with the inelegant statement, "Je dis," he is saying in effect, "I speak, I announce my power as a poet to challenge that deafening noise which is analogous to the blindness that I see before me, and that I fear even in myself." For the "eternal silence" that his words temporarily displace can be none other than that of the grave, also a place of "noir illimité." By linking sight and sound, darkness and deafness, to the celestial-infernal axis of urban experience, Baudelaire refigures in the most elemental sensory terms the search for heavenly answers beyond the unreal city. And within this transcendent frame rages the ongoing battle to open a space of light and harmony amid the urban storm.

Like Wordsworth, Baudelaire is shaken by the uproar of the workaday city: there are the earthshaking tremors of traffic in "Les Sept Vieillards" and "Les Petites Vieilles," roadworks sounding like a hurricane in "Le Cygne," the bellows and howls of the street in "Les Aveugles" and "A une passante," even brass bands in "Les Petites Vieilles." The images of urban noise that pervade *Tableaux parisiens* recall the archetype of Babel. But Baudelaire's Parisian bedlam is the medium for expression, unlike London's "babel din" in *The Prelude*, which is destructive of it.[32] In place of the Wordsworthian longing for the silence of midnight streets, Baudelaire professes a Blakean willingness to listen and hear, however unsettling the experience. Yet what he hears are not harlots' curses but the tumultuous siren-song of the seductive, inspiring metropolis.[33]

In the poet's contest against urban chaos and death, the archetypes of Babylon and New Jerusalem, and their emblems of harlot and virgin, provide the metaphors by which he structures his response to the city. Baudelaire exploits what Wordsworth shuns, not only by situating himself in the thick of urban cacophony but also by undermining the oppositions of heaven and hell through a poetic prostitution and a holy matrimony with the crowd. Indeed, Baudelaire's equating of art and prostitution reveals that his thematics of encounter and the striving for poetic form can be understood to meet in another way, in the verbal and bodily "figure" of the woman passing on the street. This dynamic tension between changing city, imaged as a woman, and the poet's desire for control over "her," lies at the heart of *Tableaux parisiens*.[34]

"A UNE PASSANTE"

In "A une passante," the poet explores the unreality of urban experience through the quest for a woman whom he figures triply as an image of death, desire, and writing. Out of the noise of the roaring street, he articulates a classic vision of the search for elusive meaning in the modern city. In her transience and beauty, the *passante* plays both harlot and virgin, evoking irrecoverable loss as well as personal, poetic fulfillment. For in the press of the crowd, the poet comes to know the particularly urban shock that Benjamin has named "love at last sight"—the "farewell forever that coincides . . . with the moment of enchantment":[35]

La rue assourdissante autour de moi hurlait.
Longue, mince, en grand deuil, douleur majestueuse,
Une femme passa, d'une main fastueuse
Soulevant, balançant le feston et l'ourlet;

Agile et noble, avec sa jambe de statue.
Moi, je buvais, crispé comme un extravagant,
Dans son oeil, ciel livide où germe l'ouragan,
La douceur qui fascine et le plaisir qui tue.

Un éclair . . . puis la nuit!—Fugitive beauté
Dont le regard m'a fait soudainement renaître,
Ne te verrai-je plus que dans l'éternité?

Ailleurs, bien loin d'ici! trop tard! *jamais* peut-être!
Car j'ignore où tu fuis, tu ne sais où je vais,
O toi que j'eusse aimée, ô toi qui le savais!

[The deafening street was howling all around me. Tall, slender, in full mourning—majestic sorrow—a woman passed, lifting, swaying her garland and hem with a sumptuous hand; (she was) agile and noble, possessing the (sculpted) legs of a statue. Convulsed like a madman, I drank deep in her eye, a livid sky where the hurricane brews, the sweetness which fascinates and the pleasure which kills. A lightning flash, then night! Fugitive beauty, whose glance made me suddenly reborn, will I see you again only in eternity? Elsewhere, very far from here! too late! *never*, perhaps! For I know not where you are fleeing, and you don't know where I am going, O you whom I would have loved, O you who knew it!][36]

Out of the dissonant throng that threatens death to the poet's words, a woman emerges who promises rebirth and deliverance. She dresses in black but brings light and happiness to the poet who instantly falls in love with her. When she vanishes, the absence of her dark form plunges the poet into night. Her deep mourning proves inextricably linked to the very silence and loss that her sudden appearance seems to defer.

Both formally and thematically, "A une passante" has been carefully prepared for by "Les Aveugles."[37] Employing the same sonnet form, the earlier poem sets up a network of polarized visual and auditory images upon which this poem builds. What may at first appear as a transition from blindness in "Les Aveugles" to deafness at the start of "A une passante" turns back upon itself as the two states of sensory deprivation are interrelated. For if blindness was defined by deafness in the first poem, "eternal silence" functioning as an analogue for black night, deafness gives way to sightlessness in the second, when amid the "rue assourdissante" the poet is blinded by the sudden vision of the *passante*: "Un éclair . . . puis la nuit!"

The poet thus finds himself in the darkness inhabited by *les aveugles*, a darkness further underscored by the *passante*'s clothing. When the poet asks if he will never see her again except in eternity,

the auditory image of "silence éternel" extends into one of mortality. Similarly, her beauty, "fugitive" like herself, counterpoints
only temporarily the "ripeness for eternity" of the shriveled *petites
vieilles*. In this context, "eternity" begins to seem more like the dark
night of the grave than a heavenly reunion of the lovers.

If "death is the mother of beauty," as Wallace Stevens has written, for Baudelaire it is also the fountain of desire. The object of the
poet's yearning enters the poem marked by an earlier loss and
made beautiful by the sign of it in her dress. (She may be a widow,
her arrival here anticipated by the poet's meditation on Andromache in "Le Cygne.") Although the immediate drama of the
poem depends on the instantaneous finding and losing of someone
whom the poet "would have loved," her appearance in mourning
makes her an image of all that is *already* lost—"trop tard!" In fact,
Baudelaire originally concluded the tenth line with "m'a fait *sou-
venir* et renaître" ["made me *remember* and be reborn"] (1: 1023; my
emphasis). The poem thus becomes a reenactment of the painful
separation of death, alienation, and exile, a last desperate chance
to recover what seems to have irrevocably passed.

Given its placement in *Tableaux parisiens*, "A une passante" represents the finely poised climax of the poet's search for meaning in
the mortal world of the city streets, for it is bracketed by poems of
blindness and death whose fatality it metaphorically engages and
defers. Its promising yet punishing eye contact improves upon the
dark prospects of "Les Aveugles" even as it postpones fulfillment
until eternity. Moreover, it is the last poem of *living* encounter,
since "Le Squelette laboureur," which succeeds it, presents a joyless vision of the hereafter. If the black-clad *passante* trails the scent
of mortality along with her beauty, in "Le Squelette" the figure of
death appears to the poet unequivocally when, in a bookstall by
the Seine, he finds himself studying the engraving of a flayed
corpse, condemned for all time to harsh labor in the fields. In the
same way that the poem acts as *passant* by accosting the reader of
"Les Sept Vieillards," here the poem, like the "cadaverous" medical book which "sleeps like a mummy" in its box, confronts the
reader with a grotesque vision of the afterlife. Retrospectively, "Le
Squelette laboureur" announces just how liminal—how delicately
balanced between life and death, and the possible meanings of the
life to come—is the moment evoked in "A une passante."[38]

Death-ridden though it may be, desire fills the foreground of the
poem, for to call back the *passante* is a sign of life, the sign of a quest
to turn the fatal entropy of the urban world into a lasting poetic

order. Like Baudelaire's Painter of Modern Life, the poet here is "un *moi* insatiable du *non-moi*, qui, à chaque instant, le rend et l'exprime en images plus vivantes que la vie elle-même, toujours instable et fugitive" ["a *self* insatiable for the *non-self*, who, at each instant, renders and expresses it in images that are more alive than life itself, which is always unstable and fleeting"] (II: 692). Willing to lose his life to gain it, the poet risks "the pleasure which kills" in order to preserve the fleeting beauty that revives him. Whereas the *petites vieilles* were mocked by passing drunks, the *passante* makes the poet drunk with the murderous delight that he drinks from her eye. As the very image of urban ephemerality (Baudelaire describes both life and woman as "fugitive"), the *passante* becomes the representative object of the poet's voracious desire to still life's endless motion. Only in his poem can she achieve a permanence and reality "more alive than life itself."

The turbulent crowd is the precondition for the poem that tries to defeat its transitory nature. Yet the poet who is fixated on the crowd may have difficulty in "fixing" the position of a single one of its members. "A une passante" highlights the difficulty of achieving the poet's ideal "marriage" with the multitude, as he shifts his attention from the bliss of "number" to the individual.[39] The fact that his passion has been noticed ("ô toi qui le savais!") suggests that the poet's marriage with the *passante* has been momentarily consummated.[40] But equally, the decision to dwell "dans le fugitif" ["in the fugitive moment"] (I: 691) implies the impermanence of "holy prostitution" and the "insatiable" need to find others ("non-moi") with whom he can repeat this apparently unique experience.

In "A une mendiante rousse," the poet actually does meet, face to face, the combined figure of the prostitute and the beggar whose professions haunt the other poems of encounter. The lengthy, mannered address that the poet makes to this suppliant suggests a far more leisurely contact than the meeting with the *passante*. Yet it, too, cannot be prolonged. The poet's courtly wishes—that she have the most splendid clothes and lovers instead of her present rags and puny poet—are all he has to offer:

> Tu vas lorgnant en dessous
> Des bijoux de vingt-neuf sous
> Dont je ne puis, oh! pardon!
> Te faire don.

[You go admiring from afar cheap jewelry that I can't, forgive me! give you.]

Without the means of monetarily satisfying the young woman, he must satisfy himself with her skinny, naked beauty that peeps through the holes in her dress: "la robe par ses trous / Laisse voir la pauvreté / Et la beauté." Her economic inaccessibility, which in a sense renders the whore a virgin whom the poet longs to woo, stands out ironically against the situation in "A une passante," where the obstacle is lack of knowledge, not money.

Yet a further contrast clarifies the relative instability of these two figures. In "A une mendiante rousse," Baudelaire divests worldly Babylon of its riches, while endowing the *mendiante* with a kind of redemptive, sexualized spirituality:

> Que des noeuds mal attachés
> Dévoilent pour nos péchés
> Tes deux beaux seins, radieux
> Comme des yeux.

[May poorly fastened bows unveil for our sins your two beautiful breasts, radiant as your eyes.]

What first draws the poet to the young beggar-woman—her dress whose holes reveal both poverty and loveliness—becomes the basis for a saving, radiant, heavenly "gaze" cast by her eye-like breasts.[41] The slim *passante*, on the other hand, attracts by the elegance of her mourning attire, then by a devastating, disorienting glance. The poet's impulse to control what he desires may be forestalled by his own poverty; but in comparison to the *passante*'s shattering apparition, the *mendiante* permits him to enjoy a certain possessive equanimity: her scanty rags have granted him specular knowledge of her body. Freed by the success of his own gaze to make her body look back forgivingly, he is able to send her on her way with resignation: "Va donc, sans autre ornement / . . . / Que ta maigre nudité, / O ma beauté!" ["Go therefore, without any other ornament . . . than your skinny nudity, O my beauty!"].[42] The poet's anguish at having to relinquish contact with the *passante* is another matter. She illustrates perfectly that combination of ungraspable qualities that Baudelaire ponders in "The Painter of Modern Life": "La femme est sans doute une lumière, un regard, une invitation au bonheur, une parole quelquefois . . ." ["Woman is undoubtedly a light, a look, an invitation to happiness, a word sometimes . . ."] (II: 714). The progression of terms suggests that the textuality of the urban woman may be her most chimerical aspect. Amid the "immense dictionary" that Baudelaire calls modern

life in the same essay (II: 686), the *passante* is a word whose signification remains uncertain, evasive. Less palpable than the linguistic paving stones with which the poet contends in "Le Soleil,"
the feminine stranger functions as an unknown *parole* within the
langue of the city. She is an image of the city as text, a single signifier whose meaning is made possible by the crowd or *langue*
around her, from which she temporarily emerges.[43]

Although Baudelaire explodes the usual idea of strangeness by
instantly loving and knowing the *passante*, the concept itself is already fraught with contradiction. For we "recognize" the stranger
by the absence of all familiar marks, by her carrying within her the
negative traces of an absent community of those people whom we
do know.[44] The poet thus responds to the "familiarity" of the Other
at the same time that he notes her strangeness in the past and her
inability to be known in the future. Like an unmarked grave, even
the image of loss refuses fixity. All he knows is what each of them
knew of the other—his love and her awareness of it. Never fully
present, the *passante* signifies the differential nature of the text in
which she appears. Although she cannot help emerging as a focal
point that grounds, if just momentarily, the play of desire she sets
in motion, only rereading the poem (or writing it) will reunite her,
the poet, and what she represents.[45]

And yet the "éclair," or "lightning flash," that devastates the
poet may provide the means to this reunion. For the image conveys
not only his instantaneous comprehension of the *passante*, but also
the way in which the poem itself can have meaning for his readers.
Benjamin writes that the link between the signifier and the signified can be glimpsed only through a kind of magical semiosis
"through which, like a flash, similarity appears. For its production
by man—like its perception by him—is . . . limited to flashes. It
flits past."[46] Like the encounter with the *passante*, the speed of
reading produces a momentary fusion, between word and thing as
between man and woman, and it is similarly evasive and ephemeral. The *passante*—something or someone that "flits past"—represents an elusive consummation that both enables meaning and
suddenly wrenches it from us.

LOOKING INTO ETERNITY

The lightning flash of the *passante*'s glance returns us to Baudelaire's assertion that "la femme est sans doute une lumière, un
regard." The doubleness of her gaze, its danger and rewards, sug-

gests an even more complex specular interaction than those presented in earlier poems of the *Tableaux parisiens*. Lacan writes that
in situations where glances are exchanged, the subject sustains
himself "in a function of desire" by imagining the debilitating gaze
of the Other upon him, thus helping to render himself immobile.[47]
What seems passive—the self as object of the gaze—is really active; the self is an accomplice of the gaze. In "A une passante," the
poet complicitously accepts his own blinding, the castration of his
would-be piercing phallic glance, as the price of his momentary
jouissance with the *passante*. He defers until the poem's end the ad-
mission of her awareness of his gaze in order to feel all the more
intensely, directly, and unselfconsciously the power of her flashing
eye. Can such (willingly) lost potency ever be restored?

The question becomes one of poetic as well as sexual fertility. In
the encounter poems, the "I" who sees and is seen, and who attempts to reinscribe that look in the poem, takes a double risk. He
hazards his own personal success within the narrative he unfolds,
as well as his potency as author and shaper of the textual city that
his persona inhabits. Thus the poet's double task, in Lacanian
terms, is to deflect the fatal eye of the *fascinum*—which simultaneously engenders the play of signification and cuts off the poet's
power to control it—and yet to enjoy its identity-dissolving effects,
although not beyond the point of being able to re-enact the experience in language. The final satisfaction of poet and reader depends
on just this balanced semifrustration of narrative desire. To pursue
and name the *passante* would destroy her appeal just as surely as
prolonging her gaze would incapacitate the poet. What potency his
words possess results in no small part from his overwhelming
sense of estrangement which, as in "Le Cygne," engenders "ma
mémoire fertile." If the poem is the mark of a possibly eternal deprivation, it is also the scene of perpetual re-engagement where the
wounding gaze is never fully parried, withdrawn, or forgotten.

For this reason, the situation in "A une passante" would seem to
conform to Benjamin's definition of the aura: "Looking at someone
carries the implicit expectation that our look will be returned by the
object of our gaze. Where this expectation is met . . . there is an
experience of the aura to the fullest extent."[48] Nonetheless, Benjamin fears, the aura is endangered by the relentless proximities of
modern life: "la rue assourdissante autour de moi hurlait."[49] In
Benjamin's scenario, Baudelaire fences his way through the crowd,
struggling to maintain distance while simultaneously letting down

his guard to receive the counterthrusts that painfully produce his greatest insights. And as a result of this desperate yet creative combat, it is finally the *poet*'s aura that has been (virginally) lost in the *Tableaux parisiens*: "He indicated the price for which the sensation of the modern age may be had: the disintegration of the aura in the experience of shock. He paid dearly for consenting to this disintegration—but it is the law of his poetry." [50] Connecting the central ideas of shock and aura, Benjamin argues that to be receptive to shock is to allow one's aura, one's self-defining sense of distance and integrity, to be broken down.

The urban anonymity that makes individual city dwellers appear less individual and important, less part of the enormous community they inhabit, must inevitably diminish their auratic distance and uniqueness. Yet Benjamin appears to recognize "A une passante" as an exception: "What this sonnet communicates is simply this: Far from experiencing the crowd as an opposed, antagonistic element, this very crowd brings to the city dweller the figure that fascinates." [51] What Benjamin does not mention is how closely related are the "antagonistic" and generous elements in the crowd: the crowd gives only because, in the very same gesture, it takes away. The howling street sets up the need for unalienated contact that it will both supply and then foil, by its very motion, in a single moment. Ironically but economically, the crowd that destroys the aura can replenish it, by furnishing yet keeping at a distance "the figure that fascinates": the *passante* who is the image of the aura, more honored in her loss than in her observance. [52]

Seeking to demystify the lyric poet's relation to the modern world, Benjamin is in fact engaged in creating his own myth of the poet who surrenders all he has in order to expose the corrosive forces of the contemporary city. For the notion of the aura is itself based on a nostalgic reading of earlier eras and activities, repressing the realization that Baudelaire's words generate their own aura of de-aurification. [53] Under poetic and critical scrutiny the crowd too has developed an aura, in that it both augments and threatens the uniqueness of the object seen against its clamorous, ever-encroaching background. What Baudelaire actually describes, then, is not the aura's disintegration, but rather its reinscription in new forms, under new material conditions. Regenerating the aura in the moment of its violation, the auratic gaze returned by the poem regains for the poet the price he has paid for his own atomizing experience.

And in fact, the objects of the poet's desire, the aura and the *passante* (who images both its essence and its erosion), become themselves commodities. As Terry Eagleton remarks, "In the aura as in the imaginary, there occurs a mystifying interplay of otherness and intimacy; and this is nowhere more marked than in the commodity, which combines the allure of the mythically untouchable madonna with the instant availability of the mythical whore."[54] Virgin-madonna and Babylonian whore—the two poles of urban figuration—return as a means of defining the (male) experience in the alienating yet seductive crowd. Baudelaire's "holy prostitution" of the artist takes a final turn here, back to the cash nexus, a turn already incorporated in his view of the writer as prostituting himself in the literary marketplace. In an endless cycle of consumption and replenishment, poet and *passante*, aura and commodity offer themselves to the eye of the consumer, provoking desires whose satisfaction will ever be elsewhere.

But if Benjamin saw in the decay of the aura an opportunity to reveal how constrained by social conditions the art object is, he was reluctant to admit the possibility of its remystification through a process of commodification in which the aura, by virtue of its resilient excess, becomes not the first victim of modern capitalism, but its chief attraction, its best selling point.[55] This is the ultimate shock Baudelaire's poems deliver, that the poet's experience of the crowd can only be figured, finally, in terms of that excess, as the provocative economies of prostitution, textuality, and unreality keep the last buyer at bay through a promiscuity of signification that can never be owned. Thus the multiple meanings of the *passante* that stimulate the interpretive possessiveness of auratic theory also serve as a warning. Only by the lightning flash of the eye is the chasm illuminated and crossed, but like the *passante* herself it is a bridge that vanishes, even as it shows the way.

For Benjamin the semiotic flash works to repair, in an instant, the ancient linguistic rift of Babel. Indeed, Benjamin sees history itself as a kind of *passante* that can be apprehended only momentarily: "The true picture of the past flits by. The past can be seized only as an image which flashes up at the instant when it can be recognized and is never seen again."[56] The meeting with the *passante* therefore becomes a crisis in history, the struggle of the time-bound with the timeless, "for every image of the past that is not recognized by the present as one of its own concerns threatens to disappear irretrievably."[57] In this larger sense, the grieving, disappearing *passante* represents man's own lost past, which must be re-appropriated in the present moment, relived rather than forgotten. The *passante* thus functions as the image of both collective and individual memory, of the need to recapture what is most important, most elusive, and most poignantly missing from the very start. For Benjamin, her lightning flash is all the history we can recover, and the only way—fleetingly—we can recover it.[58]

Benjamin's effort to rescue a moment from the past leads him to assign Baudelaire's whole ethos as a writer to the experience of Parisian life during the Second Empire. Can poetic texts be thus restricted? Geoffrey Hartman argues that Benjamin's linking of the shock experience to the modern city persistently "excludes a rival perspective, the religious, that continues to haunt the features exposed by a socioeconomic interpretation."[59] In "A une passante," Hartman maintains, "something modern, a Parisian street, is made old again," as poet and *passante* reenact the Edenic drama of sexual knowledge.[60] From this vantage point, the presence of the howling city is not so much determinative as predetermined: the *passante* bringing the gift of herself through the urban uproar mourns for the initial fall of the first parents into sexuality, alienation, and death, and for the fall of the first great city, Babel, into division.

Yet the shared knowledge of the poem's lovers, in which Hartman finds a complicity stronger "than sexual possession itself,"[61] may prove to be a *felix culpa*, a fall back into the history that makes possible the poet's spiritual rebirth in the *passante*'s sight. For he finds her only because of the atomizing conditions he represents as the poem's urban genesis. The deep-rooted association of the city with sex, sin, and knowledge that Hartman adduces corroborates rather than refutes Benjamin's assertion that the poem reveals "the stigmata which life in a metropolis inflicts upon love."[62] For Hartman, the city symbolizes this situation; for Benjamin, the city provokes it. But there is no reason to say that Baudelaire does not elide the two—as Benjamin quietly does in his choice of the theologically loaded "stigmata" to describe the imprint of urban life felt in the poem. Thus "religious" and "socioeconomic" readings may not so much exclude as complement each other. The very notion of the *passante* depends upon modern social forces—large cities in which circulate an endless supply of strangers—but the poem's resonance builds equally upon the archetypal cities beyond time where all desires are ruined or redeemed.

Baudelaire recognized the divided nature of his quest. He had translated Thomas De Quincey's *Confessions*, which tell, in words and sentiments that strikingly prefigure those of "A une passante," of De Quincey's anguished search for the prostitute Anne: "If she lived, doubtless we must have been sometimes in search of each other, at the very same moment, through the mighty labyrinths of London; perhaps, even within a few feet of each other—a barrier no wider in a London street, often amounting in the end to a separation for eternity!"[63] For Baudelaire as for De Quincey, the unreal situations of the city continually force the juxtaposition of the temporal moment and eternity, deferring the simplest of contacts in this world to the timeless plane of the next.

As the way out of the dilemma of time and history ("Ne te verrai-je plus que dans l'éternité?") and yet the means of forcing one back into it ("ô toi qui le savais!"), the lightning flash of "fugitive beauté" blazes its own uneasy compromise. For in Baudelaire's aesthetic theory, "the beautiful is composed of an eternal, invariable element . . . and also a relative, contingent element" (ii: 685). Capturing this mixed vision is the duty of the Painter of Modern Life: "he is the painter of circumstance and of all that it suggests of the eternal" (ii: 687). The transient yet perpetual attraction of the *passante* makes her an elegant embodiment of this two-part amalgam of beauty. With her "jambe de statue," she appears as agelessly engaging as a piece of classical art. But the way she moves, "balançant le feston et l'ourlet," in her dark and fashionable clothing forms an equal part of her attraction.[64] The woman's special harmony consists, Baudelaire claims, "not only in her allure and the movement of her limbs, but also in her muslins, her gauzes, the vast and shimmering clouds of fabric which envelop her" (ii: 714). Pure beauty does not exist without the temporal clothing—"la mode, la morale, la passion" (ii: 685)—that is inseparable from its presence.

Just as that which supplements the woman, her dress, is seen as crucial to her unity of effect, so the dated aspects of the poem—the clothing, the language, perhaps the alexandrine meter and sonnet form—help to constitute its chief elements of attraction for the reader. What is universal here cannot be approached except through what is time-bound. Thus the flash of poetic impression melds not only word and thing but also the history and eternity of its own story. As Baudelaire postulates, all art must work this way: "The duality of art is a fatal consequence of the duality of man" (ii: 685–86).

LECHER AND WHORE

Though not strictly speaking an encounter poem, the "Epilogue" to *Spleen de Paris* can serve as summation and coda to this discussion of Baudelaire's city poetry. In this poem the poet confronts the city as a whole:

Le coeur content, je suis monté sur la montagne
D'où l'on peut contempler la ville en son ampleur,
Hôpital, lupanar, purgatoire, enfer, bagne,

Où toute énormité fleurit comme une fleur.
Tu sais bien, ô Satan, patron de ma détresse,
Que je n'allais pas là pour répandre un vain pleur;

Mais comme un vieux paillard d'une vieille maîtresse,
Je voulais m'enivrer de l'énorme catin,
Dont le charme infernal me rajeunit sans cesse.

[With happy heart I climbed the hill from which one can contemplate the city in all its abundance, hospital, brothel, purgatory, hell, prison, where every enormity flourishes like a flower. You know well, O Satan, patron of my distress, that I was not going there to shed a vain tear; but like an old debaucher of an old mistress, I wanted to make myself drunk with the enormous slut whose infernal charm rejuvenates me ceaselessly.]

The poem begins with the poet ascending a hill to view the magnitude of the city, like St. John in Revelation. But he awaits no virgin bride. The symbolic upward direction quickly reverses itself, as the poet imaginatively descends from New Jerusalem into a city that is a purgatory and even a hell, where Satan is intimately addressed as the poet's patron. This familiar otherworldly axis finds its center point midway through the poem in the third stanza, when the poet defines himself not as a repentant sinner but an old lecher enamored of his sluttish mistress. For the whore of earthly Babylon has the power, like the *passante*, to intoxicate and rejuvenate the poet, and to her he dedicates himself. The entire city has become this inconstant and unforgettable figure of desire. In the next stanza, her rumpled morning bedsheets and fine evening veils designate her varied appeal, the temporal clothing through which her eternal, "infernal" charm insinuates itself. In the contest between time and eternity, an unconstrained sexuality remains a constant feature of the poetic apprehension of the city. The poet's lustful gaze at the womanly metropolis culminates in a final confession, as "Epilogue" concludes:

> Je t'aime, ô capitale infâme! Courtisanes
> Et bandits, tels souvent vous offrez des plaisirs
> Que ne comprennent pas les vulgaires profanes.

[I love you, O infamous capital! Harlots and blackguards, often you hold out such pleasures as the vulgar masses cannot understand.]

The unheavenly climax to which the poem mounts expresses in the clearest terms Baudelaire's distinctive vision of the unreal city. Against the biblical grain exploited by Blake and Wordsworth, he has developed his own risky rapport with the fallen woman instead of her risen counterpart, preferring the promiscuous chaos of the earthly city to the ideal order of the celestial one. Immersed to the point of bliss in the crowd yet never fully united with it, he gives himself over to the secret, transitory pleasures that circulate in an underground economy of uncontrollable excess. For this reason he returns again and again, "comme un vieux paillard d'une vieille maîtresse," to the figure of the prostitute whose look always excites and whose ultimate offering is always yet to come.

Chapter Four

Walt Whitman's Urban Incarnation

Do you know what it is as you pass to be loved by strangers?
Do you know the talk of those turning eye-balls?

—"Song of the Open Road"

What language speaks through the eyes of love? Of all the poets of the city, only Whitman so readily claims to have the answer. In *Leaves of Grass*,[1] to see eye to eye is to make the world exist, and to know oneself to be inseparable from it. By recording the casual contact between strangers, Whitman tries to capture the ephemerality of the street in the substance of the poem. He boldly asserts what Wordsworth dreaded to discover, that in the city no self can be held apart from the urban whirl, and he surpasses even Baudelaire in celebrating that belief. Arguing that the observer and the objects he sees engender each other, Whitman creates a poetry of the city that attempts to transcend the limits of the text by fashioning its own physical universe. Repeatedly he affirms the existence of a bodily relationship between himself and his urban surroundings, whether persons, objects, landscapes, or even his readers. His contact with the crowd becomes the means by which he builds his own identity, his own poetic city of the self. As he proclaims in "Salut au Monde!" (1856), "I see the cities of the earth and make myself at random a part of them" (*LG* 144). Because he seeks no less than utter "adhesiveness" between poet and world, Whitman's work is animated by the desire to possess the entire city, to turn sight into speech, and the poem into a palpable entity that can, like the electric glance between strangers, bring poet and reader into physical intimacy. The "act-poem" of making love becomes the model for his communion with the reader as well as with the passer-by.

This literary, almost literal, embrace becomes the means by which he authenticates his own being in a world whose reality, he suspects, can be established only by tactile apprehension. For Whitman, the perception of an object and his sexually imagined fusion with it are almost instantaneous, but everything rests upon the tangibility of what he sees. In translating sight into signs and the "talk" of eyeballs into images of desire, he repeatedly encounters limitations of both body and text that seem to threaten that reality. In poems such as "Of the Terrible Doubt of Appearances," Whitman voices the fear that the entire basis of his apprehension, and in particular the life-giving tide of the streets, may consist of no more than "specks and flashes" or "phantoms incessant." But by striving to make his poetry unite poet, word, and world, he discovers that the glance and the poem about it may be able to reach the reader with the force of a physical embrace. Only through "the mystery of eyesight" can the poet touch and animate the passer-by, the city, the reader; and from them he demands reciprocal creation: "O city! / Behold me—incarnate me as I have incarnated you!" (*LG*, 294).

THIS NEVER-SATISFIED APPETITE

From the start of his career, Whitman was confident that he would achieve fame as an urban poet.[2] In an early poem called "Pictures," he boldly set his own portrait between those of Dante and Shakespeare, depicting himself as a laureate of the city: "—And this—whose picture is this? / Who is this, with rapid feet, curious, gay—going up and down Mannahatta, through the streets, along the shores, working his way through the crowds, observant and singing?" (*LG*, 645).[3] Although much of Whitman's early life was passed on Long Island and in the still-rural town of Brooklyn, by the time he published *Leaves of Grass* in 1855 he had spent almost fifteen years working in and around New York as a printer, journalist, and editor.[4] In the Preface to the 1856 edition he declared his affection for the city: "Every day I go among the people of Manhattan Island . . . and among the young men, to discover the spirit of them, and to refresh myself" (*LG*, 733–34). In later versions of "Song of Myself" he introduced himself as the quintessential New Yorker: "Walt Whitman, a kosmos, of Manhattan the son" (*LG*, 52). For, despite his occasional criticisms of the city, Whitman never really altered his belief that Manhattan was the center of the universe.[5]

Whitman's major city poetry belongs to the years between 1855 and 1860, during which he created the most compelling vision of the city yet seen in American poetry.[6] "Crossing Brooklyn Ferry" and the *Calamus* poems project an urban landscape thronging with crowds, permeated with longing, and insatiate for continual self-consummation. But the germ of this appetitive, sexualized city could already be found in his first great poem, "Song of Myself" (1855). With its sweeping certainties and nascent doubts, the poem anticipates the contest between appropriation and loss that underlies Whitman's entire *oeuvre*. In the sprawling catalogues of human activity that would become his trademark, Whitman seeks to encompass the city both imaginatively and sensuously. His inventory of urban life includes printers and machinists, factory girls and prostitutes, road builders, pedlars, and lunatics. The inhabitants of the city become a part of the poet who pays tribute to them, even as his identity is revealed to depend upon them: "Such as it is to be of these more or less I am" (*LG*, 44). The daily activity of the city thus produces not the strident cacophony of Babel, but the "song" of the poet who takes his identity from the multitude. As a line added later makes explicit, the poet regards himself as a harmonious textile woven of the crowd's urban multiplicity: "And of these one and all I weave the song of myself" (*LG*, 44).[7]

Yet beyond his presumption in claiming to contain multitudes within a single self, Whitman communicates what he called, in summing up *Leaves of Grass* in 1876, "this terrible, irrepressible yearning . . . this never-satisfied appetite" (*LG*, 753). The city that seems to offer him the substance he craves may, he implies, turn out to be only the echo of his own longing: "A call in the midst of the crowd, / My own voice, orotund sweeping and final" (*LG*, 76). For no city can ever be so full of life that Whitman cannot imagine wanting more of it, more from it, more than it. And this is precisely the void that must be filled by poetic assertion and literary self-completion. As he says of the relentless "procreant urge of the world," it paradoxically demands "always a knit of identity, always distinction" (*LG*, 31). The fusion between self and world is never entire, and the longing rekindles sexual, textual fires.

Thus despite Whitman's cosmic convictions and physical certitude, there remains room for literary mediation and interpretive risk:

> I know I am solid and sound,
> To me the converging objects of the universe perpetually flow,
> All are written to me, and I must get what the writing means.
>
> (*LG*, 47)

This three-line stanza, beginning with the self at the center of the universe and ending with it under pressure to decode hieroglyphic messages from an unknown author, represents concisely the ob-

stacles which Whitman will face in subsequent poems. The more
he seeks to establish his intuitive, unerring insight, his total interpenetration with the noumenal world, the more the very text that
announces his omnipresence starts to confess its anxious insufficiency. "A word of reality....materialism first and last imbueing,"[8]
he avows in 1855 (Murphy, 698). But he later revised the line to
read, "I accept Reality and dare not question it" (LG, 51), thereby
implying that he feared undoing the very authority he sought to
assert. These doubts, and the reader-oriented strategy that Whitman developed to combat them, emerge clearly by the time of the
1860 edition of *Leaves of Grass*.[9]

THE LOVE OF STRANGERS

Between writing "Song of Myself" and the *Calamus* poems,
Whitman moves from the long poem to shorter lyrics and in the
process gives a more universal cast to the inhabitants of his town
and their milieu. Forgoing detailed descriptions of his fellow citizens, as well as his mystic claims to have shared in their varied
lives, Whitman curiously achieves a more personal effect by focus-
ing instead on an archetypal moment: the poet's walk through the
heart of the city. In these poems Whitman stakes everything on the
emotional and physical contact he can establish with casual friends
and instantaneous lovers. This pursuit of perceptual certainty
through bodily knowledge not only underlies Whitman's vision of
the ideal city but also, because it inescapably involves the mediation of the text, provokes a desperate effort to recreate the material
world within the textual one.[10]
Whitman addresses his most powerful poems to unknown
strangers seen in the streets as he passes. Occupations or physical
traits do not matter; a look suffices to tell the poet all he needs to
know about the new lovers he finds wherever he turns his head—
for Whitman's supreme urban experience requires only a quick
glance, and lasts as long. The momentary eye contact between
strangers in the crowd both ignites their passion and fulfills it:

> City of orgies, walks and joys,
> City whom that I have lived and sung in your midst will one
>   day make you illustrious,
> Not the pageants of you, not your shifting tableaus, your
>   spectacles, repay me,
> Not the interminable rows of your houses, nor the ships
>   at the wharves,

Nor the processions in the streets, nor the bright windows
   with goods in them,
Nor to converse with learn'd persons, or bear my share in the
   soiree or feast;
Not those, but as I pass O Manhattan, your frequent and
   swift flash of eyes offering me love,
Offering response to my own—these repay me,
Lovers, continual lovers, only repay me.

(LG, 125–26)[11]

In "City of Orgies" (1860), Whitman fuses two of Baudelaire's
central motifs, bathing in the crowd and the "swift flash of eyes"
between strangers. In regarding the city as a vast conglomeration
of sexual desire and promise, Whitman has much in common with
the French poet, who was his close contemporary.[12] Both poets
single out eye contact with strangers on a busy street as a metaphor
for the stimulating yet disjunctive nature of modern city life. Myth-
icizing the vocation of the *flâneur*, they delight in what Baudelaire
called the "bain de multitude." But if Baudelaire discovers in each
bizarre or beautiful stranger the depths of his own estrangement
and the city's propensity to rupture human connections, Whitman seizes his satisfaction from the initial contact, ephemeral as it
may be.[13]

For Whitman, the visual interplay between poet and passers-by
embodies the essence of the city's offerings, and upon this momentary rapport all other friendships and worthwhile communities
build. Just as Baudelaire's *Tableaux parisiens* revised the popular
genre of the *tableau de Paris*, the "tableaus" that Whitman rejects in
"City of Orgies" indicate the poet's preference for rapid, repeated
encounters with his fellow citizens rather than static pictures. Processions, social occasions, and buildings seem paradoxically more
transient than the lingering intensity of glances exchanged with
sudden lovers in the streets.[14] As he writes in "Song of the Broad-
Axe" (1856), "How the floridness of the materials of cities shrivels
before a man's or woman's look!" (*LG*, 190). Casual but loving contact is the most permanent feature of the city, a city where the
word *orgies* has no negative connotations, but is rather synony-
mous with that quintessential urban activity, walking, and its result, joy. This intimacy between lasting friends and instant lovers
lies at the heart of Whitman's celebration of the city; it forms the
irreducible core of his poetic effort to convey that community to his
readers.[15]

Whitman's roving eye delights not only in what Baudelaire

called "the bliss of multiplying numbers." Sometimes it fastens on
a single member of the crowd, perhaps someone already looking
his way:

> Among the men and women the multitude,
> I perceive one picking me out by secret and divine signs,
> Acknowledging none else, not parent, wife, husband, brother,
>   child, any nearer than I am,
> Some are baffled, but that one is not—that one knows me.
>
> Ah lover and perfect equal,
> I meant that you should discover me so by faint indirections,
> And I when I meet you mean to discover you by the like in you.
>
> "Among the Multitude" (1860; *LG*, 135)

The poem is rare among Whitman's descriptions of the passing
glance, for it shows the poet being caught in the gaze of another.[16]
The divinity of the eyesight that bears a look of love, the instant
rapport between sharers of a gaze that transcends all other personal attachments—these characteristic qualities of the encounter
are now being reported by the object of scrutiny. But the poet is far
from helpless in this visual field, far from being discomfited by it;
rather, he claims credit for the situation ("I meant that you should
discover me so by faint indirections"). He salutes the onlooker as
his lover and equal, and announces that he will discover him in return. Yet there is an element of narcissism in these echoing, reciprocal actions, as though the poet were looking in a mirror. Do such
optic excursions enable the poet to reach out to others? Or is he
just gazing at his own reflection? The poem hints at the voiceless
signs by which homosexual lovers recognize each other;[17] if the
gaze penetrates to no sexual difference, the image of this "perfect
equal" may produce just such a sense of mirroring self-admiration.
The actual contact that could confer separate if similar identities
upon poet and Other is deferred beyond the poem's end: "And I
when I meet you mean to discover you by the like in you."

Many of Whitman's poems pursue the endless stream of potential lovers that the city streets provide.[18] Yet in only one does Whitman match the finely poised ambiguities of Baudelaire's "A une
passante." Though he could not have known Baudelaire's poem,
his own "To a Stranger," written the same year (1860), provides an
uncannily direct reply:

> Passing stranger! you do not know how longingly I look upon
>   you,

You must be he I was seeking, or she I was seeking, (it comes
    to me as of a dream,)
I have somewhere surely lived a life of joy with you,
All is recall'd as we flit by each other, fluid, affectionate,
    chaste, matured,
You grew up with me, were a boy with me or a girl with me,
I ate with you and slept with you, your body has become not
    yours only nor left my body mine only,
You give me pleasure of your eyes, face, flesh, as we pass,
    you take of my beard, breast, hands, in return,
I am not to speak to you, I am to think of you when I sit alone
    or wake at night alone,
I am to wait, I do not doubt I am to meet you again,
I am to see to it that I do not lose you.

                                      (*LG*, 127)

Here the city, the presence of the crowd, and the eye contact between poet and stranger are so much a part of the moment that
they are assumed and never mentioned. In contrast to "A une passante," where no words are possible in the deafening street, Whitman asserts that there is no need for words: "I am not to speak to
you." Sight alone is enough, enabling the poet "to see to it" by his
act of poetry and memory that the moment will not be lost. While
Baudelaire cries hopelessly, "Fugitive beauté . . . ne te verrai-je
que dans l'éternité?" Whitman tells his *passante*, "I do not doubt I
am to meet you again." And yet, Whitman's stranger does *not*
know the depth of his longing, while Baudelaire is convinced that
the *passante does* know how the poet feels about her. Baudelaire's
sense of loss is all the more poignant for what he and the *passante*
have shared, once and finally; Whitman's satisfaction lies rather in
the prospect ("I am to think of you when I sit alone or wake at
night alone") and in the poem's memorializing of that possibility.
Both poets make the poem a site of possession, but Baudelaire
commemorates the past, while Whitman looks to the future.
    Perhaps it is this anticipation that lends Whitman's encounter,
for all its immediacy, an air of unreality, a quality of wish fulfillment:

You must be he I was seeking, or she I was seeking, (it comes
    to me as of a dream,)
I have somewhere surely lived a life of joy with you,
All is recall'd as we flit by each other, fluid, affectionate,
    chaste, matured.

"As of a dream" the two halves of the fantasy, the yearner and the yearned for, come together in a hazy cloud of euphoria. In comparison to the particularized object of Baudelaire's poem—dressed in mourning, swinging her skirts as she walks, displaying a finely sculpted leg—Whitman's object of desire is discreetly sexless and undefined. The stranger may well be, in fact, like a brother or sister ("You grew up with me, were a boy with me or a girl with me"), further complicating the nature of the poet's longing.

Yet his "chaste" feelings can hardly be platonic. In three other Calamus poems, "Behold This Swarthy Face" (LG, 126), "A Glimpse" (LG, 131), and "What Think You I Take My Pen in Hand" (LG, 133), Whitman's urban lovers do make physical contact, sharing kisses, holding hands, and parting with loving hugs in the midst of a crowd. "To a Stranger" strives to achieve that established relationship for its participants as well: the intensity of the poet's conviction that the stranger is not really strange ("I ate with you and slept with you") attempts to preclude the unfulfilled desire it expresses. Not only do the eyes and imagination find their consummation in the instant of crossing, but also does the body: "You give me pleasure of your eyes, face, flesh, as we pass, you take of my beard, breast, hands, in return." Here Whitman turns "the talk of the turning eye-balls" into a mutual offering, a transformation of self into Other: "your body has become not yours only nor left my body mine only;" it is, in William Carlos Williams' phrase, an "interpenetration, both ways." Possessing the body of the stranger in both the past and present moment, the poet announces his belief that the future will be his as well.

What initially appears as an instant, untroubled rapport with the anonymous Other becomes by the end of the lyric a psychic drama of desire as fraught with tension and contradiction as Baudelaire's sonnet. Even Whitman's enjoyment of the transience of the event seems contravened by his claim that he has already had "pleasure" of the stranger, and intends to do so again. The poet's quest for knowledge of the Other extends into both an intimately shared past and an anxious, wakeful future, leaving little room for the casual, present-tense encounter that the poem at first seems to represent. It is thus not so much a question of his stilling the stranger's motion as of their moving together in unison, and through all stages of life. Yet because all this passing, parallelism, and parting are mediated for us by the poet's aggressive omniscience, it is finally as difficult to believe that he has possessed the secrets of the stranger's life and body as it is to doubt it. The poem turns its gaze back on the reader, and only its first line seems certain: "you do not know how longingly I look upon you."

The possibility that you or I might be the passing stranger whom Whitman addresses attests to the evident power yet indeterminate depth of the poet's desire, his quest to possess even the crowd of his readers. If the reader is Whitman's *passant(e)*, then the text is the fluid city in which they temporarily meet. The very indefiniteness of the "you" enables the poet to pull the reader into his textual crowd, swelling the ranks of the admirers he rejoices in having around him. But while Whitman's direct appeal to his unnamed auditor brings the reader closer to him as he strolls his poetic Mannahatta, another, complementary trajectory emerges: the poet is trying to break out of the text and into the city of his audience. As he says explicitly in another poem of 1860, "I spring from the pages into your arms" ("So Long!" *LG*, 505).[19]

Whitman usually takes care not to give this impulse too much rein, for it dangerously suggests that the poem may be more an inscription of emptiness than a cry of ecstatic repletion. Instead of containing multitudes, the poet may be exposed as a vast hollowness that craves them. The significantly titled "Poem of Joys" (1860) demonstrates not only how closely Whitman associates the urban throng with sexual desire but also how painfully unrequited he sometimes feels his love to be:

> O for the girl, my mate! O for happiness with my mate!
> O the young man as I pass! O I am sick after the friendship of
>   him who, I fear, is indifferent to me.
>
> O the streets of cities!
> The flitting faces—the expressions, eyes, feet, costumes!
>   O I cannot tell how welcome they are to me;
> O of men—of women toward me as I pass—The memory
>   of only one look—the boy lingering and waiting.
>
> (Pearce, 261)[20]

The familiar "joys" of streets, faces, eyes, all in constant flux, are present; but they are compromised. Even more strongly than "To a Stranger," the passage confesses the ache amidst the excitement, the "sick" yearning for more satisfaction, more recognition, more love than "only one look" can provide. Enticing faces flit past at the boundary of the self, marking the lingering pain of their distance as well as the spontaneous pleasure of their brief proximity. In such moments Whitman, like Baudelaire, appears to depend upon the crowd for his own self-animation, the ardent vitality of his life ignited by the eyes and bodies of others around him and by the memory of unnamed possibility: "the boy lingering and waiting." In later versions of the poem, Whitman canceled these lines, perhaps because they gave away too much, not just about his sexual preferences, but about his yearning to be noticed by a city that did not always heed his advances. Here he has no "continual lovers" who "repay" him, as in "City of Orgies," nor can he maintain the emotional balance and mirrorlike coolness of "Among the Multitude."

But this is not his typical stance. Whitman prefers to stress his delight in belonging to the crowd, omnivorously devouring it. His awareness that others are as lonely as he is permits him to discover a paradoxical emotional unity in the very isolation that prevents their embrace.[21] A line from "Poem of Joys" celebrates that comforting revelation: "O the joy of that vast elemental sympathy which only the human soul is capable of generating and emitting in steady and limitless floods" (LG, 177). Such sentiments enable him to take a Baudelairean bath of multitude in the torrents of "elemental sympathy" that his own sense of human community produces. This belief is what justifies the earlier hyperbolic fantasies of "Song of Myself":

> My lovers suffocate me,
> Crowding my lips, thick in the pores of my skin,
> Jostling me through streets and public halls, coming naked
>   to me at night.
>
> (LG, 81)

The suffocating, jostling proximity that for Wordsworth obliterates the self and its creativity provides Whitman with the very means of poetic life. This erotic bravado, publicly oversatisfying the private desires that prompt it, strikes the elaborate balance between sexual urges and textual gratification upon which Whitman's best poetry relies. It is almost inevitable, then, that his ideal city should be built around the free and open love of its citizens, easing the chronic tension between eye and Other.

IDEAL CITIES

In the 1876 Preface to Leaves of Grass, Whitman retrospectively asserted that his poetic intentions had been utopian, that his poems were meant to lay the basis for a sexually healthy—and therefore vibrant—body politic:

> to make a type-portrait for living . . . joyful and potent, and modern and free . . . male and female, through the long future—has been, I say, my general object. . . . I also sent out LEAVES OF GRASS to arouse and set flowing in men's and women's hearts . . . endless streams of living, pulsating love and friendship.
>
> (LG, 752–53)

A number of poems published in 1860 are specifically dedicated to representing Whitman's ideal urban society. He crystallizes his vision of universal love in the short poem, "I Dream'd in a Dream":

> I dream'd in a dream I saw a city invincible to the attacks
>   of the whole of the rest of the earth,
> I dream'd that was the new city of Friends,
> Nothing was greater there than the quality of robust love,
>   it led the rest,
> It was seen every hour in the actions of the men of that city,
> And in all their looks and words.
>
> (LG, 133)

In this new, unconquerable city of brotherly love, the ephemeral looks and words of lovers have become the tangible proof of the city's greatness. Whitman's dream permits the repressed sexuality of the present to become the future city's central life force.[22]

In contrast to the poems about personal interaction in the contemporary city, those about the visionary cities of the future contain no second-person address, no direct appeal to readers and lovers. Rather, they take that close relationship as already established, and make it the basis for the ideal cities yet to come. "I will make the continent indissoluble," Whitman proclaims:

> I will make inseparable cities with their arms about each
>   other's necks,
>   By the love of comrades,
>   By the manly love of comrades.
>
>   "For You O Democracy" (1860; LG, 117)[23]

In this amorously utopian version of manifest destiny, the poet imagines cities rapturously embracing, for the happy contact by which individual citizens participate in the human community ought to guide their *polis* as well. Similarly, in "I Hear It was

Charged against Me" (1860), the poet claims that he is "neither for
nor against institutions" but that he "will establish in the Mannahatta and in every city of these States" what he calls "the institution of the dear love of comrades" (*LG*, 128). Poems like these make
it clear that Whitman is not proposing to restructure urban political
life, but is rather, like Blake or Lawrence, offering a vision of how
society could begin to reshape itself from the individual outward.[24]

Ultimately Whitman's city emerges as a kind of prelapsarian
Eden where hearty, unselfconscious citizens can love without inhi-
bition. Innocent of Adam's fall into sexual guilt and of Babel's fall
into urban alienation, the men and women of these cities live
openly and communicate easily. In "Ages and Ages Returning
at Intervals" (1860), the poet presents himself as primal, fertile,
unconstrained:

> I, chanter of Adamic songs,
> Through the new garden the West, the great cities calling,
> ·
> Bathing myself, bathing my songs in Sex,
> Offspring of my loins.
>
> (*LG*, 107)

In an era when his literary contemporaries frequently saw the city
as a rising Babylon,[25] Whitman becomes bard of a sexually regenerated New Jerusalem. To recreate natural paradise in utopian urban
form has been an American dream since the Puritans sought to
build "a city upon a hill," but Whitman is unique in insisting on
"bathing my songs in Sex" as a means of doing so.

Like the author of Revelation, Whitman replants the original
garden of Eden in a final, harmonious city.[26] But his conception of
the ideal city, sexual though it may be, does not depend on St.
John's opposition of spirit and flesh—the virgin bride reflecting the
purity of the city and the shameless whore of sensuous satisfaction forever excluded from it. Revelation refuses to forget the Fall;
Whitman, however, proposes a far more radical community that
would repair the rift by sanctifying all sexual behavior. His ideal
city has neither a jeweled wall for protection nor a radiant center to
be worshiped; there is only a sharing of love that already exists,[27]
and everyone in the "new city of Friends" participates in this democratic process.

For this reason the Whore of Babylon has no symbolic role to
play in Whitman's poetry, although the individual fallen woman
appears with some regularity. In "To a Common Prostitute" (1860),

he casually greets her: "be at ease with me—I am Walt Whitman, liberal and lusty as Nature," and he brings her into his network of visual exchange: "I salute you with a significant look that you do not forget me" (LG, 387). While Baudelaire admits his fatal weakness for the temptations of the prostitute, Whitman treats her as only one more urban unfortunate through whom he can test his powers of empathy. "I walk with delinquents with passionate love," he says in "You Felons on Trial in Courts" (1860); "I feel I am of them—I belong to those convicts and prostitutes myself, / And henceforth I will not deny them—for how can I deny myself?" (LG, 386). Or as he proposes in "Native Moments" (1860): "O you shunn'd persons . . . I will be your poet" (LG, 109).

But in one poem, "The City Dead-House" (1867), Whitman does regard the woman of the streets in the larger framework of the otherworldly city. Compassionately musing on the body of a dead prostitute brought into the morgue, he refuses to pit this originally "divine woman" against the virgin purity of the New Jerusalem, but instead envisions her as still partaking of it. The poet values that "immortal house" of her body more than "all the old high-spired cathedrals" (LG, 367). Even so, her ravaged form has become the wrecked "tenement of a soul—itself a soul," symbol of urban dereliction and despair. It is "dead, dead, dead," not from a narrowly defined moral failing but because the real curse of Babylon lies in the absence of love that encourages prostitution in the first place. The poet pays homage to his subject's divinity here in the present city because both her profession and her sufferings will have ceased in the new garden to come.

And yet Whitman also contends that there is no need to wait, for his ideal city does in a sense already exist. He calls it "Mannahatta." In a poem devoted to exploring the resonances of the word, he reveals that the name evokes the archetypal city imagined in his most joyous poems, actualizing the landscape even as it is spoken:[28]

I was asking for something specific and perfect for my city,
Whereupon lo! upsprang the aboriginal name.

Now I see what there is in a name, a word, liquid, sane,
     unruly, musical, self-sufficient,
I see that the word of my city is that word from of old,
Because I see that word nested in nests of water-bays, superb,
Rich, hemm'd thick all around with sailships and steamships,
     an island sixteen miles long, solid-founded,

Numberless crowded streets, high growths of iron, slender,
   strong, light, splendidly uprising toward clear skies,
· ·
The mechanics of the city, the masters, well-form'd, beautiful-
   faced, looking you straight in the eyes,
Trottoirs throng'd, vehicles, Broadway, the women, the shops
   and shows,
A million people—manners free and superb—open voices—
   hospitality—the most courageous and friendly young men,
City of hurried and sparkling waters! city of spires and masts!
City nested in bays! my city!

                                   "Mannahatta" (1860; LG, 474–75)[29]

In "Mannahatta" the primal garden of the past, the thrilling crowds
of the present, and the loving harmony of the future have already
merged. In contrast to the unreal city of New Jerusalem, the actual
city of New York, imaginatively transformed into "Mannahatta,"
belongs to the here and now and can be physically enjoyed as an
everyday reality—the "simple produce of the common day," in
Wordsworth's phrase. The city encapsulates itself in a word, but
just as the poet perceives in its letters the "high growths of iron"
rearing up and the sparkling bays nesting them, so the word
becomes the physical, sexual being, rising up before the eyes—
spoken, as in Genesis, into existence. The "beautiful-faced" inhabitants "looking you straight in the eyes" complete this landscape of
consummation, marrying observer to scene through the intense
pleasure of a flashing glance.

   Whitman does indeed "see what there is in a name," for he
never uses the words New York in his poetry, always Manhattan or
Mannahatta. As notes he made for a lecture indicate, he wished to
distinguish between the literary city, a city of imagination linked in
name and spirit to the pure beginnings of the island (a place of
"swift tides and sparkling waters"), and the contemporary, often
inegalitarian center of American commerce. If Mannahatta is "musi-
cal, self-sufficient," capable of expressing all that he loved about
his city, New York regrettably commemorates the name of the "ty-
rant" Duke of York who later became James II. The one name represents the best to which free and democratic citizens might aspire,
the other implies moral servitude and misuse of the city's natural
abundance.[30]

   In its poetic incarnation as Mannahatta, then, Whitman's city
appears less a mundane New York than a sexualized, modernized
New Jerusalem. The components of the actual city—buildings,

crowds, traffic, shipping, the routine yet memorable gestures of countless individuals—give Whitman's poetry its tremendous energy and specificity. At the same time, the city's potential and excitement, its vibrant melding of natural beauty and man-made wonders, lend it the mythic quality that Whitman declares his poems will perpetuate. The conflicting concerns of mid-nineteenth-century New York as a political and economic entity are rarely permitted to intrude, for the tension in Whitman's city poetry lies elsewhere. In striking contrast to other writers of the city, Whitman's struggle is not so much to create the ideal city as to preserve it.

THE TERRIBLE DOUBT OF APPEARANCES

In *Leaves of Grass*, Whitman seems to entertain two major fears that threaten his passionate glances and perfect communities. He worries that the material world in which he delights may turn out to be unreal, and that the self, defined though the body, may lack substance. A distressing sense of unreality haunts Whitman, as it does Blake, Wordsworth, and Baudelaire. Yet it derives not from an alienated perception of everyday urban life but from the fear that what appears so radiantly to constitute it may in fact be an illusion. If Whitman's world is built on an immediate sensuous apprehension capable in its most rapturous moments of ecstatically fusing poet and crowd, reader and city, then what if the perception itself is unreliable? Whitman vacillates between a tremendous confidence in the power of his poetry to answer his deepest emotional and physical needs, and the lurking doubt that even the material world is unreal—making it impossible for him to actualize his text through an appeal to the presence of the city or the body of the reader.

Critics have maintained that Whitman's confident mastery and intense love of the city are increasingly undercut, in successive editions of *Leaves of Grass*, by the recalcitrance of the real world, as New York's materialism distanced it further and further from the democratic utopia projected in his writing.[31] This is an important issue in Whitman's biography and overall development. But his poems themselves reveal a deeper, more fundamental concern with the relation of the poet's own body to the city, and his ability to authenticate them both through the alleged corporality of the text. To satisfy himself, he must transform "calamus" from a literary into a literal phallus, and engender the physical city in his fertile words.[32]

The poems "Not Heaving from my Ribb'd Breast Only" and "Of the Terrible Doubt of Appearances" appeared back to back in the 1860 edition, and the transition between them exemplifies the divorce Whitman sensed between body and text, desire and fulfillment. The first concludes boldly by demanding whether the "pulse of my life" has any greater manifestation "than in these songs" (*LG*, 119). And yet the second poem opens by speaking "Of the terrible doubt of appearances, / Of the uncertainty after all, that we may be deluded." And once speculation starts, everything is called into question:

> May-be the things I perceive, the animals, plants, men, hills,
>   shining and flowing waters,
> The skies of day and night, colors, densities, forms, may-be
>   these are (as doubtless they are) only apparitions, and the
>   real something has yet to be known,
> . . . .
> May-be seeming to me what they are (as doubtless they
>   indeed but seem) as from my present point of view, and
>   might prove (as of course they would) nought of what they
>   appear, or nought anyhow, from entirely changed
>   points of view.
>
>   (*LG*, 120)[33]

As this increasingly convoluted excursion into relativism and phenomenology indicates, Whitman's doubts were far clearer to him than the answers he could come up with.[34] But he eases his mind and salvages the poem by a characteristic recourse to what he feels is most certain in his world: "To me these and the like of these are curiously answer'd by my lovers, my dear friends." The answer is "curious" because insufficient—"I cannot answer the question of appearances," the poet admits—but it nonetheless provides tangible evidence that world, body, and self are secure: "He ahold of my hand has completely satisfied me" (*LG*, 120). Dr. Johnson tried to refute Bishop Berkeley by rebounding from a stone, and in *In Memoriam*, Tennyson resolved a decade of religious doubt by feeling the imagined pressure of Arthur Hallam's hand. Whitman anchors *his* world by holding tight to his "dear friends."[35]

One of Whitman's earliest poems, "There Was a Child Went Forth" (1855), explores the poet's insecurity less abstractly, connecting it to the flux of urban life. The poem maintains that each self develops from its initial moments of consciousness through a kind of visual osmosis:

There was a child went forth every day,
And the first object he look'd upon, that object he became,
And that object became part of him for the day or a certain
    part of the day,
Or for many years or stretching cycles of years.

(LG, 364)[36]

Differing from most writers and psychologists, Whitman imagines
the child-object union as continuing into adulthood and into poetry. But in the poem's last stanza several disturbing questions
intrude:

> the sense of what is real, the thought
>   if after all it should prove unreal,
> The doubts of day-time and the doubts of night-time, the
>   curious whether and how,
> Whether that which appears so is so, or is it all flashes and
>   specks?
> Men and women crowding fast in the streets, if they are not
>   flashes and specks what are they?

(LG, 365)

The lines evoke the ghost-like processions in the unreal cities of
Baudelaire and Eliot, and give urban form to Emerson's observation, "All things swim and glitter. Our life is not so much threatened as our perception."[37] Here the crowd that usually offers Whitman a means of self-definition seems instead to produce that sense
of disorientation Wordsworth experienced in London. The human
"flashes and specks" also anticipate a passage in *Democratic Vistas*
(1871) where, after customary praise of "the splendor, picturesque-
ness, and oceanic amplitude and rush of . . . great cities," Whitman suddenly demands: "Confess that to severe eyes, using the
moral microscope upon humanity, a sort of dry and flat Sahara appears, these cities, crowded with petty grotesques, malformations,
phantoms, playing meaningless antics."[38] The older Whitman
would vainly call upon the power of literature to dispel these
ghosts, but in "There Was a Child" he attempts to repair his loss of
perceptual faith by an appeal to solid actuality: "The streets themselves and the façades of houses, and goods in the windows, /
Vehicles, teams, the heavy-plank'd wharves" (*LG*, 365). Yet in this
context of uncertainty the very nominative qualities that generally
make his poems so concrete seem to invoke a phantom world that

dissolves the mortar of their urban substance. Once the questions have been asked, a kind of Cartesian enchantment makes even the most acute sensations suspect.

Whitman's poetic dominance of the city he describes depends upon an immense will-to-power over a multiplicity of urban lives and entities. In a sense, he continually operates in what Jonathan Raban has called the "soft city" of the imagination, a landscape created and controlled by individual perceptions rather than the exigencies of economics or the built environment.[39] In "Of Him I Love Day and Night" (1860), the mere dream of a friend's death makes "Chicago, Boston, Philadelphia, the Mannahatta . . . as full of the dead as of the living" (LG, 446). And not only the condition of cities but the value and coherence of the world itself depend upon the mental attitude of its beholder:

> I swear the earth shall surely be complete to him or her who
>   shall be complete,
> The earth remains jagged and broken only to him or her who
>   remains jagged and broken.
>
> "A Song of the Rolling Earth" (1856; LG, 223)

In comparison to the many modern poets, including Baudelaire, Eliot, and Williams, who see the world as "jagged and broken," Whitman often seems to envision a primeval wholeness. But he has difficulty preserving that unity against internal doubts and swarming multitudes. The spectral quality of the crowd haunts him even in the exuberant "Song of the Open Road" (1860). The repression and duplicity that every city contains give birth to "Another self, a duplicate of every one, skulking and hiding it goes,[40] / Formless and wordless through the streets of the cities." The result is "hell under the skull-bones" (LG, 158). The end of the poem offers the same wishful response to these fears as "Terrible Doubt": "Camerado, I give you my hand!" (LG, 159).[41]

But how are we to take it? The texts that should furnish Whitman with proof of his own substantiality are themselves part of the problem. In "Song of Myself" he is already denigrating the second-hand experiences of "the spectres in books" (LG, 30), and in later poems, he openly addresses the perplexed antagonism between poet, city, and text. Asking himself what good are "cities fill'd with the foolish," or "the plodding and sordid crowds I see around me," the poet responds:

Answer.
That you are here—that life exists and identity,

That the powerful play goes on, and you may contribute
a verse.

"O me! O life!" (1865; LG, 272)

This oracle restates a central tenet of Whitman's poetry, that life, sheer physical presence ("you are here") presumes identity. But he does not make the leap which his most confident poems would lead us to expect: that identity can be achieved through writing, by "contributing a verse." Rather, he interposes a middle layer of drama and illusion. Conscious of the artificiality of "the powerful play" of life, the poet can only add his lines to its all-encompassing script. There appears to be an irrecoverable distance between city and text, body and writing, which Whitman's cosmic scenario labors heroically to conceal, transcend, or even obliterate.

The desire to break out of the page and into the world—or to capture reality and possess it substantively within the poem—obsesses Whitman from the very beginning of his career. In "Song of Myself" he writes:

> My words are words of a questioning, and to indicate reality;
> This printed and bound book....but the printer and the
>   printing-office boy?
>
> . . . .
>
> The well-taken photographs....but your wife or friend close
>   and solid in your arms?

(1855; Murphy, 726)

How to transform the "well-taken photographs" of each of his objects into something "solid" in order to resolve "questioning" into "reality" becomes Whitman's most pressing task. We must possess the printer—appropriately, in the case of the poem's first edition, Whitman himself—as well as the book. The poet must combine the moments of seeing, writing, and reading into a palpable experience, always available to the grasp.[42]

His strategy is compellingly simple and literarily impossible: to demonstrate the reality of the body and the city, and the imminence of the city of friends, through the immediate, solid, sexually tactile presence of the poem. He must equal the achievement Emerson attributed to Montaigne—"Cut these words, and they would bleed; they are vascular and alive."[43] The city and the poem must become as real to us as our own bodies, a conclusion Whitman states decisively in "Kosmos" (1860):

> Who, out of the theory of the earth and of his or her body
> understands by subtle analogies all other theories,
> The theory of a city, a poem. . . .

(LG, 392–93)

This belief that city, body, and poem share the same substance informs all of Whitman's efforts to prevent his Mannahatta from dematerializing into "specks and flashes." By presenting the text as an extension of his body, as a physically charged intermediary between the reader's and his own, Whitman tries to minimize its role as abstract communication even as he freights it with the flesh of sender and receiver. As he made clear in the Preface to *Leaves of Grass*, 1856, "the body of a man or woman [is] the main matter . . . the body is to be expressed, and sex is" (*LG*, 739).[44]

And thus the poet longs for "the real poems (what we call poems being merely pictures)" (*LG*, 103). The reader soon learns that such poems are meant to be as tactile and provocative as the naked body:

> This poem drooping shy and unseen that I always carry, and
> that all men carry
>
> . . . .
>
> Arms and hands of love, lips of love, phallic thumb of love.

"Spontaneous Me" (1856; LG, 103–4)

The entire masculine thrust and seminal force of Whitman's poetry about the city strive to overcome the body-text division. The aim is no less than to *embody* the text through the power of "Beautiful dripping fragments. . . . The oath of procreation I have sworn" (*LG*, 103, 105). When the unseen phallus becomes the self-actualizing poem, the stated purpose of *Leaves of Grass*, "to put *a Person* . . . freely, fully and truly on record" (*LG*, 573–74), takes on a literal dimension. It also lends a special urgency to those wishful, triumphant words from "So Long" (1860): "this is no book, / Who touches this touches a man" (*LG*, 505).

THE SOLIDITY OF THE TEXT

If Whitman counters the suspected unreality of self and city by asserting the physical and sexual presence of the text, he resists in principle the idea of the self-sufficient, modernist poem-as-object. His book is not a book, he claims, even amid the desperate self-referentiality of his writing. Fighting the limitations of language,

the poet seeks his own way out of this impasse by insisting that his
pages are more than just print, and yet, paradoxically, that within
his printed lines the corporeal world can be created and contained.
"Starting from Paumanok" (1860) boldly employs Whitman's strategy of asserting the solidity of his subject while calling attention to
the textuality of his medium:

> See, steamers steaming through my poems,
> See, in my poems immigrants continually coming
>   and landing
>
> · · · · · · · · · · · · · · · · · · ·
>
> See, in my poems, cities, solid, vast, inland, with paved
>   streets, with iron and stone edifices, ceaseless vehicles,
>   and commerce
>
> · · · · · · · · · · · · · · · · · · ·
>
> See, lounging through the shops and fields of the States,
>   me well-belov'd, close-held by day and night.
>
> (LG, 27)

As he describes the populating and building of cities, Whitman
commands the reader to participate in this urban construction by
visualizing the presence of immigrants and pavements, lovers and
poets. "Speech is the twin of my vision," Whitman remarks in
"Song of Myself" (LG, 55), and the task of the poem is to animate
them both, the one authenticating the other. The poet may opti-
mistically claim at the same time that "With the twirl of my tongue
I encompass worlds" (LG, 55), but the eyes are at least as important, not only recording impressions and speaking silently to
strangers, but opening the text to the reader. Hence the stern in-
junctions to "See!"—for all the talk of embracing, genuine contact
with the reader is possible only through sight.

The solidity of body and city in his poems, Whitman recognizes,
depends on the reader's receptivity and willingness to share the insights which the poem records. More perhaps than any other poet,
Whitman deliberately invites the participation of the audience in
his work, as the inordinate number of imperatives and apostro-
phes attests. He exhorts us and coaches us, hoping to transmit successfully the bodily sensations encoded in the text. For it is only by
the reader's involvement, only by our feeling the effect of Whitman's lines upon our own bodies, that words and body meet again.
And when the poet senses that the connection has been made, as
in "Starting from Paumanok," he marvels at the world which his
words have brought into being:

This then is life,
Here is what has come to the surface after so many throes
   and convulsions.

How curious! how real!

(LG, 16)

At its fullest pitch Whitman's poetry radiates a resounding conviction of its own solidity, of its ability to give the reader the physical world, not merely words about it. In "Song of the Open Road"
(1856), the accumulated force of the bold declarative sentences
gives the written city a personality and substantiality not to be
denied:

You flagg'd walks of the cities! you strong curbs at the edges!
You ferries! you planks and posts of wharves! you
   timber-lined sides! you distant ships!
You rows of houses! you window-pierc'd façades! you roofs!
You porches and entrances! you copings and iron guards!
You windows whose transparent shells might expose
   so much!
You doors and ascending steps! you arches!
You gray stones of interminable pavements! you trodden
   crossings!
From all that has touch'd you I believe you have imparted to
   yourselves, and now would impart the same secretly
   to me,
From the living and the dead you have peopled your
   impassive surfaces, and the spirits thereof would be
   evident and amicable with me.

(LG, 150)[45]

"Latent with unseen existences," the city's inanimate objects seem
to offer him their surfaces and souls, just as he offers himself to
them. In their composite existence, saturated by the city, Whitman
discovers a bond "amicable" with his own all-encompassing nature. Here he salutes the material world that has helped give him
his own being and identity—a situation that could be summarized
in the phrase "Objects gross and the unseen soul are one" (LG,
216). Impregnated with secret meanings by constant use, the apparently opaque materials of the city are actually "transparent
shells" ready to expose the rich inner life beneath the impassive
surface.

Like Montaigne, Whitman shows that "composing a self" involves the individual *and* the world. Indeed, one might call Whitman a mystic structuralist because of his continuing recognition, for all his romantic egotism, that the self is not a privileged center of consciousness, apart from the material world. Only through a network of interrelations with everything around him does the poet enjoy his consciousness of the city. The interplay of exterior stimuli and the senses of the onlooker comprise a single reality of which subject and object are simply mutually enabling elements. Thus, in the Preface to the 1855 edition of *Leaves of Grass*, Whitman praises the animating power of the poet's glance: "What the eyesight does to the rest he does to the rest. Who knows the curious mystery of the eyesight?" (*LG*, 716). Then in "A Song for Occupations" (1855) he takes the city as an example of how perception engenders its object:

> All architecture is what you do to it when you look upon it,
> (Did you think it was in the white or gray stone? or the lines
>   of the arches and cornices?)
>
> (*LG*, 215)

But this union is a two-way street. For if architecture depends on the perceiver for its actuality, so the poet needs to be seen by others to live fully, just as his poems need to be read to activate the process by which they try to enter the physical world. In order to make the city live in his poems, he must implore its aid in authenticating him; its engendering gaze must repay his:

> —submit to no models but your own O city!
> Behold me—incarnate me as I have incarnated you!
>
> (*LG*, 294)

With its merging of noumenal and phenomenal worlds, Whitman's poetry operates on what could be called a principle of reciprocal absorption; as the 1855 Preface concludes: "The proof of a poet is that his country absorbs him as affectionately as he has absorbed it" (*LG*, 731). City and poet bring each other to life, a quasi-divine act of creation repeated daily in the streets and poems of New York–Mannahatta. Imposing the body of the poet on the text of the city, Whitman's quest to encompass the urban world remains an intensely personal, ecstatically sexual enterprise: "What cities the light or warmth penetrates I penetrate those cities myself" (*LG*, 148). This amorous, unending interplay between object and observer, city and self, grants the poet his peculiar genealogy as the child and begetter of all he experiences, the genuine progeny of the city he builds.

"CROSSING BROOKLYN FERRY"

Whitman's greatest poem of the city, "Crossing Brooklyn Ferry" (1856), triumphantly meets the challenge of merging city and text, and it does so by joining site and sight, "I" and eye, to the moment of the poem's incarnation by the reader. Turning from present-day to future audiences of *Leaves of Grass*, Whitman transforms the reader into the longed-for passer-by of his landscape, validating himself, his poem, and his city through the reader's own physical situation, through the exchange of glances out of and beyond the page. Caught in the poet's vision, the reader changes from present stranger to future lover, and enters the ideal city of friends. While Whitman may not be able to guarantee the poem's "presence" as an extratextual entity, he can claim that immediacy by exploiting the poem's undeniable textual presence to the reader, and the reader's present-tense relation to it.

Whitman's preoccupation with the city's surface and depth, its textual reflection and physical reality, make it appropriate that he should begin his poem by confronting the mirroring surfaces of sea and sky. The first two lines enlarge the notion of visual rapport with a passing stranger to include the landscape itself:

> Flood-tide below me! I see you face to face!
> Clouds of the west—sun there half an hour high—I see you
>   also face to face.

(LG, 159)[46]

Just as the poet eliminates the difference between himself and others through a single glance, he now sees eye to eye with all the external world. The reiterated phrase "face to face" evokes St. Paul's relation to God, and implies that Whitman's experience of the city is providentially sanctioned, and more celestial than earthly. The poet inspects his subject, not through a glass darkly, but by looking directly into the natural manifestation of the Divine countenance—which, reflected in the water, will turn out to be the poet's own.[47]

Far from being a timeless, static moment, everything is in motion around the ferry—tide, shipping, sea-birds, snapping flags above shore and sail. And yet few poems approach the sustained liminality of "Crossing Brooklyn Ferry"; even as landscape, poet, and reader all surge toward one another in countless ways, each seems balanced on a fulcrum. While the ferry traverses the river from Manhattan's business district toward Brooklyn's hills, poem and poet rest poised between city and country, day and night, amid earth, air, and water, with the fourth element, fire, visible in the setting sun and the brightening flares of foundry chimneys.

The reader, too, partakes of this motion and balance. The next few lines prepare for another and even more important crossing:

> Crowds of men and women attired in the usual costumes,
>   how curious you are to me!
> On the ferry-boats the hundreds and hundreds that cross,
>   returning home, are more curious to me than you suppose,
> And you that shall cross from shore to shore years hence are
>   more to me, and more in my meditations, than you might
>   suppose.
>
> (LG, 159–60)

Poet and reader begin to engage in a double motion, not just across the river in their respective eras, but across time and text, toward each other.[48] The shifting referent of "you" here indicates the line of the poet's attack: first he names fellow participants in the present scene, then an unsupposing contemporary reader, and finally ferry riders and readers of the years to come. In place of the delocalized encounter usual in lyric poetry, Whitman situates the reader as part of a specific urban landscape, the poet's own. As it develops, their bond will depend increasingly on their common experience of the scene they share, each inseparable from the harbor and its sights. The mirroring relationship that being "face to face" with water and sky implies thus prepares for the subsequent effort to bring poet and reader to a similar understanding.

Drawing his own breath from the objects around him—"The impalpable sustenance of me from all things at all hours of the day"— the poet dissolves his being into the city's: "The simple, compact, well-join'd scheme, myself disintegrated, every one disintegrated yet part of the scheme" (LG, 160). The myriad phenomena that seemed to Wordsworth to melt into an incomprehensible mass from the heat of the throng retain for Whitman their individuality even as they show their common substance. The enduring differences of the crowd are the means to and proof of the identity which assimilates them; the "certainty of others" cannot be denied, making urban perception a sort of divine rosary: "The glories strung like beads on my smallest sights and hearings, on the walk in the street and the passage over the river" (LG, 160). The "scheme" in which they share comprises the poem as well as the city and its citizens, and through it Whitman intends to bring them all to an awareness of their underlying union with the landscape.

Thus, in section 3 the poet insists on the converging parallels between his life, his city, and those of the reader:

> It avails not, time nor place—distance avails not,
> I am with you, you men and women of a generation, or
>   ever so many generations hence,
> Just as you feel when you look on the river and sky, so I felt,
> Just as any of you is one of a living crowd, I was one of
>   a crowd
> ·
> I too many and many a time cross'd the river of old
> ·
> Saw the reflection of the summer sky in the water,
> Had my eyes dazzled by the shimmering track of beams,
> Look'd at the fine centrifugal spokes of light round the
>   shape of my head in the sunlit water.
>
>   (LG, 160–61)

Like ripples spreading outward from his haloed head, the next twenty lines describe clouds, bay, ships, sailors, and shore as day deepens into night. Each line begins with or implies verbs of sight: "watched," "saw," "look'd." At this stage, visual interaction is primary, the intensity of the poem's sight becoming the reflection of the self-reflection that poet and reader see in the landscape. Like the paintings of John Kensett or Martin Heade, or the sporting pictures of Thomas Eakins, such as *Max Schmidt in Single Scull*, these passages depict a luminist world resting perfectly at the intersection of time and eternity.

But at the center of the poem, in section 5, vision gives way to the quest for a more immediate and physical rapport. Playing on the double sense of the question "What is it then between us?" Whitman provokes the reader to consider the nascent relationship they share while also discounting any obstacle to it: "Whatever it is, it avails not" (LG, 162). Through an increasingly passionate appeal to mutual experiences and desires, Whitman thrusts himself upon his audience, even those "ever so many generations hence."

Yet as in other poems expressing this textual-material tension, he voices his fears about his unreality and solitude, in order to overcome them:

> I too walk'd the streets of Manhattan island, and bathed in
>   the waters around it,
> I too felt the curious abrupt questionings stir within me,
> In the day among crowds of people sometimes they came
>   upon me,
> In my walks home late at night or as I lay in my bed they
>   came upon me,
> I too had been struck from the float forever held in solution,
> I too had receiv'd identity by my body,
> That I was I knew was of my body, and what I should be
>   I knew I should be of my body.
>
> (LG, 162)

It is only through the body, finally, that the poet can address the sexual and metaphysical questionings that have risen from the city to disturb him, and through which, in his isolation, he can feel his connection to countless others like him.

This is Whitman's strongest move, to draw boldly upon the reader's own body and personality to give substance to himself. As he ingenuously puts it in the 1876 Preface, "I meant LEAVES OF GRASS . . . to be the Poem of Identity, (of *Yours*, whoever you are, now reading these lines)" (*LG*, 752). Anticipating that the reader may not always possess an identity and outlook conducive to reproducing the poet's own, he counters by skillfully insinuating just how "whoever you are" might feel deep down inside. Thus, in "A Song for Occupations" he remarks reassuringly, "If you meet some stranger in the streets and love him or her, why I often meet strangers in the street and love them" (*LG*, 212). This typical allusion to the fellowship of shared emotions cleverly assigns to the reader habits that actually belong to the poet. In practice, the intimate effect of Whitman's appeal transcends its shakiness as a rhetorical strategy. Built entirely on this principle, section 6 of "Crossing Brooklyn Ferry" not only contains Whitman's most convincing attempt to prove that he too "knew what it was to be evil," but also provides one of his most eloquent descriptions of casual urban love and longing: "I too," he says,

> Was call'd by my nighest name by clear loud voices of young
>   men as they saw me approaching or passing,

Felt their arms on my neck as I stood, or the negligent
   leaning of their flesh against me as I sat,
Saw many I loved in the street or ferry-boat or public
   assembly, yet never told them a word.

(LG, 162–63)

In the guise of recognizing in the reader traits indelibly his own,
Whitman manages to convey what "identity by my body" might
mean for the person who inhabits it beyond the scope of a poem.

   With common ground now established, the two brief stanzas of
section 7 take the decisive step:

Closer yet I approach you,
What thought you have of me now, I had as much of you—
   I laid in my stores in advance,
I consider'd long and seriously of you before you were born.

Who was to know what should come home to me?
Who knows but I am enjoying this?
Who knows, for all the distance, but I am as good as looking
   at you now, for all you cannot see me?

(LG, 163)

Here for the first time the reader is assumed to be thinking of the
poet who has lain patiently in wait for so long. Calling attention to
but dismissing the fact that he is present only by his words, Whitman assigns to the reader responsiblity for any absence: the reader
is blind, while the poet can see, reveling as usual in the pleasures
of sight.

   The crucial, consummatory visual contact has finally been made.
But the poet remains hidden from the reader, and the circuit of
sight must be completed indirectly by the landscape they both look
upon, separately yet together. When the poet's glance shifts momentarily back to his surroundings at the start of section 8, the climax is reached: "Ah, what can ever be more stately and admirable
to me than mast-hemm'd Manhattan?" (LG, 163). Nothing, comes
the answer, except the people of the city, his readers, whom he
now knows through the landscape and who are therefore inextricably bound to it, participating with him in its divinity as intimate
friends:

What gods can exceed these that clasp me by the hand, and
   with voices I love call me promptly and loudly by my
   nighest name as I approach?

What is more subtle than this which ties me to the woman or
    man that looks in my face?
Which fuses me into you now, and pours my meaning
    into you?

                                        (*LG*, 164)

By returning to the archetypal "face to face" communion of poet
and city with which he began, Whitman miraculously cures the
blindness of the text and "fuses" sexually as well as spiritually with
"the man or woman that looks in my face"—the reader. The amorous relationship with the city and its inhabitants that they now
have in common makes them both contemporaries and lovers;
the look they exchange through the page collapses their distance
in time and space. Moreover, it annihilates textual as well as temporal gaps between them, and "pours my meaning" beyond any
doubts into the reader. The rest of the section displays satisfaction
after consummation: "We understand then do we not? / What I
promis'd without mentioning it, have you not accepted?" (*LG*,
164). The lines emphasize the mystical nature of the union effected;
we can note the steps leading to it, but cannot really specify how it
has happened. Because Whitman courts the reader by indirection
and glances, they meet only by a kind of peripheral vision, when
each regards the city rather than the other.

    Yet the final section leaves no doubt as to the outcome. Poet and
reader return to the panorama of harbor, town, and sky, now in
full rapport with it. Other writers may engage our interest by in-
vesting their images with enough symbolic resonance to make us
feel that we too share their urban sensibility. But Whitman makes
himself and the reader co-eternal with the city, joined with it in a
permanently orgasmic union:

Flow on, river! flow with the flood-tide, and ebb with the
    ebb-tide!
Frolic on, crested and scallop-edg'd waves!
Gorgeous clouds of the sunset! drench with your splendor
    me, or the men and women generations after me!
Cross from shore to shore, countless crowds of passengers!
Stand up, tall masts of Mannahatta! stand up, beautiful hills
    of Brooklyn!
Throb, baffled and curious brain! throw out questions and
    answers!
Suspend here and everywhere, eternal float of solution!

Gaze, loving and thirsty eyes, in the house or street or public
   assembly!

                                                                    (*LG*, 164)

The admonition to the "loving and thirsty eyes" points to the
source of this giant procreation: flooding tides, drenching clouds,
erect masts and hills, and ejaculating mind all leap almost visibly
from the poet's animating glance. For Whitman, city life does not
exist apart from his perception of it,[49] just as his own life would be
empty without the city to stimulate poetry and even thought itself.
Mingling with the material of his creation, the poet becomes a
god, the mirroring environment of the opening lines now spontaneously providing halos for him and his city of saints: "Diverge,
fine spokes of light, from the shape of my head, or any one's head,
in the sunlit water!" (*LG*, 165).[50]
   Corona'd all, poet, reader, and citizens of Mannahatta become
members of a harmoniously pastoralized city of the Saved.[51] The
four elements serve as the four-square walls of this New Jerusalem:

Fly on, sea-birds! fly sideways, or wheel in large circles high
   in the air;
Receive the summer sky, you water, and faithfully hold it till
   all downcast eyes have time to take it from you!
. . . .

Burn high your fires, foundry chimneys! cast black shadows
   at nightfall! cast red and yellow light over the tops of
   the houses!
. . . .

Thrive, cities—bring your freight, bring your shows. . . .
                                                               (*LG*, 164–65)

As the godlike poet sets the city in motion with his exultant imperatives, Revelation's divine marriage of heaven and earth con-
verges with the Wordsworthian marriage of man and nature, body
and soul, to create an urban-pastoral synthesis, the prosperous, in-
dustrialized new garden of the West.[52] Arrayed for the holy union,
the entire city participates in the wedding. Assuming the roles of
bride and groom, the "beautiful hills of Brooklyn" meet the "tall
masts of Mannahatta" that stand up to greet them at the poet's
command. In the prefatorial letter to the 1856 edition of *Leaves of
Grass*, Whitman speaks of "the divinity of sex" (*LG*, 738), and to
the degree that "Crossing Brooklyn Ferry" merges city and nature,
poet and reader, through that medium, the entire scene becomes a

celestial landscape perfumed with the scent of the bodies that enclose and sustain the soul: "You necessary film, continue to envelop the soul, / About my body for me, and your body for you, be hung our divinest aromas" (*LG*, 165).

Earlier in section 6, in the context of "gnawing" uncertainties, the poet had confessed that he too played "the same old role" (*LG*, 163) in the self-conscious drama of life. But having now penetrated through the text to reader and landscape, he returns to the troubling image with renewed enthusiasm. Now he both accepts the divisions between self, object, and city that might encourage this inauthentic theatrical activity, and at the same time suggests that they have lost their power to mediate, to keep each apart from its essence:

> Live, old life! play the part that looks back on the actor
> or actress!
> Play the old role, the role that is great or small according as
> one makes it!
> Consider, you who peruse me, whether I may not in
> unknown ways be looking upon you.
>
> (*LG*, 164)

As he commands a moment later, "Appearances, now or henceforth, indicate what you are" (*LG*, 165). Reversing the opening passages where the poet scrutinizes the reader, the writer admits that to us he is only a text. Accepting that *his* role is to be perused, Whitman leaves to his readers the task of imagining the "unknown ways" that the poet's presence and empowering vision can reach us. The mutual exchange between eyes and mirroring sky and sea serves as a model for the loyal reciprocity that ought to obtain between them: "Receive the summer sky, you water, and faithfully hold it till all downcast eyes have time to take it from you!" Like the water he traverses and imprints with his own reflection, Whitman has been entrusted with impressions he must preserve until all the "downcast eyes" of his reading public remove them from him. As long as the bay mirrors the world above it, the poet can count on his poem being charged with elemental "questions and answers" (*LG*, 164) that the reader, through personal rapport with the scene, will then be able to draw from it.

The conclusion of this interchange carries with it the heightened awareness that all inanimate objects manifest as much of the heavenly as the poet's silhouette in the water. The assimilation of matter and mind by one another is complete:

You have waited, you always wait, you dumb, beautiful
   ministers,
We receive you with free sense at last, and are insatiate
   henceforward,
Not you any more shall be able to foil us, or withhold
   yourselves from us,
We use you, and do not cast you aside—we plant you
   permanently within us,
We fathom you not—we love you—there is perfection in
   you also,
You furnish your parts toward eternity,
Great or small, you furnish your parts toward the soul.

                    (LG, 165)[53]

Creating a self commensurate with the city, and a city inseparable from the self, Whitman nevertheless does not claim to have mastered or subsumed the phenomena he addresses: "We fathom you not." The plural subject confirms that Whitman has decisively joined himself to the former "you" of the reader, both becoming fellow admirers of the harbor scene that lies open to them. The receptive "free sense" with which in turn they admit the "dumb, beautiful ministers" of the material world into their lives is the relaxed outcome of the poem's gradual but importunate processes of commingling observer, text, and world. Nonetheless, the fact of their being "insatiate henceforward" indicates that the old longing must continue, as part of the inevitable thrust of life, even in divine conditions. Though poet has crossed to reader, the rest of the scene guards its liminal quality, adding subject and object to the list of items suspended in transit. The city and its objects, although unable to withhold their substance from the desire of the poet who wishes to internalize them, still remain independent "parts toward eternity." With the realization of permanence and perfection, the poem claims for itself a lasting status in the field of entities penetrated by sight and born of the body. As the imagination and body are projected onto the urban landscape which has become cosmic, and material phenomena are planted within, the poem partakes of world and word in its own "unknown ways," the ever-retraceable record of the soul's embrace of the city.

Whitman himself was at times skeptical of the reality of this encounter. But through his amorous "face to face" apprehension of the city's stones, streets, and passing strangers, and his absorption of them in return, he builds in his poetry the almost palpable city of Mannahatta, a modern, secular, and sensuous New Jerusalem fabricated from the contemporary materials of thriving New York. Defying textuality by announcing it, he asserts the solidity of his city by claiming the reader's body for his own. Seen in this light, Whitman's program for self-incarnation appears both less assured and more daring than previously imagined. If his frank sexuality as a "lover of populous pavements" (LG, 15) makes him more thoroughly sympathetic to modern city life than Blake, Wordsworth, or even Baudelaire, his "terrible doubts" about the substance of his vision bind him to all the poets of the unreal city, and foreshadow the fractured cityscapes of The Waste Land and Paterson.

In a letter written in 1889, two years before his death, Whitman addresses for a final time the relation between his poems and the city, setting out in the process what would later become the underlying principle of William Carlos Williams' epic. He summarizes the bond with a characteristic appeal to the sexual conjunction that was always, for him, at the heart of both urban and literary existence:

> I can hardly tell why, but feel very positively that if any thing can justify my revolutionary attempts & utterances it is such ensemble—like a great city to modern civilization, & a whole combined clustering paradoxical identity a man, a woman.[54]

The worth of Leaves of Grass as innovative poetry, Whitman concludes, lies in the book's being itself like a city. In its variousness, its desires and frustrations, its sense of being separate from yet joined to the lovers on the other side of the page, it embodies the "whole combined clustering paradoxical identity" of male and female that marks the "ensemble" of Whitman's work. By the force of the analogy, Whitman completes a circuit that he had dedicated his poetic career to closing—from the physical body of the poet to the body of his work, and ultimately, mysteriously, to a city of sexual beings of whom he counts himself one. If the city is the concrete image of his life's work, then his life itself may seem to merge with that irresistible metropolis which, "insatiate," he takes such pains to make solid in his writing. That he can "hardly tell why" this incarnation should occur is the appropriate sendoff to such a city of texts, for they successfully resist logic each time they insist on "the mystery of the eyesight" and the tactile rewards it yields.

Chapter Five

The Waste Land and
Urban Renewal
T. S. Eliot's Poetics of Surrender

Unreal City, I have seen and see . . .
—*The Waste Land*, original draft

In contrast to the shock of fresh perception that animates the landscapes of other city poets, T. S. Eliot's *The Waste Land* (1922) presents a bleary vision of a city already seen.[1] It is a city made unreal by repetitive, worn-out sights of places, people, and texts. "My personal landscape is a composite," Eliot once remarked (ILP, 421), and in *The Waste Land* he fashions an amalgam of "slumminess" and urban woe based on his experience of blighted life in St. Louis, Boston, Paris, and post–World War I London.[2] The absence of vital contact and stimulating encounters among the citizens of the waste land bespeaks the extent of Eliot's despair over the brutalizing monotony of urban existence. This absence also accentuates his difference from Wordsworth, Baudelaire, and Whitman: amid the swarming crowds he fails to find a glimpse of the entrancing, unknown Other through whom he might discover the "real" city of genuine communication.

At first, Eliot's metropolis reveals itself only as an insubstantial tissue of texts, perverse personae, and fragmentary relationships representing the ruin of Western civilization. Sexual dysfunction, social alienation, and spiritual despondency—all conspire to prevent the poem's various persons and voices from true interaction. As image and recorder of the divorce of self from Other, self from self, the blind, two-sexed Tiresias wanders Eliot's London. The fractured yet central figure of the poem, he functions as a negative version of the *passant*, enacting with his loveless trysts and sightless eyes a grotesque parody of Baudelaire's moment of discovery. Condemned to watch endless rehearsals of the same tired scenes, Tiresias points to the poet's own infertility: unable to generate insights for himself, he must scavenge earlier texts and recycle the words of others. The *passant* experience missing in the poem signals a lack not only of human interaction, but also of poetic receptivity and fecundity. The failure to see Others anew becomes textual as well as sexual. The "unreal emotions" of both urbanite and poet block imaginative access to the unwasted city that might flourish before an inviting glance.

And yet the poem contains the seeds of its own rejuvenation. For, despite the near-extinction of the *passant* in the world of *The Waste Land*, by the end Eliot transforms the unexpected encounter into an image of the regenerative shock that occurs in the act of reading itself. Indeed, he regards his own reading of poetic texts as if it were a sudden meeting with a stranger. In both his prose and poetry, Eliot explicitly prescribes "the awful daring of a moment's surrender"—a Baudelairean yielding to texts and to others—as the only means of living fully and creatively. The meeting with the Other thus becomes nothing less than a double-edged image of the poet's—and his reader's—relation to all reading, all history and culture. In order to make his meaning seminal rather than barren, the poet's openness to the city and the crowd—progressively more important in the poetry of Wordsworth, Baudelaire, and Whitman—must here manifest a parallel surrender to the fecund instant of reading wherein literary and urban texts combine. The startling potential of the passing stranger thus translates in Eliot's own work into a catalyst for textual production.

Still, not until *The Waste Land*'s final section does the poet discover how to achieve the self-sacrifice toward which the entire poem yearns, an act that renews poetically the city of human emotion stunted by sexual and imaginative sterility. But in the process he and his readers learn how to revitalize the waste land and how to produce poetry—how, in effect, to make the "unreal city" real again.

"UNREAL EMOTIONS, AND REAL APPETITE": THE ANTI-*PASSANT*

According to Eliot, the "plan" of *The Waste Land* is based on the legend of the Holy Grail as presented in Jessie L. Weston's *From Ritual to Romance*.[3] The legend "postulates a close connection between the vitality of a certain King, and the prosperity of his kingdom; the forces of the ruler being weakened or destroyed, by wound, sickness, old age, or death, the land becomes Waste, and the task of the hero is that of restoration."[4] Eliot's poem hinges on this mythic association of the ruler's strength and potency with that of his city, but extends it to include every inhabitant. Each one becomes a sterile Fisher King, bringing desolation to the waste land of London, which in the poem serves as a synecdoche for the degradation of Western civilization.

A series of squalid sexual episodes enervates the city. The purity of the river Thames, representing the lifeblood of London, is polluted by the sleazy successors of nymphs and nobility, by seedy foreign merchants, by the affairs of bored typists and lowly clerks, by the submissions and rapes of modern-day Thames-daughters, the latest whores of Babylon. The unthinking reproduction of the lower classes that leads to abortion (for Lil and Albert) is no better—or worse—than the childless sterility of the rulers (Elizabeth and Leicester) that dries up the land.[5] "Responsive to the momentary need" (*WLFT*, 31), all this sexual activity can never transcend mere physical satisfaction. Loveless gratification breeds misery and further hunger.

In the absence of authentic love and communication, the city becomes Babel as well as Babylon, its polyglot voices raised in a brutal discourse of sexual aggression: "'Jug Jug' to dirty ears" (103). Failed readings, broken lines, even nonsense syllables of sadly dated onomatopoeia ("twit twit twit / Jug jug jug jug jug jug") stutter out the story of the city's multiple sexual disorders—not only the impotence of the Fisher King, but the violence and callousness of rape, prostitution, and joyless intercourse.

This vision of the city conveys more than the "disillusionment of a generation" with postwar Europe and its *mores* that many readers have found in the poem (*SE*, 324). Eliot identifies contemporary London with all cities, past and present, and with a continuing, transhistorical sexual dysfunction that includes "Jerusalem Athens Alexandria" as well as Elizabethan London and Dante's Florence.[6] Since the modern city shares its woes with earlier ones, its wasted condition clearly symbolizes rather than causes the sexual failure of its inhabitants. Eliot thus diverges markedly from writers like Wordsworth, Dickens, and Tennyson, who see the modern city itself as the source of the perversion of human life. Eliot is actually closer to Blake and, oddly enough, to D. H. Lawrence,[7] wishing to revitalize life through a more perfect sexual response: "the land becomes waste and the task . . . is that of restoration." For, according to the original manuscript of the poem, it is "unreal emotions, and real appetite" (*WLFT*, 27) that are laying waste the city. The insistent presence of appetite ensures, until the very end of the poem, the unreality of the city. Eliot's use of the same adjective, "unreal," to describe both sex and city demonstrates how thoroughly he conflates the two.

If Eliot's city is unreal, it is in part because the quintessential urban experience, the encounter with the *passant*, does not take place. This vitalizing shock of recognition which lies at the heart of city life and city poetry, has been effaced, or at least repressed and deferred, in the waste land. Its inhabitants are not invigorated by fresh eyes; on the contrary, they cannot escape their all-too-familiar partners. The blind prophet Tiresias is unable to exchange an animating glance with another, not only because he literally can't see, but also because he has already seen too much. For him, the Other can never be unknown: with his gift of prophecy, he has foreseen all, "foresuffered all." Tiresias acts as a repetitive voyeur, an anti-*passant*. Everything in his city seems stale and lifeless; the original draft of the poem finished the line "Unreal city" with the words "I have seen and see" (*WLFT*, 31).

Tiresias surveys the deficiencies of the entire city, metaphorically assuming the role of Fisher King whose impotence is responsible for the present desolation of his once-fertile kingdom. Critics have complained that the withered and ineffectual prophet is barely present in the poem, or that he serves only to show how little anyone can make this wasted world cohere.[8] But Tiresias's history provides compelling grounds for regarding the seer as the central figure in the poem. He collects all the fragmentary consciousnesses in *The Waste Land*, becoming, as Eliot himself explains, "the most important personage . . . uniting all the rest" (*NWL*, 218).

Eliot's use of Tiresias points, significantly, to another incarnation of the Fisher King, Oedipus Rex, a man whose country's woes result from his sexual crimes. Although Oedipus is never mentioned directly in the poem, his words enter its arid echo chamber in Section III. Repeating Oedipus's cry of anguish at the plight of Thebes, "O City city," the narrator reiterates the connection between city, sex, and the pollution of the land.[9] In both *Oedipus Rex* and *The Waste Land*, tainted sex is the source of civic and private misfortune, producing a dessicated, diseased city in the desert. Like the inhabitants of the modern-day urban waste land, Oedipus must learn to know others so that he can know himself. He kills his father, a passing stranger, at a crossroads, a proto-city, and tries to evade his past by seeking a form of urban anonymity in Thebes.

Although he outwits the Sphinx and comes to rule the city, his knowledge of his own wife, the queen, is merely sexual; he has married his mother.

Tiresias reluctantly exposes this perverted story as the root of the blight on Thebes. But although he and Oedipus are antagonists in Sophocles' drama, they are in fact versions of one another: after discovering his horrifying relation to his parents, Oedipus blinds himself and becomes a valued seer; Tiresias's tawdry knowledge has been gained from his own sexual irregularities. For, in Ovid's account, which Eliot cites (NWL, 218), Tiresias struck with his staff two snakes that were coupling, and was turned into a woman. After seven years he repeated the action and was returned to his former state. Since he had experienced both male and female sexuality, Zeus and Hera asked him to settle their dispute over which sex took the most pleasure in lovemaking. When Tiresias decided for the female, Hera blinded him in anger, but Zeus compensated him with long life and the gift of prophecy.[10] With the loss of sight, both Tiresias and Oedipus undergo a symbolic castration in punishment for their unprecedented sexual knowledge, and in both cases their potency is partially, but only partially, restored by the power of the seer, a "second sight."

If, as Jessie Weston writes, "the woes of the land are directly dependent on the sickness, or maiming, of the King,"[11] then Tiresias, like Oedipus, serves as a maimed "king" of the waste land. Thus, when Eliot notes of his unhappy characters that "the two sexes meet in Tiresias" (NWL, 218), the union is not a fertile one. Tiresias introduces himself to the reader by repeating his story in two brief lines: "I Tiresias, though blind, throbbing between two lives, / Old man with wrinkled female breasts, can see . . ." (218–19). The physical details indicate his masculine impotence and his female barrenness, while "throbbing between two lives" suggests that he has been condemned to repeat his sexual alternation indefinitely. His appearance at the twilit "violet hour," halfway between day and night, further emphasizes his liminality. Pulsing like the "taxi throbbing waiting" in the lines that precede his entry, Tiresias is also half-human, half-machine, embodying the representative "human engine" and its mechanistic sexual practices.

And yet "though blind" he "can see." This is perhaps the worst curse of all for, as Eliot notes, "What Tiresias *sees*, in fact, is the substance of the poem" (NWL, 218). A prophet's greatest anguish lies in foretelling disaster without being able to avert it, and Tiresias must preview then sustain all the ruin the poem encompasses:

I Tiresias, old man with wrinkled dugs
Perceived the scene, and foretold the rest—
I too awaited the expected guest.
. . . .

(And I Tiresias have foresuffered all
Enacted on this same divan or bed;
I who have sat by Thebes below the wall
And walked among the lowest of the dead.)

(228–30, 243–46)

Having prevented the natural reproductive act of the snakes, Tiresias now relives the parched intercourse of a "wasted" human society. Just as the mythic Tiresias is forced to read the pleasures of sex for the gods and to suffer for it, so the seer of *The Waste Land*, as Eliot's mouthpiece and "spectator" (NWL, 218), must envision for the poem's audience the sexual deficiencies of the modern world-city.

The bored Tiresias comes to symbolize the futility of prophecy: he foresuffers, re-perceives, and foretells innumerable acts of sexual sordidness, but there is no penetration to his gaze. Like the bold stare of the young man carbuncular or the glance in the mirror of the typist, upon whose rendezvous these lines comment, Tiresias takes in nothing new. All passers-by are already known, the unshockingly familiar corpses of a once-living tradition. As the weary rereader of the city's lifeless texts, Tiresias moves through the city like a negative *passant*, very much an *hypocrite lecteur* fallen prey to the most insidious vice of all, a timeless Ennui that can never break through to a new version, a new vision.[12]

Tiresias may be the poem's primary embodiment of the figure of the anti-*passant*, but he is not the only one. Other characters function as extensions of Tiresias, equally "unreal" in that they have neither offered understanding nor found true sympathy in any human relation. The young man carbuncular, for example, comes to the listless typist as an *expected* guest, to whom the sexual self-offering is merely mechanical (like an "automatic hand"), a stopping short reminiscent of that in the hyacinth garden earlier in the poem (35–42). His groping assault and the unlit stairway to her flat insist on the debilitating blindness of the assignation. In contrast, the Baudelairean meeting with the *passante* is a bold emotional and visual exchange: "Moi, je buvais, crispé comme un extravagant, / Dans son oeil." But Eliot's meetings involve a failure of sexual and psychological commitment, connoted by blindness: "I could not /

Speak, and my eyes failed." In *The Waste Land*, characters do not surrender to mysterious strangers, for every meeting has already been presaged and "foresuffered."[13]

Preceded by the rancorous conversations of upper- and lower-classes in Section II, and the polluting promiscuity at the start of Section III, the narrator's appointment with Mr. Eugenides is another instance of a barren urban rencontre:

> Unreal City
> Under the brown fog of a winter noon
> Mr. Eugenides, the Smyrna merchant
> Unshaven, with a pocket full of currants
> C.i.f. London: documents at sight,
> Asked me in demotic French
> To luncheon at the Cannon Street Hotel
> Followed by a weekend at the Metropole.
>
> (207–14)

The noon-time hour and suggestion of luncheon expose the "real appetite" of the unreal city, while the disreputable speech and appearance of Mr. Eugenides accord with his suspicious proposition, his dubious business and origin. Because the guarded conditions of exchange, "documents at sight," substitute an inspection of goods and invoices for trust and eye contact, the rendezvous promises little satisfaction.[14] Rather than authenticating personal relations, the seedy commercial self-interest of this encounter further debases them.

The same pattern holds true for the fruitless adventures of the "Thames-daughters." The potentially exciting strangers of the city, the original nymphs, are departed, and the remaining ex-virgins confess a triple seduction that bespeaks only defilement, not love. Their stories recapitulate the theme of sexual exploitation and the emotional deadness half responsible for it. The tale of their seductions carries the reader on a bleak pilgrimage along the undrinkable river downstream from Richmond and Kew, past Moorgate, toward the lower-class holiday resort of Margate near the mouth of the Thames. The journey ends with a pathetic scrap of autobiography:

> 'On Margate Sands.
> I can connect
> Nothing with nothing.
> The broken fingernails of dirty hands.

My people humble people who expect
Nothing.'

(300–305)

The nastiness of the hands and fingernails make this scene one of
the most brutal in the poem. Eliot's characteristic fragmentation
of the body seems particularly self-reflexive here, since the poet
composed part of the poem while resting at Margate from a ner-
vous breakdown. The dirty hands (figuratively, the poet's as he
writes) recall the dirty ears, "jug jug," earlier juxtaposed with Philomel's rape and mutilation. The Thames-daughters reenact the
typist's seduction, and one rape stands for all ("all the women are
one woman" [NWL, 218]). Partly an excuse, partly resignation,
the lines "My people humble people who expect / Nothing" speak
of the violation that life in the unreal city continually inflicts. The
victim accuses but accepts the consequences of the "momentary
need." And so the speaker's connecting "nothing with nothing"
suggests not only the poem's fractured form, but the absence of
sympathetic connections which the poem relentlessly records.

This discontinuity of experience underlines the helplessness of
Tiresias to organize the atrophy and entropy he reviews. As one
who sees both past and future, and has been both man and woman,
Tiresias mirrors the transhistorical "city mind" of *The Waste Land*,
just as Eliot's imagined "mind of Europe" contains the full sweep
of literary tradition (*SE*, 6). Because Eliot substitutes this universal
consciousness for an individual one, alienation and noncommuni-
cation are turned from personal torments into aspects of the collective psyche of the culture at large. But the blind prophet can give
voice only to shattered fragments—quotations, echoes, and par-
odies evocative of other times, other texts—condemning the poem's
isolated characters to form broken parts of the same identity, the
same problem. As J. Hillis Miller contends, this triumph of expand-
ing the private self to incorporate all of history may really be a defeat, since "the quality of the life of the mind of Europe is exactly
the same as the experience of the solitary ego."[15]

Worse yet, this solipsistic self is hollow at the core. Because
Tiresias is ever at the margins of his own history, his "uniting"
presence actually signals a void at the heart of what he sees. Although he has the protean ability to assume other forms, to register all minds through his own, the different voices competing in
the poem continually displace the would-be central one, forcing
the reader outward to other texts, other readings.[16] In this respect

Tiresias embodies what Joseph Riddel calls the "moving image" of the modern long poem, subverting the idea of a unified, "closed" text, and thus he "resists the possibility of a text commanded by any one of its elements: a controlling theme, a privileged point of view." [17] The fleeting quality of Tiresias's presence in the poem and Eliot's describing him as "a mere spectator and not indeed a 'character'" (NWL, 218) ensure his role as a mobile anti-*passant* who further dislocates the city he stalks. Poetically as well as mythically, the Theban sage appears more a random perceiver than a shaper of the events he witnesses. What has been viewed as an aesthetic failure, then, the inability of Tiresias to organize clearly the events of the poem, should be seen as part of the poem's technique, inevitably following from the inability to see directly, to read creatively, to feel openly. [18]

Yet if the relationship of Tiresias to the shards of life and culture that make up the poem is not a determinative one, it is nonetheless crucial since his "sight" is "the substance of the poem." Though he may not be the shaper of events, he is necessarily an interpreter of them, a mediator between poet, poem, and audience. This "will to read" is the most potent of the desires expressed in the poem, a substitution for the natural sexual forces Tiresias disrupted when he parted the snakes, a condemnation to secondary or belated reading and knowledge. "What Tiresias *sees*" is a disintegrative repetition of what his experiences with the serpents and Oedipus have already shown him, the blinding shock of sexual difference. As Jacques Lacan suggests, sight is a means of sexual appropriation, but as it discovers differences from itself, the effect is one of castration, of setting loose the play of signification and of subverting personal identity based on the denial of such differences. [19] Thus the consummatory plenitude of vision can sometimes represent, as it does for Whitman, an effacing of differences, a union of inside and outside, consciousness and world. But for those blinded by the knowledge of what they have seen, as Tiresias is, signification floats free and intervention appears impossible. Tiresias's efforts at seeing and reading are perforce ineffectual and repetitive, lacking a creative "I" to control or to comprehend them. [20]

The readers of *The Waste Land* thus confront the interpretive and reportorial strategies of Tiresias-as-narrator, plunging into a presentation of the city as a collection of fragments which are in turn further fragmented ("so rudely forc'd") by readers through the violence of their own (now secondary or tertiary) readings of texts that were blindly read, in bits and pieces, to begin with. In the ensuing

Babel of the poem's voices, the urban uproar of recycled emotions and words takes precedence, and a Tiresias incapable of original seeing reveals the author's crisis of creativity by echoing the tradition, not re-forming it into something new. Cut off from the primal experience of urban shock, life and text stunt the productive natural order of surrender, recovery, and, finally, expression.

THE SHOCK OF READING

Leaving the bubbling beverage to cool
Fresca slips softly to the needful stool,
Where the pathetic tale of Richardson
Eases her labour till the deed is done.
(WLFT, 23)

The Waste Land is a poem about reading—wasted, wasteful, yet ultimately cathartic and redeeming. Its wealth of literary allusion and quotation, its self-conscious rereading of previous literature, its notes from the author directing us toward sources that would reproduce his own anterior reading—all of these features mark the poem as a text extraordinarily implicated in the processes of literary production and consumption. But the myriad, ever-proliferating "readings" of the poem since its publication in 1922 have had the paradoxical effect of downplaying this very issue. As Richard Ellmann notes, "Today footnotes do their worst to transform innovations into inevitabilities. After a thousand explanations, *The Waste Land* is no longer a puzzle poem, except for the puzzle of choosing among the various solutions."[21] Given this situation, a look at Eliot's own views of reading may enable us better to appreciate the "puzzle" of the poem as a textual construct—not just as the product of Eliot's reading, but more important, as the product of interaction between reader and text. Because Eliot describes that interaction in terms closely connected with urban encounters, reading itself has the potential to become a redemptive version of the shock experience of the *passant*.

Eliot's remarks about the act of reading in the 1929 "Dante" essay serve as a guide through the layers of textuality that both surround and constitute *The Waste Land*. They emphasize the almost physical impact of the text upon the reader, and the idea of yielding to its force:

The experience of a poem is the experience both of a moment and of a lifetime. It is very much like our intenser experiences

of other human beings. There is a first, or an early moment
which is unique, of shock and surprise, even of terror (*Ego
dominus tuus*); a moment which can never be forgotten, but
which is never repeated integrally; and yet which would become destitute of significance if it did not survive in a larger
whole of experience; which survives inside a deeper and a
calmer feeling.

(SE, 212)

Eliot's sensation as he reads a text closely parallels the "shock experience" in the crowd that Walter Benjamin identifies as the key feature of Baudelaire's city poetry.[22] Like the glimpse of the *passant* or
a sexual initiation ("our intenser experiences of other human beings"), the act of reading begins in an unforgettable moment of
"shock and surprise" which persists and deepens, to become a significant part of the self. This "early moment" of terror forms a decisive aspect of Eliot's writing, so much so that he shares with Baudelaire an aesthetic of shock that animates both the poet's reading
and his subsequent creation.

The relation between reading and urban experience is more than
a mere analogy. For Eliot is alluding to the most famous and revelatory urban encounter in literary history, that of Dante with
Beatrice. In *La Vita Nuova*, Dante explains how the shock of seeing
Beatrice in the street prompted a dream in which "a lordly man,
frightening to behold" appeared on a cloud of fire, holding Beatrice
in his arms and announcing "*Ego dominus tuus*"—"I am thy master."[23] Later identified as Love, the "dominus" that the reader must
accept amid his terror is the yearning for another, fostered by the
surprise meeting with the passer-by.

A letter written by Eliot to Stephen Spender in 1935 further elucidates this traumatic yet stimulating process:

you don't really criticize any author to whom you have never
surrendered yourself. . . . Even just the bewildering minute
counts; you have to give yourself up, and then recover yourself, and the third moment is having something to say, before
you have wholly forgotten both surrender and recovery. Of
course the self recovered is never the same as the self before it
was given.[24]

As Baudelaire or Whitman offer themselves to the passing stranger,
so Eliot submits to the poem, turning reading into an image of poetry making, of the receptiveness that makes the consummation of
art possible.

Like the meeting with the *passant*, the encounter with the text and the consequent, related acts of criticism and creation are rendered in sexual terms. The reader gives up control to an author and experiences a climactic "bewildering minute" in doing so. With self-recovery comes the need to say something before the act is forgotten. But nonetheless "the self recovered is never the same as the self before it was given." Innocence lost, body impregnated, or outlook transformed, Eliot's reader does not just discover something to talk about, but becomes changed in the process. Why should the reader want to undergo such sweet surrender? Eliot's reason, the need or desire to criticize, seems insufficient unless we accept the sexual, generative logic of the passage—this self-abandon to the poetic tradition is the means to poetic procreation. Only by playing a willing Virgin to the power of the Word does Eliot feel he can be delivered of his emotion.

Poetically speaking, the transformed poet's relation to his literary experience is similar to that of the new poem's relation to its tradition.[25] Both acts of surrender produce a new self, a new art out of the engagement of the old order.[26] The three generative stages of the *reading* process that Eliot describes thus constitute equally the stages of a critical and then creative *writing* process.[27] Just as the poet in Baudelaire's "A une passante" sees, loves, and loses the passing stranger all in an instant and then writes a poem about it, so Eliot's textual but explicitly equivalent shock ("like our intenser experiences of other human beings") follows surrender with recovery and then the representation of the experience before it fades. As the emblematic figure of the reading experience, the *passante* that fascinates Baudelaire plays an integral part in Eliot's city poetry.

This is not accidental, for in Baudelaire Eliot discovered the most seductive part of the urban tradition to which he yields himself:

It is not merely in the use of imagery of common life, not merely in the use of imagery of the sordid life of a great metropolis, but in the elevation of such imagery to the *first intensity*—presenting it as it is, and yet making it represent something much more than itself—that Baudelaire has created a mode of release and expression for other men.

("Baudelaire," 1930; *SE*, 377)

The reading of Baudelaire functions as a microcosm of the process of reading in general: the phrase "first intensity," which Eliot underscores, indicates an immediacy of feeling akin to the surrender

of poet and critic. As a "mode of release and expression" Baudelaire's poetry stimulates that sense of "shock" and then of "having
something to say." Reading Baudelaire enables Eliot to create the
kind of fruitful criticism and poetry that he associates with the intimate act of reading.[28] Baudelaire's representation of the city, "the
sordid life of a great metropolis," makes possible Eliot's own "release" and subsequent acts of urban creation.

For the poet's own experience alone is insufficient. His personal
response to his native American city must be grafted onto the sensibility of Baudelaire to make his urban poetry possible:

> From Baudelaire I learned first, a precedent for the poetical
> possiblities, never developed by any poet writing in my own
> language, of the more sordid aspects of the modern metropo-
> lis, of the possibility of fusion between the sordidly realistic
> and the phantasmagoric, the possibility of the juxtaposition
> of the matter-of-fact and the fantastic. From him . . . I learned
> that the sort of material that I had, the sort of experience that
> an adolescent had had, in an industrial city in America, could
> be the material for poetry; and that the source of new poetry
> might be found in what had been regarded hitherto as the im-
> possible, the sterile, the intractably unpoetic.
>
> ("What Dante Means to Me" [1950], *TCTC*, 126)

Eliot insists that it was Baudelaire who showed him the way to
handle his own urban experience, providing a model he had not
been able to find in English.[29] But the "sterile" images he wishes to
fecundate with the aid of Baudelaire obstinately retain their barren-
ness for most of *The Waste Land*. In the end it is only by submitting
to the shock of that experience, as already described by Baudelaire,
that Eliot becomes able to vivify and raise to "the first intensity"
the "impossible" inertness of the urban landscape. The major obstacle to this, however, is that Eliot's foremost reaction to his own
sordid cities lies in the perception of them as unreal.

UNREAL CITY, UNREAL POEM

Any reading of *The Waste Land* as a "city" poem must explore the
central concept of the "unreal city" that Eliot derived from his
reading of Baudelaire.[30] As Eliot confesses:

> It may be that I am indebted to Baudelaire chiefly for half a
> dozen lines out of the whole of *Fleurs du Mal*; and that his sig-
> nificance for me is summed up in the lines:

Fourmillante Cité, cité pleine de rêves,
Où le spectre en plein jour raccroche le passant . . .

I knew what *that* meant, because I had lived it before I knew
that I wanted to turn it into verse on my own account.

("What Dante Means to Me," TCTC, 126–27)³¹

Eliot can successfully read Baudelaire ("I knew what *that* meant")
by virtue of his own lived experience, and this reading in turn
opens the way for him to express that Baudelairean unreality, the
"fusion between the sordidly realistic and the phantasmagoric."
The confessional remarks in "What Dante Means to Me" that link
Eliot's lived experience to Baudelaire's lines complement the note
in *The Waste Land* (NWL, 60) that points to those same lines as a
source for the "Unreal city" of the poem. Both citations support
Eliot's contention that the mediation of the intertext is both catalyst
and condition for all poetic or critical production: "No poet, no artist of any art, has his complete meaning alone. His significance, his
appreciation is the appreciation of his relation to the dead poets
and artists" (*SE*, 4).

It is the shock of reading the dead poet Baudelaire that enables
Eliot to put his own impressions into words—"to turn it into verse
on my own account." Thus he can transform Baudelaire's opening
lines of "Les Sept Vieillards" into his own "city full of dreams":

Unreal City,
Under the brown fog of a winter dawn,
A crowd flowed over London Bridge, so many,
I had not thought death had undone so many.
Sighs, short and infrequent, were exhaled,
And each man fixed his eyes before his feet.
Flowed up the hill and down King William Street,
To where Saint Mary Woolnoth kept the hours
With a dead sound on the final stroke of nine.

(60–68)

Everyday London has become hallucinatory: it is a "composite" landscape where obviously symbolic features, like Dantesque crowds of
the dead flowing over London Bridge, threaten to dematerialize the
"real" city and crowds. The specificity of place gives substance to
the dream-vision even while making the city's physical structure
seem spectral, imaginary.

For in building upon a poet whose representation of the urban
landscape, in another country and century, was far more psycho-

logical than topographic, Eliot does not seek a specific rendering of contemporary London. Baudelaire's poetic city is historical Paris only by virtue of the title *Tableaux parisiens* and a few topical references; he projects imaginative pictures of a city whose essence he has thoroughly distilled.[32] Eliot recognizes that Baudelaire's techniques are not designed to convey the unique flavor of a particular city, but rather to express what is common to all urban experience: with his "stock of imagery of contemporary life" Baudelaire, Eliot says, "introduces something new, and something universal in modern life" (*SE*, 377).[33]

Curiously, Eliot's mention of specific sites in the city contributes little toward grounding the poem in an original "lived" experience. Perhaps under the influence of Joyce's *Ulysses*, Eliot makes extensive use of London geography to link the mythic with the quotidian. But the constant interpenetration of topographical and literary landscapes highlights the process by which the "real" comes to seem "unreal"—how, for example, the reader's apprehension of apparently solid London bridges is filtered through verses of Dante and nursery rhymes. Indeed, the more real, the less so; editing the original draft of the poem, Pound wrote "Blake" in the margin next to "King William Street," implying that by locating mythic events in contemporary London Eliot was following Blake's method in *Jerusalem* and other poems (*WLFT*, 9). Therefore, even when Eliot's topography would seem to be at its most concrete—in the name of an actual street—the very first reader of the poem, living in London with Eliot, responded to his words as a literary code, one that deflected attention to and gained resonance from its interaction with the larger intertext of urban poetry.[34]

Eliot's other references augment this dematerializing effect, while at the same time allying Eliot with Baudelaire's belief that the modern city must be measured against the city of God.[35] Since the "Unreal city" passage appears at the climax of the first section of *The Waste Land*, "The Burial of the Dead," the context of the Anglican burial service implies that the earthly metropolis is impermanent and illusory; the City of London especially, with its deadening financial obsessions, is merely an ephemeral commercial Babylon. The allusion to Dante's damned goes further, denominating an infernal image of the New Jerusalem to come. In consequence, nature and society too have lost their reality: the work-bound automatons are "undone" by a prophetic death-in-life because the organic rhythms of life are disrupted by atomistic urban time. The disjunction of natural processes culminates in the "unreal emotions" of human intercourse, tied to clocks, time, and machines, that plague the entire city-poem.[36]

Two quotations used in the manuscript help clarify the otherworldly perspective from which Eliot's London seems unreal. After the line in which Madame Sosostris sees "crowds of people, walking round in a ring" (56), Eliot originally wrote "I John saw these things, and heard them" (*WLFT*, 9). His quotation from Revelation 22:8 links these crowds—who later reappear in the first "Unreal city" stanza—to the citizens of Babylon, the worldly city of fornication and greed soon to be destroyed. Then, in the poem's second "Unreal city" section, which describes the meeting with Mr. Eugenides, Eliot had written, "Not here, O Glaucon, but in another world" (*WLFT*, 31). He was alluding to the passage at the end of Book ix of *The Republic*, in which Glaucon comments that the ideal city cannot be found on earth, and Socrates responds that "it is laid up as a pattern in heaven, where he who wishes can see it and found it in his own heart."[37] By using Plato, Eliot stresses the metaphysical quality of the "real" heavenly city, as opposed to the secondariness and impermanence of the earthly "unreal" city. Since, as Valerie Eliot points out, it was this passage that "inspired the idea of the City of God among Stoics and Christians, and found its finest exponent in St. Augustine" (*WLFT*, 128), Eliot indirectly invokes the major Christian and classical sources for the concept of the heavenly city. Thus, at the points where the "unreal city" appeared in the poem's original draft, Eliot took care to refer to the "real" otherworldly city by which it had been judged and found wanting.[38] The removal of such references in the final version obscures only slightly the reasons for the "unreality" of a London that is clearly Babylonian in the symbolic resonance of its "fallen" condition.[39]

Eliot's note to the phrase "Unreal city" cites Baudelaire's lines in which the poet himself becomes the *passant* accosted by the specters of urban life (NWL, 60). In this way Eliot links the passing stranger to his own unreal city. But the stranger who emerges from this text is a literary, not literal, passer-by. The single multiplying character of Baudelaire's *vieillard*, fantastically proliferating like the city he symbolizes, inspires Eliot to envision the various characters of *The Waste Land* merging into one another. Perhaps more important, the way in which Baudelaire's speaker must unwillingly witness the repugnant self-repetition of the old man anticipates the relationship between the narrating Tiresias, who has "foresuffered all," and the "swarming life" of London (*WLFT*, 31) that Eliot's multiple personages represent. Like the poet, Tiresias rereads and relates experience rather than participating in it at first hand.[40]

Eliot's statements about the process of reading confirm what his poetry already demonstrates, that there is no direct line to be traced from the poet's urban experience to the poem of the city. Indeed, the form of the poem, from epigraph to endnotes, expresses the mediation of texts and reading to the point of obliterating whatever specific events may have generated it.[41] For Eliot, his encounter with Baudelaire was more striking than any actual encounter the city could provide. *The Waste Land* therefore registers an important shift in the poetic response to the city, one that becomes even more pronounced in Williams. However figural the situation ultimately might prove to be, in the nineteenth century the urban poet of *Tableaux parisiens*, *Leaves of Grass*, or *The Prelude* represents his encounter with the Other in a mimetic way, as an incident spawned by the new social and physical conditions of the great city. But in the twentieth century the poet encounters the Other—and the city—as *already written*, as a figure already displaced into quotation, pastiche, collage, poetic text. Eliot destabilizes time, space, and mimetic effect so that his metropolis becomes a polyphonic, multivoiced, unabashedly literary artifact.[42] In "Le Cygne," Baudelaire says that "tout pour moi devient allégorie"; but for Eliot, the city and its inhabitants do not *become* allegory—they are already figurations of the clash between literary culture and urban consciousness.

In the psychosexual literary history that Eliot's writing enables us to trace, Baudelaire thus plays a double role: first as the captivating *passant* to whose spell the young Eliot willingly surrenders, and second as a ghostly forefather or "spectre en plein jour" who in his turn accosts the passer-by, in this case the impressionable poet and reader. In the first instance the meeting with the older poet serves as a revelation, opening new vistas; but in the second the stern forebear will not release his grip, and seems to determine every word his *hypocrite lecteur* would like to utter.

This metaphoric encounter between the poet and his predecessor informs the actual meeting of the narrator and Stetson which takes place in the continuation of the "Unreal city" passage quoted above:

> There I saw one I knew, and stopped him, crying: 'Stetson!
> 'You who were with me in the ships at Mylae!'

> (69–70)

Unlike those who fix their eyes before their feet, the narrator comes face to face with one of the specters of the unreal city. The shock of recognition suddenly enables him to step aside from the numbness of the masses flowing over London Bridge. Yet it is not a genuine *passant* experience, for that requires a brush not merely with the unexpected, but with the unknown. The figure of Stetson (apparently based on a clerk with whom Eliot worked at Lloyds Bank)[43] is both strange *and* familiar: he is the shade of a sailor whom the long-lived narrator had once fought beside in the First Punic War. Nonetheless, in his double identity as modern man and ancient warrior, Stetson is alien enough to shock, prompting the narrator to reveal his deepest fears:

> 'That corpse you planted last year in your garden,
> 'Has it begun to sprout? Will it bloom this year?
> 'Or has the sudden frost disturbed its bed?
> 'O keep the Dog far hence, that's friend to men,
> 'Or with his nails he'll dig it up again!
> 'You! hypocrite lecteur!—mon semblable,—mon frère!'
>
> (71–76)

The ghostly deadness of the city, fraught with literary echoes, provokes this aggressive confrontation, releasing a torrent of questions and exclamations that betray the narrator's anxieties about the human, vegetative, and especially literary sterility in which he finds himself imprisoned. While his inquiry about the planted corpse and his expectation that it will sprout suggest a vegetation ritual, they also relate to fertility in another way, designating the corpse or "corpus" of the literary tradition to which the poet must offer himself. His talent must germinate within this seedbed so that they will be able to "bloom" together.

The "corpses" scattered throughout the poem—"quotations from, allusions to, or imitations of, at least thirty-five different writers," according to Edmund Wilson's count[44]—are waiting to "sprout" into new lives and verses. As Eliot remarks, "not only the best, but the most individual parts of [the poet's] work may be those in which the dead poets, his ancestors, assert their immortality most vigorously" (*SE*, 4). But when they suffer from the frost of unreal urban blight, the dormancy of the dead only intensifies the poet's own fear of sterility, his knowledge of himself as frustrated brother of Baudelaire's *hypocrite lecteur*.

Eliot's sternest comment on reading, the quotation from "Au

Lecteur," signals his sense of the inescapably literary mediation of
life and art, and in particular his reliance on Baudelaire as a medium for expressing his own urban experiences. Eliot's narrator addresses these borrowed words to Stetson. But by virtue of their
original use (as Baudelaire's address to *his* complacent readers), as
well as their bold assertion of camaraderie and hypocrisy, they encompass both the present poet and his readers. Forcing both creator and consumer of the poem to face their own belatedness and
inauthenticity, Eliot underscores the textual interdependency of
poet, tradition, and audience. Since the line closes the "Unreal
city" passage, it identifies the metropolis of *The Waste Land* with a
failure of both sex and text, of literal and literary fecundity.

Connecting the contemporary urban landscape to a pervasive
spiritual and sexual morbidity, and tersely alluding to the complex
interaction between poet and reading, the scene functions almost
as a microcosm of the entire poem. For, finally, the city of *The
Waste Land* is unreal because it is made of words. Founded on Baudelaire and pieced together with quotations from dozens of other
writers, it is a metaphoric construct whose self-conscious art betrays its artifice. As Tennyson's Merlin says of Camelot, "the city is
built / To music, therefore never built at all." [45] Even the biblical or
platonic authority that establishes the heavenly city's metaphysical
substance is ultimately textual. If Eliot claims that the poet must
find an "objective correlative" to transform his emotion into art,
here his expression is so heavily mediated by borrowings that its
only source seems to lie in words already written. The poem's disembodied voices, allusions, and imitations suggest a desperate
struggle for self-definition amid the recognition of its impossibility. [46] Unless creative readings can reassemble its scattered corpus, the poem will remain textually unreal, unpresent to itself. [47]

In a later discussion of the poetic tradition, Eliot remarked how
the progress of poetry also marks a deterioration of its promise, for
each poem ends a possibility for expression by subtracting from as
well as adding to the great reservoir of all literature (*OPP*, 66). *The
Waste Land*, for all its references to a richly varied cultural tradition,
forms with its fragments a lament for lost poetry and potency. It
announces a new sterility of creation in which the "anxiety of influence" prevents new poems from being born, condemning poets to
repeat dislocated pieces of the old ones. [48] Even more than Whitman's "beautiful dripping fragments" of phallic poetry, Eliot's
quotations seem disembodied, cut off from their contexts, fraught
with a Lacanian sense of floating signification. Together with failed

sexuality and spirituality, failed art preoccupies the poet of *The Waste Land*.

It might be argued that Eliot's weaving of quotations is sufficiently innovative in itself. But as Roy Harvey Pearce comments on Eliot's adaptation of Webster and Baudelaire in the "The Burial of the Dead," the creativity must come from somewhere beyond the text. The poet acts "as recorder, not creator":

> If the reader . . . has perhaps begun to sense how the carefully wrought consolidation of allusions does indeed argue for the creative presence of the poet, the last line transforms this argument into one for rather the creative presence of the reader. . . . Such private identity as the reader has is made out to be a product of his discovering something whose power, import, and significance derive from a source other than himself.[49]

The empowering source that circumscribes both poet and reader is the tradition, crushingly alluded to in the citation from Baudelaire that concludes the "Unreal city" stanza. Baudelaire's words singled out his poems, and now designate Eliot's, as objects "already read" even as they are written, thereby destroying the reader's imagined intimacy with the text, the sense of being spoken to by a poem that completes itself only in the reader's presence.

What, then, of the positive "self-sacrifice" of creative reading, which Eliot's criticism calls for? The appeal to Stetson does not appear strong enough to help the speaker to break out of himself, or away from the forces that enervate the entire city. With everything already read and written, with the crowds parading in numb self-enclosure, the text itself seems to be closed off from invigorating perception, just as Eliot and F. H. Bradley assert the self to be: "My experience falls within my own circle, a circle closed on the outside" (NWL, 411). Seeking genuine feeling and experience, the poet and reader uncover only quotation upon quotation, *semblable* meeting *frère*, a duplicity mirrored by a secondary text and mirroring secondary selves.[50] To read *The Waste Land*, then, is to retrace the path of Eliot's reading of Baudelaire and his other predecessors, noting the connections and crossings, the submissions, recoveries, and interpenetrations.

The sidewalk struggle between poet and precursor is not confined to the unreal city of *The Waste Land*. Twenty years later in "Little Gidding" (1942) Eliot would write of the eerie meeting with "a familiar compound ghost / Both intimate and unidentifiable" with whom he "trod the pavement in a dead patrol." Here, in "the sudden look of some dead master," the encounter with the *passant* that is partially submerged in the earlier poem comes explicitly to the surface.[51] Still haunted by a "compound" of dead poets— among whom the urban shades of Dante and Baudelaire must be prominent—and still surrounded by a blasted city, Eliot continues to look in wartime London for a way to comprehend the desolate present through his importunate literary past. In his criticism Eliot represents poetic influence as an intimate exchange, and thus this climactic moment of confrontation almost inevitably takes the form of a face-to-face meeting in the City. But emblematic of the obstacles impeding this final understanding, the street itself is defaced, and the poet's gaze deflected:

> In the disfigured street
> He left me, with a kind of valediction,
> And faded on the blowing of the horn.

Eliot had first written "dismantled street," but in changing the adjective to "disfigured" he chose to emphasize the conjunction of visage, vision, and mutilation that characterized his troubled rapport with the spectral past and the present self it might mirror.[52] The rhetorical "dis-figuring" of the Baudelairean street remains the preoccupation of Eliot's urban poetry, and his ongoing quest is to find the image and the eyes that will set him, ultimately, face to face with his reading and his city, and refigure that street once more.

THE UNKNOWN STRANGER

The process of refiguration requires Eliot to confront another face of the compound ghost, one he does not want to see. For Baudelaire's is not the only shade that prowls Eliot's unreal city. The specter of Walt Whitman also haunts *The Waste Land*, surreptitiously accosting poet and reader as they traverse the streets of the poem. In conceiving of Tiresias as an omniscient urban overseer, one capable not only of looking into any private room but also of claiming to have felt with his own body all that transpires there, Eliot could not evade the precedent of Whitman, author and peripatetic urban everyman.[53] Like Whitman, who declares, "I am afoot with my vision," Tiresias makes the rounds of the city, paying as much attention to hidden sexual relations as to the crowds in the street. And like Whitman, Eliot believes intensely that the vitality of the city can be measured in terms of its sexual health. But because Whitmanesque plenitude, eye contact, and enthusiastic prophecy about the rewards of the future stand in such pointed opposition to "what Tiresias sees," his provocative presence must be—unsuccessfully—repressed.[54]

Eliot's multiple characters, actions, occupations, and contentious, self-mirroring, first-person voices make *The Waste Land* a sort of cacophanous "Song of Myself." The spirit of Whitman seems to inform the only hopeful moment in the first four sections of the poem:

> O City city, I can sometimes hear
> Beside a public bar in Lower Thames Street,
> The pleasant whining of a mandoline
> And a clatter and a chatter from within
> Where fishmen lounge at noon . . . .
>
> (259–63)

The apostrophe to the City suggests that Eliot, who worked in the financial district of London, "the City," and pondered its relation to the metropolis at large, might also have felt himself to be a kind of Oedipus, lamenting the city's condition and searching poetically for a cure.[55] And here he unexpectedly, momentarily finds it in the pleasant music and easy masculine rapport of the public bar. Unconstrained by a Baudelairean "brown fog of a winter noon," the fishmen lounge in Whitmanesque fashion, unperturbed by the malaise of the city. Using Whitman's distinctive spelling, Eliot originally wrote "lounge and loafe" (*WLFT*, 37), thus echoing even more closely Whitman's well-known line, "I lean and loafe at my ease."[56]

Both poets associate sight and sexual vigor, and for both, perception helps determine the reality of the city, and even the wholeness of the poem and the poet representing it. But Whitman creates his city through the power of perception ("all architecture is what you do to it when you look upon it") and through a sense of his own vitality, while in Eliot the urbanite has the complementary power to destroy his city. For although both narrators perform the same function, wandering the city and appraising its condition, Whitman's self-projection is buoyantly youthful, rejoicing in male comradeship, the "swift flash of eyes offering me love," while Eliot's Tiresias is old, eyeless, androgynous. Because Tiresias's vision is barren and blind, the city and especially its sexual life wither and become repugnant to him. Both poets display the control of imagination over the city, in terms that may be read sexually, phallically; but one uses his vision to build his city—"Stand up, tall masts of Mannahatta!"—while the other devastates his—"London Bridge is falling down."

Eliot was never entirely comfortable with Whitman as poet or precursor, and in order to praise Baudelaire's conception of sexuality at Whitman's expense, he seriously misreads the latter: "Whitman had the ordinary desires of the flesh; for him there was no chasm between the real and the ideal, such as opened before the horrified eyes of Baudelaire." [57] Or the horrified eyes of Eliot, for that matter. Thus the Anglicized native son renounces his too-common father in order to adopt a fastidious foreign patrimony. Compared to what Eliot sees as the limitation of Whitman's sexual "frankness," Baudelaire "was at least able to understand that the sexual act as evil is more dignified, less boring, than as the natural, 'life-giving,' cheery automatism of the modern world" (SE, 380). Eliot seeks to show how this kind of intercourse is cut off from the spiritually oriented values that could give it meaning, even an infernal one. Because he refuses to recognize similar strains in Whitman's anxious quest for a sexually healthy city, Eliot turns away from his unascetic, often ecstatic, example.

Eliot's preoccupation with myths of vegetation and the Grail implies a desire to substitute sex for religion as a regenerative force amid the spiritual drought. But as The Waste Land demonstrates, he is painfully aware that this currency too—particularly in its clamorous Whitmanesque version—has been debased. Thus he takes the desperate position that "damnation itself is an immediate form of salvation—of salvation from the ennui of modern life, because it at last gives some significance to living" (SE, 379). In his effort to describe an authentic encounter with something beyond the self, Eliot associates the self-giving acts of reading and sex; and here he is even willing to conceive of eternal punishment as a way to combat Baudelairean ennui, to jolt the poet into life in a lifeless world. The boredom he flees has a literary as well as a sexual history, for "Ennui" is also the monstrous central figure in "Au Lecteur." To escape it, then, would be to discover a way out of the impasse faced by all the *hypocrites lecteurs* of the vapid modern city.

But Eliot seems reluctant to take the risks this escape requires. By foregrounding conventional religious purgation at the end of Section III ("O Lord Thou pluckest me out / O Lord Thou pluckest // burning" [309–11]), the poet reveals his own reading, his own battle against ennui, to have been only half-hearted. For what he must do, and what his poem *does* do, almost in spite of him, is to offer himself more boldly to the "shock and surprise" of reading. He must turn from the familiar, "lived experience" of Baudelairean texts, and embrace what for him is the real unknown Other, the ghost he has most resisted, the poetry of Whitman. Not by the damnation he comprehends and is attracted to, but by the sexual surrender that he resists, will he finally redeem his city and poem. Such a process demands the participation not only of the poet-as-reader but also of the readers of the poet. To transcend the half-liberating experience of Eliot's reading of Baudelaire—an original "release" followed by a debilitating transformation into repetitive *lecteur*—we must help bring to life the other corpses buried in Eliot's still-dormant text. In spite of Eliot's unwillingness, the reader comes to see Whitman, with a shock of recognition, as a hidden *passant* who helps to overcome the poem's unreality.

It is only through the continuing friction of its intertexts that the poem begins to suggest how moments of potential discovery might be truly embraced rather than blindly, ineffectually repeated. Just as the urbanite's sense of belatedness and waste is due to a mis-guided withholding of self from experience, so the poet's barren-ness stems from his inability to yield to the texts he inherits. Full acceptance of what it means to be an *hypocrite lecteur* provides a way of transcending initial impotence. Forced to act as a startling stranger, the reader, like the poet, must be willing to make the dan-gerous commitment to the text, to become for it the *passant(e)* that will shock it into life, even as it shocks back. To reverse the inverted waste-land sequence of saying or seeing nothing through refusal to sacrifice, creative readers must give themselves up to their own texts, and the ghosts therein. Only by meeting as sudden strangers can they recover that "bewildering minute" of shock and terror that spontaneously engenders both criticism and poetry. The bur-ied invocation of Whitman in Section III suggests a random fellow-ship that, if composed of receptive poets and readers, might dis-place Tiresias's emblematic dominance of the city's sterile readings.

In fact, the figure of Whitman finally does break through. But this regenerative voice is not heard until the poem's final section. The purifying fires ignited at the end of Section III by the citation of Buddha and St. Augustine begin to force the poem toward a crisis. City and body, exhausted flesh and shattered community, fuse in the purgatorial conflagration: "Burning burning burning burning" (308). Together with the baptismal "Death by Water" of the Phoeni-cian sailor in Section IV, this elemental obliteration of physical self and city suggests at last the promise of another world beyond the unreal city. And so at the start of Section V the poem's action moves out of the city into the desert, trying to gain perspective on the meaninglessness of the metropolis, preparing to watch from afar as it crumbles under its own weight. When the poem began, a fatalistic certainty shaped the questions asked by the poet: "what branches grow / Out of this stony rubbish? Son of man, / You cannot say, or guess, for you know only / A heap of broken images" (19–22). But now new, open questions can be posed: "Who is the third who walks always beside you?" (359).

With this interrogation about the unknown stranger, with the impulse toward discovery rather than repetition, the poem reaches a turning point. The redeeming interest in the Other can now become a reality in the poem:

> When I count, there are only you and I together
> But when I look ahead up the white road
> There is always another one walking beside you
> Gliding wrapt in a brown mantle, hooded
> I do not know whether a man or a woman
> —But who is that on the other side of you?
>
> (360–365)

Concerned uncertainty is the first step toward giving, and subsequent conjectures bring the inquiring self to the verge of surrender. In contrast to Tiresias's painful consciousness of sexual difference, the sex of the mysterious figure cannot be determined; the perception of its existence is what matters. Eliot attributes the vision to polar explorers who "had the constant delusion that there was *one more member* than could actually be counted" (NWL, 360), but exegetes have long seen here a reference to the risen Christ's journey to Emmaus (Luke 24:13–16). Thus Robert Langbaum writes that "the third . . . is the unrecognized apparition born of the Antarctic explorers' despair, and the unrecognized apparition of Jesus born of the disciples' grief over the Crucifixion. In both cases the apparition was a deliverance." [58]

But there is a third figure who walks beside these two spectral interpretations. The probable source of these lines lies nearer to home, in Whitman's "When Lilacs Last in the Dooryard Bloom'd":

> Then with the knowledge of death as walking one side of me,
> And the thought of death close-walking the other side of me,
> And I in the middle as with companions. . . . [59]

Here "Lilacs" are truly breeding out of the dead land. For Eliot's Whitmanesque stranger appears immediately after the wishfully liquid song of the hermit thrush (346–57), a song that strongly echoes the warbling of Whitman's own hermit thrush who sings earlier in "Lilacs"—an image for the emotive, healing power of poetry.[60] The voice of the literary dead grows ever more importunate. But by substituting for the certainty of death the figure of the resurrected Christ, Eliot turns the poem toward the hope of a redeemed life (albeit an elusive one) beyond the desert. As a poetically potent forebear who cannot be named, Whitman is that extra companion or *member* that Eliot italicizes yet cannot quite bring into view. Under the guise of (poetic) death, a regenerative figure has entered the poem.

In another of his analogies for the act of literary creation, Eliot describes a similar process of seeking self-deliverance by trying to perceive that hidden "apparition." The poet "has something germinating in him for which he must find words . . . or, to change the figure of speech, he is haunted by a demon," and "the words, the poem he makes, are a kind of form of exorcism of this demon" (*OPP*, 106–7). The apparition is a ghost of that germinating demon trying to "sprout," attempting to come to the surface and into the line of the poet's vision. Eliot's relationship to Whitman, then, is not so much a unique *agon* as an emblem of the cooperation that must exist between dead poets and those who would make living lines from their *corpora*. By asking "who is that on the other side of you," and by allowing the voice of another to respond—in its own rhythms—to the poet's yearnings, the poem moves toward the creative commitment of the self to text and to Other that the speech of the Thunder will command.

But first, in the very next lines, the poem's third and final "unreal" passage must momentarily transcend *passants* altogether, asking a question of a new order:

> What is the city over the mountains
> Cracks and reforms and bursts in the violet air
> Falling towers
> Jerusalem Athens Alexandria
> Vienna London
> Unreal
>
> (371–76)

What *is* the "city over the mountains," and what is its relation to the other cities—ancient, modern, real—in the poem? The last line

seems to answer the first: "unreal," as if to say that all cities, in
the poem or otherwise, are not really there, not what ultimately
matter.[61] The question is set in the context of a pilgrimage, a journey through the desert. As Eliot would later write in "Choruses
from 'The Rock'" (I, 1934):

> The desert is not remote in southern tropics,
> The desert is not only around the corner,
> The desert is squeezed in the tube-train next to you,
> The desert is in the heart of your brother.

Both passages gradually converge on the reader, reflecting the
poet's sense of an urban constriction that is not merely physical,
but metaphysical. In "The Rock," the brother ("mon frère") to *The
Waste Land*'s *hypocrite lecteur* becomes a traveler through an urban
wilderness that reflects his own inner desolation.

However, in *The Waste Land* the city over the mountains is not
just one more earthly city that cannot survive the human desert
within. Rather, it becomes a mythicized urban symbol of a culture
in crisis: "Cracks and reforms and bursts in the violet air." The first
unreal city was glimpsed at dawn; the second at noon; and now, at
the "violet hour," the third must fall, unable to withstand the force
of the final violent upheaval in human relations, the tremendous
pressure of the poet's apocalyptic vision. The list of falling or fallen
cities that appears before the final "unreal"—Jerusalem, Athens,
Alexandria, Vienna, London—progresses in time and space toward the reader and poet, toward the here and now in London.
The inevitability of this clean sweep is reiterated in one of the
poem's closing lines, "London Bridge is falling down falling down
falling down" (426). The old centers of faith and culture, self-
consumed, collapse like dominoes, burying all the typists at tea-
time, all the human engines and artifacts the poem has so relentlessly surveyed. Just as the New Jerusalem—"over the mountains"
from where St. John stands to see it—arrives from heaven in the
midst of Babylon's destruction, so Eliot's vision of the "real" city
he has been seeking begins to take shape only after the unreal,
worldly city collapses.

YES IN THUNDER

Throughout *The Waste Land*, Tiresias speaks with weary re-
vulsion of a city of tainted sex. His horror of the woman's body

("female stench" [*WLFT*, 23]) and of his own ("wrinkled dugs," "dirty hands") are part of the thrust of the poem toward death rather than life: "I want to die" reads the last line of the poem's epigraph, quoting the Sybil, another seer who has lived too long. With his sexual and literary grouses against life—his inability to be a productive reader, to make the past blossom in the present, to rewrite without quotation—the poet acts as both helpless king and baffled quester in the poem, originator and victim of the blight. And so he stumbles over corpses, quotations, and images of lost virility that culminate with the broken towers, empty cisterns, and exhausted wells of the poem's fifth and last section, where they bespeak a final emptiness—only a ruined chapel and a few dry bones at the end of an apparently meaningless quest.

But as the Thunder speaks its cryptic, redeeming word, the poem resists the death of creativity that has been the subject of its own elegy. Here, finally, through his self-instructive interpretation of a single syllable, "DA," the poet becomes the waste land's savior as well. For this transcendental utterance and the guiding words its eager listeners derive from it (*Datta*, Give; *Dayadhvam*, Sympathize; *Damyata*, Control) are the most potent words in the poem, originary acts of speech and reading that fertilize the sterile land around them. Repeating the syllables DA, DA, DA, a divine voice thunders its approval of the three readings. The Hindu fable reveals that, although no divine utterance can be completely unmediated by interpretation, creative readings are possible and can give significance to mortal life.[62]

Just how closely reading and writing, sexual surrender and purposeful living, are interconnected becomes evident here at the poem's close. Eliot has structured the climax so that the three parts of the Thunder's injunction parallel his own description of the act of reading—surrender, recovery, having something to say. The initial moments are almost identical, the free and irrevocable giving of the self, the "awful daring" that is the only true validation of love and life:

> DA
> *Datta*: what have we given?
> My friend, blood shaking my heart
> The awful daring of a moment's surrender
> Which an age of prudence can never retract
> By this, and this only, we have existed.
>
> (400–405)

The consummate risks of friendship outweigh hesitations and re-
grets, outlive obituaries and last testaments. As Eliot remarks in
the "Baudelaire" essay, any sincere action, even an evil one, is
better "than to do nothing; at least, we exist" (*SE*, 380). This release
marks the return of the generative confrontation with the Other, as
individual and as strange, non-Western text, the genuine meeting
that will confer the ability to read and see as if for the first time.
With the self-offering to "my friend," the poet of *The Waste Land*
recalls Whitman's "city of Friends," and suggests that the blindness and unreality of London-Babylon can be overcome by the love
of comrades "looking you straight in the eyes." The gift of speech
promised here, an elemental ur-syllable, blasts the Babylonian harlot's curse and blesses the usually voiceless moment of encounter.

But this action must be conjoined with the recognition of the
boundaries of the self, of the distances that each sympathetic individual must cross and, ultimately, keep:

> DA
> *Dayadhvam*: I have heard the key
> Turn in the door once and turn once only
> We think of the key, each in his prison
> Thinking of the key, each confirms a prison.
>
> (410–14)

Akin to the act of "recovery" in reading, this reestablishing of the
bounds of the self after giving suggests both the Bradleyan prison
of the subjective self ("the whole world for each is peculiar and
private to that soul" [NWL, 411]) and the means of escaping it,
through sympathy with others. Like Whitman, Eliot implies that
the prison *is* the key, self reaching Other through the loneliness
that all share, each pang of isolation confirming a common fate.

"And the third moment is having something to say, before you
have forgotten both surrender and recovery":

> DA
> *Damyata*: the boat responded
> Gaily, to the hand expert with sail and oar
> The sea was calm, your heart would have responded
> Gaily, when invited, beating obedient
> To controlling hands.
>
> (417–22)

The responsive boat is the craft of poetry, its willing heart now able
to beat obediently because of what has just been given to it ("blood

shaking my heart"). By virtue of a heartfelt invitation, a transformation begins, remaking the broken connection and fingernails of "dirty hands" into the "controlling hands" of the narrator. Now become navigator, he finds the life-giving water he needs to float the weighty vessel of his culture and poem. The feminine and masculine signs of "sail and oar" cooperate to repair the division of the sexes and unite in a creative marriage. Only the conditional tense troubles, the same "would" that Baudelaire addressed to the *passante*—"O you whom I would have loved!" This is the ghostly sign of frustrated longing, the sign of the Other as vanishing lover and insubstantial text. And yet captured in the "mémoire fertile," the lost opportunity marks with its gay remembrance the reentry of Eliot's words into the Baudelairean economy of productive desire. To the extent that we have given ourselves to the poem, the obedient heart is ours. But, compellingly, it is not quite the poet's; inviting the reader confidently like Whitman, Eliot nonetheless relies most, in this passage of discovery, on Baudelaire's dynamic tension between textual possession and personal loss.

With the rejuvenating commentary on what the Thunder said, the poet returns to life in the last moments of the poem, revealing the pervasive sterility to have been due in part to a series of imprisoning attitudes and emotions, mind-forged manacles that have shackled people to inauthentic language and joyless sex. As with Whitman, the city's redemption depends upon the spiritual condition of its inhabitants, remaining "jagged and broken" to those who feel themselves so. Sexual and literary blindness retrospectively emerge as the means by which poet and reader come to "see" what the inhabitants of the waste land have lacked. An idiom of impotence has sustained the search for the waste land's cure.

With the arid plain behind him in time as well as in space, the poet-pilot can now turn to the productive tasks of fishing and setting his lands in order. Even singing like the swallow is possible. These images of artistic action—again analogous to surrender, recovery, and expression—lend the poet the skill to build again from the shards that remain:

> These fragments I have shored against my ruins
> Why then Ile fit you. Hieronymo's mad againe.
> Datta. Dayadhvam. Damyata.
> Shantih shantih shantih

> (430–33)

These are Whitman's "beautiful dripping fragments," washed by the regenerative rain the Thunder sends. Hieronymo's madness, inseparable from the inspiration of art, permits the poet to "fit" or satisfy the reader, fulfilling the promise of delivering a new self, a new reading, instead of foisting off old ones on an ever-belated and guilty *hypocrite lecteur*. In the crazy playwright's new scenario, if poem and audience, narrator and poet, do pursue that moment of "awful daring," then "Shantih," "the Peace which passeth understanding" (NWL, 433) can become, in a poem concerned with sexual and literary rejuvenation, a final and yet originary ejaculation. Again, the father-figure of Whitman returns, his triumphant consummatory invocation of "Crossing Brooklyn Ferry" echoing in Eliot's lines. An offering that inscribes both possession and production, "shantih" is Eliot's version of the re-inseminating "blast" that Whitman's self-confessed poetic son, William Carlos Williams, will use to conclude *Paterson*, his own long poem about sexual and linguistic schism.

Tiresias vanishes, along with his wasted city, at the end of the poem, his blind and barren readings of the unreal city lost as the poem gives itself up to the ecstasy of the Thunder's primal syllable. In that arresting word, the poem meets and becomes its own *passant*, opening to the endless interpretation that the sudden juncture of heavenly sign and earthly site always provokes. Replacing the wizened and impotent prophet, the poet throbs fruitfully between two lives, assuming in his acquiescence the disseminative role of the male as well as the gestative part of the female. Yet he triumphs only retroactively, outside the poem, through rereading, for the apocalyptic end is his opening into a new world, and "the self recovered is never the same as the self before it was given." As the new self and reader discover, the final "shantih" fertilizes all the foregoing, so that what was foresuffered is now seen as mere foreplay, transforming this poem of waste into the seminal poetic performance of the twentieth century. Thus Eliot wrote to Bertrand Russell that the last part of the poem, Section V, "in my opinion is not only the best part, but the only part that justifies the whole, at all" (WLFT, 129). The completed poem complements and alters once again the whole tradition, and even its own earlier lines, becoming the validating action that brings forth new shoots from its own stony soil.

A new reading arises out of each act of self-offering, and out of each desire to "really criticize." F. R. Leavis understood this when he remarked of Eliot, "Even if *The Waste Land* had been . . . a 'dead

end' for him, it would still have been a new start for English poetry."[63] Yet the poem was a point of departure for Eliot too, radically demonstrating how the individual talent must discover its
own fecund relation to a seemingly dormant tradition. Baudelaire
and Whitman provided both a model and a challenge in this task,
becoming themselves images of the most promising encounters,
shocking figures he could not forget. By "surrendering himself
wholly to the work to be done" (*SE*, 11), as he had demanded the
poet do even before *The Waste Land* was written, Eliot found a way
poetically to re-animate the self, the world, and the words that represent them. Achieving creative victory through sacrifice—"by
this, and this only, we have existed"—he makes the unreal city real
once more by a reading built on regenerative fragments, "not of
what is dead, but of what is already living" (*SE*, 11).

Chapter Six

One Woman Like a City

Gender and Revelation in
William Carlos Williams' *Paterson*

When I finish the 'Paterson' thing . . . where do I send it? New York or Utah? It frightens me a bit and, as always, I don't think it's real; I wonder if it's really there—among those pages of words.

When William Carlos Williams wrote to his publisher James Laughlin in February 1945, the fears he confided about his new poem *Paterson* took a familiar form.[1] Were the poem and the locale it expressed "really there," or would the very words they comprised present the poet and reader with one more unreal city to puzzle out? Circumspectly imprecise, "the 'Paterson' thing" names a protagonist, a town, and a poem; striving to confirm the elusive identity of man, place, and text, it accords to each the substance and vitality of the others. But sent East or West, *Paterson* proved to be a letter of uncertain destination, and the question of its "finish"—both stylistic and thematic—turned out to be as open as life itself. For as Williams proceeded with the poem, he came to understand that "there can be no end to such a story I have envisioned."[2] Originally planned to conclude in four books (published 1946–1951), *Paterson* extended to a fifth (1958) and then to a sixth on which Williams was still working when he died in 1963. The open-ended collage form, sprawling and various as the city it replicated, found closure only with the end of the poet's life.

Unreal as it may sometimes have seemed, *Paterson* was conceived to give the opposite impression: it would palpably demonstrate that a man is like a city, and that the history of the two can be recounted in a poem giving lasting voice to their similitude. But in present-day Paterson, Williams felt, man and city had become estranged from woman and nature, the very entities that should give them meaning. And so the poem also became a quest for an ideal, redemptive marriage that could repair the division of man from woman, city from nature, and daily language from the needs of authentic speech. Divorce is the symbol that dominates the unreal in-

dustrial city of Paterson, and its alienating effects are echoed in the
babel-like roar of the waterfall on the Passaic River. The task of the
poet is to rediscover the pure tongue of his native ground, an un-
corrupted language that can heal the rifts of poem and town, reunifying the sexes and all they represent.

But beneath Williams' discourse of reconciliation lies a heavily
mediated struggle with other texts and places. Williams follows
both Whitman—seeking to possess the city through his body, by
identifying poem, poet, and town—and Eliot—trying to find a fertile authenticity of texts and language to repair the ravages suffered
by his New Jersey waste land. In the process, the genuine encounter that the poet seeks with women, land, and language is displaced and mediated by signs, letters, newsclippings, local history,
and myth. This fragmenting of a central urban mimetic experience
means that, despite the poet's desire fully to encompass and comprehend the environment he portrays, the restoration Williams
seeks cannot come about through a consummatory meeting with
passers-by or a sexually imaged embrace of the city's secrets. His
pretensions to knowledge must give way before the clamor from
within *Paterson* that challenges his mastery.

By listening to the dissenting female voices in his own poem,
Williams gradually recognizes that possession of the virgin language, like stability in marriage and texts, is an impossible, even
undesirable goal. Therefore he accepts a revelatory defeat in this
enterprise, a defeat that promises a new identity for man and city,
a continuing duality, not unity. The utopian marriage and ongoing
encounter with woman and nature will have to exist where the city
of the poem does, in the imagination. Unlike poems that search for
unity, *Paterson*, through the dialogue of its heterogeneous elements, teaches the poet to delight in the doubleness of art, sex, and
the city; he learns that reality itself must always dance in double
measure. Thus the culminating image of the sexualized city, the
woman met on the streets of Paterson in Book v, embodies both
whore and virgin, Babylon and New Jerusalem. Rewriting Revelation, Williams defies the unreality of city and text by collapsing the
oppositions upon which traditional concepts of urban "reality"
have long been based.

A POEM LIKE A CITY

I knew I had what I wanted to say. I knew that I wanted to say
it in *my* form. I was aware that it wasn't a finished form, yet I

knew it was not formless. I had to invent my form, if form it
was.

(IWWP, 74)

Complex and diffuse as it often appears, *Paterson* took shape in a
way that led Williams to reuse and revise the standard tropes of the
city poet. Williams built the poetical city of *Paterson* around its
New Jersey namesake, an actual city he lived near all his life. The
rich interplay of its long history, its striking geography, and its
down-to-earth contemporary activity would furnish him, he hoped,
with "an image large enough to embody the whole knowable
world about me" (*A*, 391). His reading of Whitman suggested to
Williams a way of making exterior events and objects interchangeable with the ideas and thoughts of the man who moved among
them:

> I began thinking of writing a long poem upon the resem-
> blance between the mind of modern man and a city. The
> thing was to use the multiple facets which a city presented
> as representative for comparable facets of contemporary
> thought, thus to be able to objectify the man himself as we
> know him and love him and hate him.[3]

The result would be an urban "Song of Myself" in which the poet's
immediate environment would "objectify" his inner life, so that
the human experience of the city would be no less tangible than its
topography and architecture: "Inside the bus one sees / his
thoughts sitting and standing" (*P*, 9).[4] In order to gain critical distance in this process of urban self-projection, Williams interposed
the persona of Dr. Paterson, a local physician and struggling poet.
But as the poem progressed, the device became increasingly transparent and Williams stepped more and more frequently into the
poem, undisguised. Poet, poem, place, and persona all merged:
Williams' association of Dr. Paterson with his town and the poem
itself became so strong that eventually he declined to distinguish
between them: "When I speak of Paterson throughout the poem, I
speak of both the man and the city" (*IWWP*, 73–74).

Mapping out the structure of *Paterson*, Williams explained in his
"Author's Note" that the four original parts represented the life-
cycle of its protagonist, "beginning, seeking, achieving and concluding his life in ways which the various aspects of the city may
embody . . . all the details of which may be made to voice his most
intimate convictions." *Beginning* his life in Book I, Dr. Paterson, the

"nine-months' wonder," familiarizes himself with the mythic and modern topography of Paterson. *Seeking* in Book II to comprehend its culture, classes, and relation to nature, he walks among lovers in the park by the river. *Achieving* a deeper understanding of city and language in Book III, the mature Paterson witnesses the fire in the local library and flees from books to the liberating but indecipherable language of the Falls. *Concluding* his life in Book IV, he refuses to consider his poem and history complete, and having followed the Passaic River to the sea, turns back inland to begin anew. Book V, added seven years later, pursues the dreams of the old poet out of Paterson and into the undying world of art.[5] In the progress and trials of his life, the man-city seeks "a new and total culture, the lifting of an environment to expression" (*SL*, 286).

By presenting the city as the body of a man and the poem as an extension of it, Williams consciously follows Whitman's example, and in Book v of *Paterson* he includes a letter from the young Allen Ginsberg ("A.G.") that acknowledges their common feeling for Whitman's urban scenes: "I do have a whitmanic mania & nostalgia for cities and detail . . . like the images you pick up" (*P*, 213). Indeed, the figure of Walt Whitman frames the action of the poem, appearing first as the male giant who represents the city at the start of Book I, and later as the swimmer who "turns inland toward Camden" (*A*, 392) at the close of Book IV.[6] In his most ecstatic moments of urban communion, Whitman would admit no distinction between himself and the city; his deep commitment to the American landscape and idiom thus makes him an inevitable model for the poet trying to recapture a lost harmony of man and environment, experience and expression. In his efforts to give voice to his surroundings, Dr. Paterson is a would-be incarnator of his urban landscape, and like Whitman he seeks to define the "elemental character of the place" through the sexual relation of his body to it. To make the poem palpable, and to re-possess both city and country through the power of this poetic embrace, is his Whitmanesque aim.[7]

But Williams' discourse of healing is built on a subtext of differentiation, not unity: it is inextricably tied to his battle with Pound and Eliot over the legacy of Whitman and the future of American poetry. It had always been obvious to Williams that the search for a new form must begin with local materials: "The city I wanted as my object had to be one that I knew in its most intimate details."[8] But this fervent belief in the poetic richness of Jerseyite subjects took shape in opposition to European counterparts. For decades

Williams had raged against Pound and Eliot for what he saw as
their refusal to cast off the baggage of other times and literatures,
and in *Paterson* he would alternately envy and assail them as es-
capists, shirkers of the real work:

> the men that ran
> and could run off
> toward the peripheries—
> to other centers, direct—
> for clarity (if
> they found it)
>   loveliness and
> authority in the world—
>
>   (*P*, 36)

To the authority and formalism of English poetic tradition, Williams opposes American history, speech, and daily life as the
most suitable materials for the American artist. Preferring "a local
pride"—the very first words of the poem—Williams rejects those
Europeanized dog-poets who "Dig / a musty bone" (*P*, 3). Calling
his poem "a reply to Greek and Latin with the bare hands" (*P*, 2)
he insists on wrestling with the still-unexploited novelty of American words.[9]

Repeatedly, Williams insisted on the "releasing quality" of local
experience (*SL*, 123), giving it universal significance: "We live only
in one place at a time but far from being bound by it, only through
it do we realize our freedom. Place then ceases to be a restriction."[10] Thus Williams took to heart the topographic lesson of
Joyce's *Ulysses*—but without the Homeric infrastructure—in his
determination to let his own time and place speak for all: "I had
been reading *Ulysses*. But I forgot about Joyce and fell in love with
my city" (*IWWP*, 72).[11] Such statements indicate the insecurity of
Williams' position, relying on Europe to help define what is most
valuable about American experience. Each time he defends Paterson, he finds it necessary to invoke the cities it is not: "What can
happen whatever the environment, whether it's Paris or London or
wherever it is, also happens here. That is why Paris and London
aren't interested—to hell with it, this is just a province. But people
live in provinces."[12] Against the mainstream modernist preoccupation with the unfathomable greatness of capital cities, Williams is
determined to be provincial, to reject their rejection.[13] Thus he also
dismisses the nearby American metropolis he might logically have
chosen as his subject: "New York City belongs to the world, and I

did not feel that I could properly handle it, in a small compass, giving it all the characteristics that I knew."[14] Explaining why he wrote about Paterson, Williams always feels compelled to say why he discounted New York.[15] The small scale of Paterson is the mark of its authenticity as the proper subject of an American poem, but its redeeming provinciality can be established only in relation to the "other centers" that Williams shunned.

Despite his lifelong argument with Pound, in *Paterson* it was Eliot and *The Waste Land* that Williams took as his particular targets, scattering jibes throughout the work: "Who is it spoke of April? Some / insane engineer" (*P*, 142). Williams regarded *Paterson* not only as a poem but as an instrument of revenge, and he was forthright about the nature of the grievance:

> out of the blue *The Dial* brought out *The Waste Land* and all our hilarity ended. It wiped out our world as if an atom bomb had been dropped upon it. . . . Critically Eliot returned us to the classroom just at the moment when I felt that we were on the point of escape to matters much closer to the essence of a new art form itself—rooted in the locality which should give it fruit. I knew at once that in certain ways I was most defeated.
>
> (*A*, 174)

Williams felt Eliot had betrayed him and his cause on two essential and interrelated issues: the subject matter of modern poetry, and the verse form it should take.[16] While acknowledging Eliot's greater reading and poetic expertise, Williams could not forgive his expatriation and his lack of interest in putting his ability to use in a decisively American manner.[17] If *The Waste Land* sandwiched dozens of allusions to world literature in between references to contemporary London and Hindu scripture, *Paterson* would reject this approach by loyally sticking to Jersey history and such Paterson landmarks as the castle, the park, and the public library.

Williams quarreled with Eliot not just on his own account but also in defense of the idea of a true American poetry, first made possible by Whitman: "I shall never forget the impression created by *The Waste Land* . . . . I had not known how much the spirit of Whitman animated us until it was withdrawn from us. Free verse became overnight a thing of the past." For Williams it was necessary to keep the spirit of Whitman alive because it was he who "facing the breakers coming in on the New Jersey shore" first sensed "the great mystery" of "a new language akin to the New World."[18] According to Williams, Eliot had never understood the need for a

new poetic measure based on the free verse that Whitman had pio-
neered, rooting foreign rhythms in local soil. Faced with Whitman's unfinished work, Williams argued, "It is up to us, in the new
dialect, to continue it by a new construction upon the syllables"
(*A*, 392). But Eliot seemed to be working at cross purposes: "Whitman as a symbol of indiscriminate freedom was completely anti-
pathetic to Mr. Eliot, who now won the country away from him
again." [19]

Williams' struggle with Eliot over the ghost of Whitman relates
directly to the identity of *Paterson* as a city poem. [20] Fulfilling his
duty to Whitman, Williams wants to create for himself and American poetry a new language, a "new contribution," through which
he can articulate the natural voice of the Passaic Falls as well as the
daily urban life lived beside it: "to *make* a poem, fulfilling the re-
quirements of the art, and yet new, in the sense that in the very lay
of the syllables Paterson as Paterson would be discovered, perfect
. . . particular to its own idiom" (*A*, 392). But in attempting to sur-
pass *The Waste Land* and return American poetry to its legitimate
native course, Williams finds himself reinscribing the European
Other he seeks to vanquish. His many references to Eliot keep before the reader the divorce of language from locality that *Paterson*
strives to repair. [21]

To deal faithfully with the disjunctions of contemporary American life meant presenting the beautiful and innocent alongside the
perverted and deformed, in much the same way that the daily
newspaper juxtaposes the catastrophic and the trivial, the brutal
and the humane. [22] Readers of *Paterson*'s "newsclippings" must, in a
process similar to that of reading *The Waste Land*, piece together the
mosaic bits of the town's collective life, or be overwhelmed by the
apparent chaos. And as with the encyclopedic range of Whitman's
poems, the task is enormous: "a mass of detail / to interrelate on a
new ground, difficultly" (*P*, 20). *Paterson* assaults the reader with a
barrage of heterogeneous detail that simulates street experience itself: "That which is heard from the lips of those to whom we are
talking in our day's-affairs mingles with what we see in the streets
and everywhere about us as it mingles also with our imaginations"
(*Imag.*, 59).

The most distinctive formal aspect of *Paterson*, then, is also the
most original: in this poem that Williams likens to "a gathering up"
and a basket (*P*, 2), the reader confronts snatches of prose histories, letters both actual and fictitious, advertisements, medical
texts, news items, geological descriptions, and bits of dialogue, at

the same time dealing, in the more "poetic" lines, with variable feet and inventive typography.[23] *Paterson* proceeds by turning prose into poetry, dissolving the hierarchical oppositions of classical poetics in order to show that the quotidian in all its forms is material for the postmodern city poem. Williams repeatedly stressed that he did not employ "antipoetic" prose as a "heightening device": "That's plain crap. . . . The truth is that there's an *identity* between prose and verse, not an antithesis. It all rests on the same base, the same measure" (*SL*, 265)—in this case, the cadence of American speech.[24] "Poetry does not *have* to be kept away from prose as Mr. Eliot might insist, it goes *along with prose* and . . . shows itself by *itself* for what it is. It *belongs* there, in the gutter" (*SE*, 263). Poetry will lie down with prose in the urban "gutter" of the poem, as part of the attempt to "marry" city life and the poetry about it.

To achieve this multi-dimensional portrait of urban experience, Williams no longer needs to talk so extensively about the look of the streets or the rush of the crowd. The city of *Paterson* becomes a syntax, a cast of mind, a disjointed and elliptical style that has had a great influence on American poetry and especially the "New York School" since the 1950s. Many readers have been confused by this approach, claiming that there is not enough "city" in the poem to act as its organizing metaphor.[25] Charles Olson, in fact, insisted that Williams "don't know fr nothing abt what a city *is*" because Olson found in *Paterson* a superabundant detail that seemed to undo the poem's referentiality to an actual urban locale.[26] This view resists the progressive breakdown in mimetic forms since the nineteenth century and disregards Williams' constant efforts to overcome such conventions. For in *Paterson* as in *Ulysses*, "the forces of the action have become internal and in a way there is no longer a city, there is only a man walking through it."[27] Whether the poetic persona "walking through" the city-poem is Walt, Tiresias, or Dr. Paterson, he allows the urban environment to shape his thoughts, and invites the reader to experience his city from the inside out.

But while there can be no denying the city-ness of *Paterson*, it is true that Williams' preference for a "knowable" city opens up a crucial difference between himself and his predecessors. "The city I wanted as my object," Williams explained, "had to be one that I knew in its most intimate details. New York was too big. . . . I deliberately selected Paterson as my reality."[28] Implying that to know a place thoroughly is to make it real, Williams combats the unreality of the modern city by trying to avoid the immensity and mystery that earlier poets had celebrated. The intimacy of the New

Jersey town would enable the poet to track down any unknown strangers: "I wanted . . . to know in detail, minutely what I was talking about—to the whites of their eyes, to their very smells" (*A*, 391). With a curiously Wordsworthian insistence on the value of his own community, Williams tries to renounce the elusive pleasures of the *passante* by a presumptuous quest for knowledge that exceeds even that of Whitman. "Passive-possessive," Dr. Paterson stalks the park in Book II: "outside myself / there is a world, / he rumbled, subject to my incursions" (*P*, 43).

Thus in *Paterson* the sudden moment of urban revelation that plays such an important role in earlier poetry now threatens to disappear entirely. Blake, Wordsworth, Baudelaire, and Whitman record in mimetic terms the confrontation with the Other in the city streets, an experience which Eliot then transforms into an encounter with reading itself, but Williams wants to dissolve self, city, and text into one another. His all-encompassing concept of "the city / the man, an identity" (*P*, 3) erodes the boundaries between self and Other, place and poet, upon which the *topos* depends. Interiorized, the actual city and streets seem to vanish. The meeting with the Other is now so mediated by the poet's awareness of other texts and the flotsam of urban experience that such encounters, like the city itself, may be everywhere and nowhere. In the collage of *Paterson*, secondary materials have overwhelmed primary experience, for the poem is self-conscious about its status as an artifact to a degree surpassing both Whitman, who by regarding his poems as a form of bodily contact repressed their textuality, and Eliot, who admitted to the shock that *passant*-like texts could give.

But the multiple texts of *Paterson* break up the old mimesis to create a new one: instead of directly addressing the absent stranger, Williams makes the absent present through the incorporation of letters from characters both far and near (such as Pound and Ginsberg), and especially through the epistolary narrative generated by the series of letters from the frustrated poet "Cress." Her letters attacking Dr. Paterson for his incomprehension of her life act like the label of Wordsworth's blind beggar, rebuking the poet's pretensions to knowledge here in his own "knowable" world. Her voice intrudes on his thoughts during his proprietary walk in the park and, in a reversal of the usual situation, we read of her reactions to meeting the poet, not the poet's response to meeting her.

Cress and the other female voices in the poem become, for all their intimacy, images of the world that the poet cannot control. If

Dr. Paterson is a small-town Tiresias, surveying what he already knows, he discovers that local texts and persons are no easier to master than the international metropoli he has turned away from. Like Eliot he must surrender to the mysteries of his poem; as he will finally admit in Book v, "I cannot tell it all" (*P*, 236). The traditional moment of urban encounter between the poet and the *passante* gives way to a series of oppositions on a mythic, symbolic level, between male and female, country and city, America and Europe, old texts and new, the roar of the Falls and the speech of the poet.

If the turmoil of the crowd no longer helps define the poet's identity, the multiple voices of the poem's characters and texts function to constitute him as they intersect with his thoughts; they are the "outside" that the poet meets "concretely" (*P*, 43). To be a man *like* a city means not to lose oneself in crowds and texts but to out-Whitman Whitman by incorporating the entirety of Paterson; as with Aquinas's God, the center of the man-city is everywhere and his circumference nowhere. The poet becomes coexistent with his poem-place, Patersons all. But *Paterson*, like Revelation, must satisfy its quest for inclusiveness by setting its Garden in a city, and build its walls with the fallen bricks of Babylon, images of the alienation it seeks to repair. There is no "natural" way to reunite city and country in a poem, and the American ground yields European hybrids. Nevertheless, Revelation becomes an exemplary paradigm for reunifying the fragmented city of Paterson, for its urban garden on a river and its betrothal of Virgin and Lamb offer an image of how Paterson might regain its original "reality" by emulating the perfect matrimony of the New Jerusalem.

A MARRIAGE RIDDLE

A city, a marriage—that stares death
in the eye

(*P*, 106)

By envisioning the poem as a man-city, Williams sought to make his poetic city real and vital, building it on the mythic identification of a city with one man. But the equation is necessarily incomplete, for it leaves out the indecisive, ongoing encounter with those very things—woman and nature—which for him define both man and city through the fact of their difference. Ultimately, then, the man-city must take a partner:

A man like a city and a woman like a flower
—who are in love. Two women. Three women.
Innumerable women, each like a flower.

                                                      But

only one man—like a city.

                                                      (*P*, 7)

Complementing the singularity of the man, the woman is actually
"innumerable women, each like a flower," her complex variousness representing the multiplicity of the natural world out of which
the male city fashions its own civilized self. The successful city will
be a fruitful marriage between these twin emblems of culture and
nature.[29] Thus in the opening pages of *Paterson* the poet intimates
the potential union of man and nature by the close proximity of
male and female giants who, lying beside each other, preside in
their sleep over the topography they embody (*P*, 6–8).

   As early as 1923 Williams had already asserted that the identity
of man and city required completion through intercourse with the
city's female population: "His great heart had expanded so as
to include the whole city, every woman young and old there he
having impregnated with sons and daughters" (*Imag.*, 198). The
central metaphors of *Paterson* take up this Whitmanesque ambition
of sexually embracing the entire metropolis, reiterating the ancient
masculine desire to wed an environment ultimately viewed as a female space. For to the mind of the aggressively loving and beget-
ting poet, "one city, like a woman" would be a more accurate
rendering of the landscape he means to marry with the sexual
power of his words.

   And yet despite the dream of the ordered city, "SOME sort /
of breakdown / has occurred" (*P*, 51). No sooner is the poem begun
than the poet must announce that his all-enabling marriage has

            come to have a shuddering
                implication
               Crying out
      or take a lesser satisfaction:
             a few go
        to the Coast without gain—
        The language is missing them
              they die also
            incommunicado.

                                                      (*P*, 11)

As they strive for mastery of nature and unity with each other, the poet and the people of Paterson discover that instead of love, an insidious alienation has gripped the town, isolating them from their neighbors and their own best interests. As the poet testifies, "Divorce is / the sign of knowledge in our time, / divorce! divorce!" (P, 18).

This sundering of man from woman and meaning from word has been the sign of all times and cities since Eden and Babel. Since "the language is worn out" (P, 84) the poet can no longer maintain his primordial marriage with nature, with the objects and energies of the world that the female giant represents:

> And She —
>   You have abandoned me!
>
>   —at the magic sound of the stream
>   she threw herself upon the bed—
>   a pitiful gesture! lost among the words:
>   Invent (if you can) discover or
>   nothing is clear—will surmount
>   the drumming in your head. There will be
>   nothing clear, nothing clear   .
>
>   He fled pursued by the roar.
>
>   (P, 84)

The symptoms of breakdown in *Paterson* are evident in three interconnected areas: man's natural relations with his environment, his sexual partner, and his language. The troubled marriage bed of the mythic giants images both the disturbed rapport of the sexes in the city and the disruption of natural cycles, for it is also the bed of the river. The man-poet-giant who seeks to comprehend this multiple divorce contends with a language that has become part of the process of dislocation; it is female and foreign to him. "Lost among the words," he must abandon any hope of clarity as long as he is "pursued by the roar" of both waterfall and city. Searching in many directions for a way to repair the rifts in his world, the poet repeatedly engages the familiar paradigm that equates an ideal marriage with an undivided city.

For *Paterson* relaunches the archetypal quest to find the perfect structure of the Heavenly City, and to make its virgin bride and seminal Word the poet's own. Like Adam, he begins with an Eve he can neither do without nor control, and like Cain, the fallen poet searches for a new language, a new ground to regain that dis-

tant home whose loss sets him on the road.[30] This second home pre-
dictably takes feminine form, both womb and wife, a community
of men united ("only one man") in their desire to tame nature's va-
riety ("innumerable women, each like a flower"). All this the final
city of New Jerusalem promises, delivering poet and language
from the present unreality of a post-Babel world. In planning the
basic structure of *Paterson* around a revelatory marriage, the resolutely secular Williams joins the many poets and prophets who for
centuries have measured their actual, wayward Babylonian cities
against this biblical vision.

The ongoing effort to marry nature on a grand scale appears
most straightforwardly in the attempts by Paterson's residents to
harness the Falls, an historical process that Williams documents
in long prose extracts. At the root of Paterson's self-alienation lies
Alexander Hamilton's project for economic exploitation of the Passaic. Hamilton tried to capitalize on the great industrial potential of
the Falls, producing a network of flourishing factories that he
named the "Society for Useful Manufactures," or SUM (*P*, 69, 73).
But such appropriation of natural wealth without reimbursement is
reminiscent of Blake's "charter'd Thames"; it separates the city
from its natural ground, creating instead a "Legalized National
Usury System" (*P*, 74). This NUS reverses the effects of the agent
for natural growth, the sun, and must be eradicated before the city
can be reintegrated with its surroundings: "Release the Gamma
rays that cure the cancer / . the cancer, usury" (*P*, 182–83).

The plans for the layout of the city further reflect a desire to
dominate the environment, for originally Paterson was to have had
a neoclassical grid-plan drawn up by the French architect Pierre
L'Enfant, similar to his design of Washington, D.C. Seeking to mirror the divine pattern of the celestial city, the town planners attempted to impose order upon the uneven terrain of Paterson by
orienting the town and its people on well-defined axes radiating
from its civic and ecclesiastical hubs. But to dedicate any society to
rigid structures is to alienate it from the landscape that gives it life,
repeating an ancient crime against the earth. In "The Destruction
of Tenochtitlan," Williams describes how Cortez's conquest of
Montezuma violated the native American legacy of nature-city interpenetration; the act was an early instance of divorce that modern city builders have perpetuated. Since the European city of the
conquerors claims a divine model, it thus always marks an already
fallen state, one cut off from the "primal and continuous identity
with the ground itself" (*IAG*, 33–34).[31] Despite the fact that the

residents of Paterson eventually reject the foreign architect for a native one, it is already too late: "the ground has undergone / a subtle transformation, its identity altered" (P, 19).[32] The poem is replete with images of the urban dislocation of the natural world:

> a bud forever green,
> tight curled, upon the pavement, perfect
> in juice and substance but divorced, divorced
> from its fellows, fallen low—
>
> (P, 18)

The poet too cannot remain unharmed: like the bud "divorced from its fellows" he yearns to communicate in an organic language, but he has been wrenched from his native soil, both by followers of a European literary tradition, such as Eliot, and by the historical developments that have corrupted the city.

The commercial selfishness of Paterson exemplifies the basic conflicts of the natural and artificial. Thus Williams remarks that "the whole theme of *Paterson* is brought out in . . . the contrast between the mythic beauty of the Falls and Mountain and the industrial hideousness."[33] The epigraph of Book III makes the underlying alienation explicit: "Cities, for Oliver, were not a part of nature. He could hardly feel . . . that cities are a second body for the human mind, a second organism" (P, 94). If the city loses its sense of how human nature and its urban products belong organically to the natural world, Paterson as place and poem will mirror only

> .   .   .   a world of corrupt cities,
> nothing else, that death stares in the eye,
> lacking love: no palaces, no secluded gardens,
> no water among the stones; the stone rails
> of the balustrades, scooped out, running with
> clear water, no peace   .
>   The waters
> are dry.
>
> (P, 107)

This is Williams' own Waste Land, a fallen Babylon that echoes Eliot's without irony.

For despite Williams' invective against Eliot's poem, *Paterson* shares with *The Waste Land* the belief that the sexual and moral inadequacies of the city lie at the heart of a polluted landscape. Beginning in Book I with the "thousand automatons" who "walk outside their bodies aimlessly / . . . / locked and forgot in their desires" (*P*, 6), Williams repeatedly depicts the frustrated interaction of the sexes and the lack of communication and artistic insight that ensues. Although far more vibrant than Eliot's Tiresias, Dr. Paterson too has the distressing gift of discovering unreality and sexual anomie in his own town, wherever he turns. The adulteries of Dr. Paterson create their own sleazy metropolis, a devalued city expressing the degenerate life of the present day:

> Oh Paterson!   Oh married man!
> He is the city of cheap hotels and private
> entrances   .   of taxis at the door, the car
> standing in the rain hour after hour by
> the roadhouse entrance   .
>
> (*P*, 154)

In the modern city, where divorce from a sense of community, nature, or history seems commonplace, all hopes and pressures for redemption focus on sexual relations—the very area in which the divorce is most evident and painful.[34]

And hardest to escape: in Book IV the poem ventures out of Paterson to New York, but "with the approach to the city, international character began to enter the innocent river and pervert it; sexual perversions, such things that every metropolis . . . houses" (*IWWP*, 79). Small town and big city complement each other in their decadence. In Manhattan a cosmopolitan businesswoman who names herself "Corydon" and her Jerseyite masseuse Phyllis ironically enact a debased pastoral:

> Let's change names. You be Corydon! And I'll play Phyllis.
> Young! Innocent! One can fairly hear the pelting of apples
> and the stomp and clatter of Pan's hoofbeats. Tantamount to
> nothing   .
>
> (*P*, 158)

The vulgar "play" at recovering old myths of innocence, emphasized in the vacuousness of Corydon's poems, points to the formidable task *Paterson* sets for itself of repairing the breaches of nature, faith, and language that seem to inhibit every contemporary relationship.

The tangled sexual situation, with Phyllis as the teasing focus of both Dr. Paterson's adultery and Corydon's lesbianism, only underlines the distance from true Arcady. Yet this bizarre episode, too, falls back into a biblical frame. Corydon entices Phyllis with a trip on her yacht: "Let me take you on a tour   .   of Paradise!"

But Phyllis claims she is not yet ready to "die"—sexually or actually—"not even for that" (*P*, 167). She torments her lovers with
her dubious virginity (*P*, 158, 170), playing the whore who will
keep them from attaining their diminished New Jerusalem in New
Jersey.

In contrast to the unfulfilling interludes with Phyllis, what the
poet needs is a truer language of the body:

> I wish to be with you abed, we two
> as if the bed were the bed of a stream
> —I have much to say to you
>
> .   .   .   .
>
> and I am aware of the stream
> that has no language, coursing
> beneath the quiet heaven of
> your eyes
>
>   which has no speech; to
> go to bed with you, to pass beyond
> the moment of meeting . . .

(*P*, 24)

In such moments the poet, like Whitman, will "have much to say"
to his companion and will find a heavenly reward in her eyes. But
if the health of the city depends on achieving such a communion
beyond speech, Paterson is ill indeed. Listening to the sounds that
city and nature make together, the poet hears only babel: "in that
din, / Earth, the chatterer, father of all / speech" (*P*, 39).

Just as the river separates the masculine city from the female
park, the confusing "roar" of the Falls prevents the poet from
bridging the human and natural worlds. It is this breakdown of language that the disgruntled Dr. Paterson has to confront as he walks
among the Sunday crowds in the park. Like Tiresias, he stalks a
city of degraded desire, and cannot influence the degenerate behavior he observes. The drunken working-class lovers he passes
are lumpish, leering, lustful, and "flagrantly bored" (*P*, 58–59).
The *genii loci* of the place, the male and female giants, symbolize
this estrangement, for they are "married with empty words" (*P*, 83).

The extended promenade of Book II deserves attention because
of the thoroughness with which it incorporates male and female
images of the biblical quest for a reunified language, city, and marriage. Walking serves as the metaphor by which Dr. Paterson con-
ducts his sexual and poetic exploration. The poet strolls amid the

chaotic activity of his fellow man, covering ground in the hope that his presiding male intelligence can fashion from it a rational, phallocentric order: "The observation tower / in the middle distance stands up prominently / from its pubic grove" (*P*, 53). But his presence also suggests sexual violence, for "the Park / upon the rock" is

> female to the city
>
> —upon whose body Paterson instructs his thoughts (concretely).
>
> (*P*, 43)

Already defiled by its brutish citizens, the park now submits to the examination of the doctor-poet who wishes to heal their ravages with his art. Spying on lovers and probing the bushes with his eyes, he repeatedly invades the privacy of the couples whose public amorousness he disdains.

Yet "Voices! / multiple and inarticulate" (*P*, 54) continually assail him, voices that symbolize the difficulties of his own poetic enterprise. Even as the walk begins, he is reminded of the writer's deadly enemy, the inner obstacles that hobble his peripatetic desire to articulate his path through the complex Jersey landscape:

> That kind of blockage, exiling one's self from one's self—
> have you ever experienced it? I dare say you have, at moments; and if so, you can well understand what a serious psychological injury it amounts to when turned into a permanent day-to-day condition.
>
> (*P*, 45)

Throughout Book II the eloquently frustrated letters of the struggling poet Cress break into Dr. Paterson's thoughts as instances of sexual and linguistic schism. Castigating Dr. Paterson's behavior as man and poet, Cress claims that he is the source of her own writer's block. But the letters also serve as a kind of chorus restating the creative impotence Dr. Paterson himself feels. For like divorce and the exploitation of nature, "blockage" figures as a crisis of modern life, preventing the poet from speaking the natural language; he cannot achieve "the release / that should cleanse" (*P*, 34) which he needs to reestablish contact between man and nature, man and woman, word and thing.[35] Instead, the poem's texts transmit rather than diminish the divorce of true feeling from well-intended words. Dr. Paterson ignores Cress's letters only to augment their alienating effect:

it could not but follow that that whole side of life connected
with those letters should in consequence take on for my own
self that same kind of unreality and inaccessibility which the
inner lives of other people often have for us.

(P, 48)

The contagion of unreality the doctor sought to evade in his own
words spreads even in his silence.

There is a moment of hope: in his prosaic walk through the park
he cannot transmute, the poet inadvertently stumbles upon a
dance, which Williams sees as the original source of poetry:[36]

>   Mary
>   is up!
>   Come on! Wassa ma'? You got
> broken leg?
>
>   . . . .
>
>   —lifts one arm holding the cymbals
> of her thoughts, cocks her old head
> and dances! raising her skirts:
>
>   La la la la!

(P, 57)

In the immigrant Mary's dance, Dr. Paterson sees "the old, the very
old, old upon old, / the undying" (P, 57) gestures that his modern
poem cannot capture, a ritual movement around a center he is unable to find. His poem appears to lie elsewhere, in the "walking"
prose of contemporary life which escapes the old restrictions, and
he recognizes that the nostalgia for order is unnecessary and inhib-
iting. From the ancient natural vitality of Mary's dance, "suppressed : but . persistent" (P, 58), emanates a life-force that might
transform prose into poetry, breaking the artificial barriers between them. But the coarse Sunday crowds overwhelm the moment: Mary's inarticulate song amid drunken bodies cannot miraculously conceive what he later calls his "virgin purpose, / the
language" (P, 187). A prying *flâneur* rambling through the urban
refuse of the park, Dr. Paterson pursues a degraded Baudelairean
itinerary where each sight delivers less than the last.

What he does encounter, however, is another reaffirmation of
the link between sexual and heavenly cities, for there is a preacher
in the park. Spiritual descendant of St. John the Divine, the evangelist tries to restore the Word to the modern city: "Jumping up

and down in his ecstacy he beams / into the empty blue, eastward, over the parapet / toward the city" (*P*, 64). A few lines later he even seems to glimpse his New Jerusalem: "Look, there lies the city!" Telling the "great beast" of the crowd to abandon the morally crippling Hamiltonian pursuit of worldly goods, he invokes the "boundless resources" of the Almighty. Religion must tame the volatile confusion of a fallen but fertile world. But "No figure / from the clouds seems brought hovering near" (*P*, 65). In fact, the great beast, all too Babylonian in its sensuality and self-indulgence, resists his most strenuous efforts:

> There where
> the movement throbs openly
> and you can hear the Evangelist shouting!
>
> —moving nearer
> she—lean as a goat—leans
> her lean belly to the man's backside
> toying with the clips of his
> suspenders   .
>
> (*P*, 59)

Both poet and preacher are defeated in their missions, "so rivaled" are they by the vulgar sexuality of Paterson's masses. In consequence, "the poem, / the most perfect rock and temple" (*P*, 80) that should ground the life of Paterson, is insufficient to the task of ordering the chaos around it. And so "the poet, / in disgrace" (*P*, 80), unable to control the scene through the imposition of his will or the failing strength of his Eliotic "dry bones," can only project a "debased city"

> reversed in the mirror of its
> own squalor, debased by the divorce from learning,
> its garbage on the curbs, its legislators
> under the garbage, uninstructed, incapable of
> self instruction   .
>
> (*P*, 81)

Unable to harmonize the cacophony of voices in the park, the poet discovers the futility of looking for a single meaning in the "debacle" of this urban multiplicity: to the "eternal bride" of the place he confesses, "in your / composition and decomposition / I find my . . / despair!" (*P*, 75).

Near the center of *Paterson*, however, one passage shows the poet to be meditating productively on the essential insight he must actualize—the truth of his original conception that, in spite of all he has seen, the communion between man and woman must and *can* overcome the deepest divisions, including death:

> What end but love, that stares death in the eye?
> A city, a marriage—that stares death
> in the eye
>
> The riddle of a man and a woman
>
> For what is there but love, that stares death
> in the eye, love, begetting marriage—
> not infamy, not death
>
>   tho' love seem to beget
> only death in the old plays, only death, it is
> as tho' they wished death rather than to face
> infamy, the infamy of old cities   .
>
>   (*P*, 106)

In the city of divorce, death is everywhere in the exploitation of nature, the deracination of language, the failures of love. But the vision of Revelation—"A city, a marriage—that stares death / in the eye"—must be maintained. The "riddle" of marriage can be only partially understood, yet it can stare death down, it can beget and be begotten, reinstating the natural cycles divorced from human experience by "the infamy of old cities." These are Babel, Sodom and Gomorrah, and Babylon, and the true lover would face death rather than undergo the disgrace of their divisive lusts. The "new cities," by implication, like the New Jerusalem would beget a heavenly city by the union of the lover and his bride. The city founded to end the exile of Cain, caused by the failure of brotherly love, can be made whole again only by renewed commitment of male and female, overcoming death through procreation in the poet's words and flesh.

INNUMERABLE WOMEN

Yet despite the authority of their biblical resonance, the metaphors underlying Dr. Paterson's efforts toward fulfillment are based on difference and domination: they further divide the very landscape and people they propose to unite. For the age-old trek toward an ideal city derives much of its urgency, even in modern times, from the imagery of sexual conquest:

—a stone
thrust flint-blue
up through the sandstone
of which, broken,
    but unbreakable
we build our roads   .

                                (*P*, 110)

Dr. Paterson comes from a tradition that equates sexual knowledge with worldly power, and heavenly cities with virginal enclosures waiting to be entered. The woman-city must be "broken" and made malleable before she can be built upon. And so the poet's professed effort to heal divisions is simultaneously a gesture of repression that further separates him from the partner he has designated for himself. The entire matrimonial pathology of Paterson's maladies—unauthentic vows and betrothals, barren marriage beds, divorces of words and emotions—displays not just the desire for a revitalized body politic, but one in which the masculine impulses would bring the female errancies firmly under control.

But the woman resists. For because she is in fact "innumerable" rather than single, she cannot be definitively named. The language of appropriation that pervades Paterson as town and poem—exploitation of nature for industry, women for sex, emotions for poetry—cannot create a final, static ledger of oppositions. The woman refuses to remain merely a part of nature, and enters the world of culture too, speaking in her own authoritative voice: "In regard to the poems I left with you; will you be so kind as to return them to me at my new address?" (*P*, 7). Both as artist and human being, she insists on guarding her own mobility, texts, and integrity, thereby rivaling the poet's sovereignty.

This female resistance to masculine control animates the displaced encounters in the poem, and it is what makes *Paterson* unique among poems of the city. For although the man would like to be the city himself, Paterson is actually a city composed of many women, each with a life and mind of her own. Among the more prominent female voices in the poem are the unfathomable utterances of the Falls; Mrs. Cumming, who yields to that voice, perhaps leaping into the flood rather than living with her husband; the immigrant Mary, who dances in the park despite the disapproval of her companions; Cress, who counterpoints and attacks the poetic mission of Dr. Paterson; Madame Curie, who discovers the unstable element of uranium; the poet Sappho and her descendant

Corydon, who represent the translation of Dr. Paterson into a female phase;[37] and the lady of the Unicorn Tapestry, who subdues
the masculine, mythic thrusts of Paterson's art. An image early in
the poem conveys the poet's beleaguered situation: the poet re-
members a picture of the nine wives of an African chief, arranged
according to sexual priority along an "official" phallic log. Williams
ponders man's dubious authority over these women, whose sexuality can "stab at the mystery of a man"

> from both ends—and the middle, no matter
> how much a chief he may be, rather the more
> because of it, to destroy him at home.
>
> (P, 13–14)

Uneasily "at home" in his poem, the poet courts his own destruction amid the multifarious emblems of the female world he wants
to shape. His wives assail him even as he tries to give single-
handed birth (Pater-son) to himself and his city.

Thus the poet who boldly announced that he was the center of
female attention—"Say I am the locus / where two women meet"
(P, 110)—is caught in the crossfire of his own diacritical self-definition. If a man can only be his single self in the conjunction of a
number of women, where exactly does his essential identity reside,
and what can he be without their cooperation? They whom he
imagines will define him and make him whole undermine his labors, both linguistic and sexual, to extract his own unity from their
multiplicity. The idea that marriage would serve as a solution may
be part of the problem: in its composition and decomposition he
finds his despair.

The difficulties Williams faces with his metaphors of the city are
precisely those that Roland Barthes discovers in urban semiotics:
"the problem is to bring an expression like 'the language of the
city' out of the purely metaphorical stage. . . . The real scientific
leap will be when we speak of a language of the city without metaphor."[38] But of all those in *Paterson* who "leaped (or fell) without
a / language" (P, 84), only the now-silent dead who have actually
plummeted into the base of the Falls have embraced that mysterious speech. However the man-city names his task—espousing
the feminine falls, penetrating the "roar" of texts and river, finding
his meaning to "lay it, white, / beside the sliding water" (P, 145)—
he cannot enter into the purity he envisions at the heart of the roar
without reinscribing it in human babel. As Barthes says, the question is "how to pass from metaphor to analysis when we speak of

the language of the city."[39] But as the poet knows, without meta-phor he will have no "analysis," and no poetic life; his entire world and the poem that expresses it do not exist apart from the flowers and cities, men and women and waterfalls, that bedevil and yet in-carnate his words.

The poem, then, questions its own assumptions. Its own inter-nal voices insistently demand: Why *really* has this marriage failed? Is this tragedy caused by the problems the poet has so carefully de-scribed—divorce on the natural, sexual, and linguistic levels? Or is it initiated and even aggravated by his own masculine words and blindness? In short, is it his *own* fault? The problems of sex and na-ture may well be so thoroughly ingrained in Dr. Paterson's lan-guage that he has become a victim of his own search for a cure, and of one dangerous remedy in particular: the gender-based meta-phors through which he approaches the world. The tension in the poem between the poet's mythic view of man-nature interdepen-dence and modern society's perversion of it comes through most strongly in the suffering and repression of women. It may not be, then, the right course for the poet to listen for the primeval secrets of the Falls; he should hearken instead to the protests already sim-mering around the injustice of his own words, for the divorce he condemns may well stem from his own limited formulations.[40]

The poet's metaphoric dominance is clearly challenged in one particular area: despite his desire to image the city as a man and the woman as a flower, it is *the city* that keeps on appearing as a flower, while the woman refuses to be one. In his earlier poetry, Williams had followed convention in comparing the distant city to a flower-like woman whom he sought to possess.[41] Examin-ing Williams' anthropomorphic landscapes, Mike Weaver points out how in a poem of 1914, "Grotesque," Williams had made the city feminine and the country masculine: "The city has tits in rows. / The country is in the main—male" (*CP*, I: 49). Noting that Williams, even at the time of *Paterson*, "found no obstacle to refer-ring to the city of Paris as a woman's body," Weaver concludes that "what counts, here as in 'The Wanderer' and 'The City,' is the simple conjunction of opposites."[42] Trying to reverse these opposi-tions and to image Paterson as resolutely male, Williams nonethe-less found that the flower was one term of the opposition that could not be fixed: his lifelong love of flowers prompted him to strew *Paterson* with them, even comparing the poem itself—sup-posedly a man-city—to them in the last book (*P*, 212–13).[43]

Nor will the independent woman of the poem tolerate the kind

of antithesis that permits her to be plucked so casually by the poet.
In her final letter to Dr. Paterson, Cress accuses him of wanting

> to help me in such a way, I think, that my own achievements
> might serve as a flower in his buttonhole, if that kind of help
> had been enough to make me bloom.
>   But I have no blossoms to bring to any man . . .
>
> (*P,* 91)[44]

To be aided by this poet means to suffer the constraint of his
organic metaphors, to be nurtured only to ornament his poetic
lapel. Herself a writer, Cress exposes the logic of Dr. Paterson's imagery and makes explicit the male dominance that such figuration
assumes.

In an effort to elude the poet's linguistic aggression, the woman
can try to take refuge in her own imagery, domestic but decidedly
unorganic. Yet despite Cress's claim that "my doors are bolted
forever" against "professional do-gooders and the like" (*P,* 7),
Williams has by this very citation made a forced entry in the text.
For although her relations with Dr. Paterson make her doubt her
own reality, the author of Cress's letters is an actual woman named
Marcia Nardi, who corresponded with Williams between April
1942 and March 1943.[45] Critics dispute whether it is Williams' life
or his art that is more compromised by his appropriation of her
letters for *Paterson*. The publication of the letters repeats the crime
of which they accuse the poet, callously using someone else's suffering as material for art. And yet, as a part of "real life," they not
only assault the poet who has set his work apart from human emotion, but also show that work willing to be touched, even distorted,
by the incorporation of raw material from lived experience. The ar-
ranging and printing of the letters may even go a certain distance
toward demonstrating the "ultimate sensitivity" of their apparently unbending recipient.[46]

Paradoxically, then, this morally equivocal action furnishes the
poem with unexpected strength, right where many critics have
seen it at its weakest.[47] The tensions between poetry and prose, art
and life, man and woman, can be read differently depending upon
which genre, entity, or sex provides the context, and which the utterance. Looking back to the start of the poem, the rereader can see
that from the very beginning "innumerable women" have raised
their dissenting, independent voices, and Cress chief among them.
Thus her first letter, in which she writes, "I know myself to be
more the woman than the poet" (*P,* 7), need not be read as submit-

ting to Dr. Paterson's (or Williams') implication that the woman belongs to nature rather than culture. Rather, she is already testing
the doctor's own divorce of personal feeling from professional, artistic matters, by hinting that the *whole* person, and not just a part,
is involved in any genuine relationship. In asking for her poems
back without comment, "if you should find that embarrassing,"
she reveals herself not as a mere "natural" woman, but as an artist
who has not set aside human emotion.[48]

Williams apparently pondered the potential impact of Nardi's
letters long and hard before deciding to use them. Yet his reasons
for tempering his poem with such extensive passages of "real
prose" are themselves divided. On the one hand, their very literariness gave them, curiously, an attractive "authenticity." As he
said of one letter: "It is, as you see, an attack, a personal attack
upon me by a woman. It seemed a legitimate one. It had besides a
certain literary quality which was authentic, that made the thing in
itself worth recording." But on the other hand, the letter exposed a
side of his life and art that, he felt, ought to undergo the risk of
destruction: "It was a reply from the female side to many of my
male pretensions. It was a strong reply, a reply which sought
to destroy me. If it could destroy me I should be destroyed."[49]
Williams' inclusion of her damning accusations indicates how seriously he takes Cress's point about needing to rethink his polarized
definitions of art and life, male and female. The letters force him to
note that his art is not only exclusionary in conception, but also
that he should open it in practice. For if his aim is to capture the life
of the city, then the messiness of life that Cress exemplifies must
enter the poem. Thus *Paterson* becomes a poem about the act of its
own gradual realization of the need for openness—demonstrated
by an attack on how closed the poem is.

Nonetheless, his treatment of Cress's texts seems to inflict the
sterility of a waste land upon her writing, making her feel unreal:
"My own personal identity (without which I cannot write, of
course)" will be lost "until I can recapture some faith in the reality
of my own thoughts . . . which were turned into dry sand by your
attitude toward those letters" (*P*, 76). Her letter writing, which will
make Paterson's poem more "real," appears insufficient to revitalize what *she* regards as her real self, her poetry: "*Only* my writing (when I write) is myself: only that is the real me in any essential
way. Not because I bring to literature and to life two inconsistent
sets of values, as you do" (*P*, 87). Williams may be responding to
her argument when he declares later:

Pollock's blobs of paint squeezed out
with design!
pure from the tube. Nothing else
is real .   .

                                                              (P, 213)

Here both Cress and Williams seem to be in accord, that the true
reality for both of them is their art. But for Williams to accept fully
the implications of that situation means to recognize that the life of
a woman can be similar to his own.

He accomplishes this most tellingly by revising his man-city
metaphor to allow room for her. In 1948 he wrote to Horace Gregory defending the inclusion of Cress's final letter in Book II:

> The long letter is definitely germane to the rest of the text. It is
> psychologically related to the text—just as the notes follow-
> ing *The Waste Land* are related to the text of the poem. The
> difference being that in this case the 'note' is subtly relevant
> to the matter and not merely a load for the mule's back. That it
> is *not* the same stuff as the poem but comes from below 14th
> St. is precisely the key.

                                                              (SL, 265)[50]

Still sniping away at Eliot, Williams argues that the real value of
Cress's prose lies in the place of its origin—downtown New York.
A decidedly unpastoral woman, Cress—or at least her writing—is
valued for her difference. That her words are "*not* the same stuff as
the poem" implies that she has given an urban ring to her texts that
Williams has not been able to achieve himself. In the epistolary
mini-novel formed by Cress's letters, he creates a subplot for *Paterson* that subverts his assertions about women and nature and the
richness of his locale, and he begins to understand the causes of
divorce by recognizing that the old polarities will not hold. His
urban authenticity comes not from male but female, and not from
New Jersey but from New York, where he has also gone to find
Corydon, the lesbian character who represents Paterson's female
side.[51] If a man can call himself a city only at great risk, and if metaphor cannot be avoided any more than the city itself can be, then
the woman too must share that urban figuration. Perhaps, to put it
another way, the woman who had only been viewed as part of the
problem may be part of the solution—one woman, like a city.

Williams reaffirms this understanding by conceding another of
Cress's points later in the poem. His encouragement of her writing

career, she had said, was "nothing but empty rhetoric in the light
of your behavior towards me": a woman cannot achieve freedom as
a poet "until she is able *first* to 'sail free in her own element' in
living itself—which means in her relationships with men" (*P*, 87).
As if accepting her restatement of "divorce" from the female stand-
point, the poet concludes Book III with the words, "Let / me out!
(Well, go!) this rhetoric / is real!" (*P*, 145). He makes his rhetoric
real by opening the poem to the notion that women, too, depend
on redefining the relationship between the sexes.

Through the dialogue between *Paterson*'s men and women, poetry and prose, Williams begins to move toward a new definition of
the relationship between the sexes. A manuscript of the poem includes this lyric after one of Cress's letters:

> As always, Beauty, is still preserved
> by poverty and loneliness in a woman.—
> (that makes her speak) as a poet
> —or a city: in a backwash of the times
> This is no figure.[52]

Theodora Graham praises Williams' excision of the lines, noting
that "such poetizing juxtaposed with Cress's words of genuine despair could only diminish art."[53] But amid the condescension,
Williams makes explicit the basis of the new "marriage" upon
which Paterson can be rebuilt: a woman who is acknowledged to
share fully the man's role, to be both poet and city. That Williams
would claim "this is no figure" indicates his wish to imagine his
revisionary metaphor as no metaphor at all. This would be the Bar-
thesian moment of liberation—a grappling with reality, a woman's
reality, to transcend the divorce of art and life apparently inherent
in the city poet's craft.

OPEN MARRIAGE, OPEN POEM

Letters, interviews, and manuscripts show that Williams worked
hard to integrate rebellious female voices into his poem. The sustained paean to female transcendence in the "beautiful thing" lyrics
of Book III, the Sappho-Paterson-Corydon conjunction at the start
of Book IV, and the intellectual pregnancy of Madame Curie that
gives birth to discovery from dissonance later in Book IV—all these
represent Williams' effort to incorporate opposition *within* his
poem, not just to make a poem out of oppositions.[54]

But the interpolated material does not unequivocally reveal a poet in the process of waking up to the shortcomings of his sexist structurations. If *Paterson* furnishes material to undo itself, setting real urban female prose against male poetic flowering, there are still very powerful tensions operating in the poem, tensions that Williams' drive toward open forms may tend to conceal. In the same letter to Horace Gregory in which he praised the "below 14th St." quality of Cress's prose, Williams closed by commenting:

> If you'll notice, dogs run all the way through the poem and will continue to do so from first to last. And there is no dog without a tail. Here the tail has tried to wag the dog. Does it? (God help me, it may yet, but I hope not!)
>
> (*SL*, 266)

The poet still strives for mastery of the tale he has permitted another to tell—thereby revealing just how valid Cress's criticisms of him really were. Since the poet doesn't intend to allow the tail to wag the dog, isn't he continuing to exploit the poem's recognition of his own exploitation? How ordered is *Paterson*'s disorder, how much revised are the revisionary metaphors? What was a personal problem for Cress has become a formal problem for Williams.

In the wake of the embattled exchanges between the sexes, an uneasy truce reigns in the poem. The poet "uses" Cress for poetic material, even while—and by—admitting it. Only by a curious imposition of freedom on the materials through which he strives to undo the man-city metaphor can Williams render it more complete. A poem so perplexed thus illustrates not so much a conversion to feminist thinking as an "open marriage" reinscribing the male-female, art-life struggle.[55] Since the textualized Cress continues, by virtue of her status as prosy outsider, to serve as life to Williams' art, her own epistolary skill, the proof of her "authenticity," remains unvalued.[56] Williams' note to himself that "*She* has the last word" is patently untrue.[57] If true marriage looks death in the eye, the poet's nuptials with Cress occur not in text but in the reader's own imagination, in the interplay of male and female principles.

This marriage needs to be rethought in another way. Cress has perhaps altered the poet's sexual consciousness about women and flowers, art and life, but only indirectly has she challenged the biblical paradigm of the ideal city that holds these concepts in place. In his extended meditation on virgins and whores, Williams attacks the very distinction upon which the heavenly and earthly cities of Revelation are based, by discovering identity, not polarity, between the two designations. His own poetic quest forces this realization upon him—one always has to whore the "virgin purpose" of language to make art. All purity put to use is no longer pure, and within his schema all art may be imaged as sexual violence of the kind Cress protests: "every married man carries in his head / the beloved and sacred image / of a virgin / whom he has whored" (P, 234). In order to establish relations with the woman thus rediscovered, he must work toward a new definition of sexual innocence and experience, one that can free female metaphors from exhausted stereotypes.[58]

The scenes in the library in Book III of *Paterson* illustrate how the poet reconsiders in tandem the virgin-whore and his dream of a unified poem; the open marriage and altered city evolve together with the notion of an open poem. If frenetic energy and a will are required to establish dominion in the sexually restless park, then the library seems at first to provide a soothing "cool of books," translating the "hot" turbulence of experience into the measured articulation of masculine knowledge (P, 95). But Dr. Paterson is tormented by voices; the city and texts he inhabits resist his obstetric operation, his attempt to deliver language from urban corruption:

> Do
> you still believe—in this
> swill-hole of corrupt cities?
> do you, Doctor?   Now?
>
> Give up
> the poem. Give up the shilly-
> shally of art.
>
> What can you, what
> can YOU hope to conclude—
> on a heap of dirty linen?
>
> (P, 108)

The passage suggests the adulterous Dr. Paterson's painful consciousness of how he has created the "dirty linen" of his own art and life. Satisfying sexual communion and poetic closure seem more impossible than ever, casting doubt on the "shilly-shally" of his entire quest.

But perhaps it is not that his bedsheets and proofsheets are soiled, but that he has to learn not to expect to find them in any other condition. He asks himself what he would have become if he had spent his life in brothels, allowing himself to become the creation of the two whores of his artistic maturation—one an image of natural America, the other of cultured Europe. Both "offer the same dish / different ways," and so he resolves to "Let the colors run"—to blur the two and shamelessly follow the whores, like Toulouse-Lautrec: "And so he recorded them" (*P*, 110). Eschewing a final order, a perfect clarity, he decides he must let metaphors and genders mix, virgin become whore, and nature marry culture.

Yet that marriage depends on a rape—on his exploitative obsession with what he calls "beautiful thing," a complex image of female sexuality apparently derived from the doctor's own experience of a black woman whom he treated, and found still seductive, after she had suffered a gang rape. Williams first recorded this composite urban woman in "Paterson: Episode 17": streetwalker and drunken prey, she manages to remain an unforgettably attractive "sacrament" capable of winning the poet's devotion. In *Paterson* she is "the whored virgin, sacrificial victim of modern city violence."[59] She can end all name-calling ("You smell / like a whore") when she transcends mere chastity by showing the doctor the paradox of her flesh—the "astonishing virtue of your / lost body" (*P*, 105). Yet she is also a dove who touches with fire (*P*, 96) and a "dark flame, / a wind, a flood—counter to all staleness" (*P*, 100). Her holy spirit momentarily lends to the poet a tongue of flame to combat the babel roar of the library and town. Impossible to grasp, she weds the actual fire in the library to the notion of sexual violence and phoenix-like renewal: "The radiant gist that / resists the final crystallization" (*P*, 109).[60]

Thus the virgin-whore becomes the poet's weapon to harrow the hell of the burning library with her own white heat. Paterson's divorce from the quick of its own life is greatest in this tomblike institution: "The Library is desolation, it has a smell of its own / of stagnation and death" (*P*, 100). Over time, the city has accreted a human history, contained in and symbolized by the library, that falsifies Paterson's natural potential. The poet fears succumbing to this dead weight of knowledge—or even capitalizing upon it, as Pound and Eliot did. Instead, he declares, he will begin again, "decrying all books / that enfeeble the mind's intent" (*P*, 102). Tearing the covers off these moribund artifacts, the poet takes the offensive, declaring that "the writing / is also an attack," like Cress's letters, on the enslavement of city and culture. In its purest form the poem becomes "a fire, // a destroying fire" (*P*, 113). It soon assumes the fury of an apocalyptic conflagration:

> Blow! So be it. Bring down! So be it. Consume
> and submerge! So be it. Cyclone, fire
> and flood. So be it. Hell, New Jersey, it said
> on the letter. Delivered without comment.
> So be it!
>
> (*P*, 97)

In "Hell, New Jersey," the New Jerusalem that Williams' letters seek can be located in the aftermath of fires like those that sweep Babylon in Revelation. These are not the purgatorial fires of *The Waste Land*, but a regenerative force that the poet finds aesthetically satisfying. Welcoming this liberating destruction ("so be it"), Williams' poem unleashes a creative violence of its own, rejoicing in a new life born of rape and urban immolation: "Beautiful thing / —the whole city doomed! And / the flames towering" (*P*, 116). Since both men and cities have wrongly tried to dominate the (female) language that sustains them, the rising flames will level "towering" pretensions to knowledge that go back to the library at Alexandria and before that to the building of Babel.

And yet the "Poet Beats Fire at Its Own Game!" (*P*, 118) only by emulating its aggression, by consuming the "Beautiful thing! aflame" for his own purposes. As a "defiance of authority" (*P*, 119), the woman / fire appears for Williams to melt down the oppositions that keep man and woman, city and country, apart. But as with Cress, there is a human cost to this poetic strategy. Williams admires the resilience while capitalizing on the pain of the female body "reflowered there by / the flame" (*P*, 118). With this vision of the whore made virgin by the incineration of lifeless words, the poem resists the logic of natural laws and social conventions: "the waterfall of the / flames" now attains the primitive purity of the Falls to become a "cataract reversed" (*P*, 120).

In Book III the "poet (ridded) from Paradise" (*P*, 108) comes to terms with his worldly material by textualizing urban and sexual violence, turning a problematic destructive power into a question of poetic form that can acknowledge mortality: "Only one answer: write carelessly so that nothing that is not green will survive" (*P*, 129). Freed from the necessity of measuring by the archetypal heavenly city, the poet is not only "ridded" of Eden but also of the crippling nostalgia that attempts to recover it. The earthly city and the woman who represents it can be realized only by recognition of earthly limits. As Williams remarks of Book IV, "At times there is no other way to assert the truth than by stating our failure to achieve it. If I did not achieve a language I at least stated what I would not say. I would not melt myself into the great universal sea (of love) with all its shapes and colors" (*SL*, 304). What counts is particularity and process: the variegated poem in the act of its writing and reading, the multiform woman in the act of knowing and being known. Williams indicates how easily one can overlook his simple but essential point when he quotes Pound's dismissive remark to him: "Your interest is in the bloody loam but what / I'm after is the finished product" (*P*, 37).

The "finished product" is impossible, Williams comes to understand, and an undesirable goal in any case: "My whole effort . . . is to find a pattern, large enough, modern enough, flexible enough to include my desires. And if I should find it I'd wither and die."[61] The poem, like the city, must continually "begin again, again, here" (*P*, 200). As the famous passage "The descent beckons" asserts, "No defeat is made up entirely of defeat," for the heavenly "world lost" becomes a new "world unsuspected" (*P*, 77–78). The difficulty of making a fresh start is compounded by an uncomprehending audience; even the poet's wife may say, "What I miss . . . is the poetry, the pure poem / of the first parts" (*P*, 171). In order to create the impure poetry that will most closely approximate the "pure poem" of Paterson as it is, he must "Waken from a dream, this dream of / the whole poem" (*P*, 200). In the refractory jumble of word and world, clear-cut categories and organic wholes inevitably disintegrate, for in a poem built on the model of the earthly city, even the elements, like sexes and metaphors, are unstable:

> Uranium, the complex atom, breaking
> down, a city in itself, that complex
> atom, always breaking down
>
> (*P*, 178)

VIRGIN AND WHORE: IT IS ALL FOR YOU

The first four books of *Paterson* conclude by resisting closure with the urgent refrain, "the sea is *not* our home" (*P*, 201). Life is not simply a river that flows inexorably to the sea. The Whitmanesque figure who has followed the course of the Passaic River to the ocean turns back inland to plant his seed along its banks, rededicating poetry to the indigenous life of New Jersey. In Book v, published after a hiatus of seven years, Williams recommences his work with a new "last" book that almost forgets the land and city of its origin. But by moving the scene of his poem from prosaic Paterson to the Cloisters Museum in New York, the aging doctor enters "A WORLD OF ART / THAT THROUGH THE YEARS HAS / SURVIVED!" (P, 209). In what is his most unified book, the metaphors of marriage, woman, and city that Williams made increasingly elastic in the later books of Paterson are now applied to the life of the imagination.[62] Here the pervasive duality of virgin and whore becomes the major theme, skillfully woven into several scenes describing the Unicorn Tapestries.[63] But the climax of Williams' revisionary figuration of the city comes in a single, sustained passage drawn not from art but from life—the poet's glimpse of a passing stranger.

Dedicated to Toulouse-Lautrec, maître of the whorehouse, Book v was originally to be titled "The River of Heaven."[64] These intimations of Babylonian decadence and redemptive purity suggest how thoroughly in this book Williams assimilates the vision of St. John for his own purposes. Adopting the language of the Evangelist, Williams inserts himself into the Apocalypse: "I, Paterson, the Kingself / saw the lady" (P, 234). His sight of the virginal New Jerusalem is doubly determined, for Williams reads Revelation through the tapestries depicting the unicorn legend, into which he also thrusts himself as the central figure. In Christian symbolism, the unicorn that is tamed by a virgin, killed by hunters, and finally revived to be enclosed in a garden provides an image of Christ's virgin birth, sacrificial death, and resurrection. Paul Mariani observes that "in Williams' retelling of the myth . . . the Unicorn in search of the Virgin becomes the artist's imagination in pursuit of the Woman. And the corollary to that pursuit is the unabashed, naked pursuit of the poem in search of the virgin language which must of necessity be whored."[65] Thus, in viewing himself as the unicorn, Williams becomes not only He who governs the Celestial City, the Lamb who marries the Virgin Bride, but also the phallically horned whorer of virgins who ultimately seduce him into their enclosures. He can find the language of poetry and identity only in the lap of the virgin who leads him astray.

By linking himself to the artist-beast who is pursued by the dogs of his own desires, and defeated by the surrender of his virgin ideal, Williams again finds himself caught on the importunate horn of his gender-based metaphoric dilemma. The unicorn kicks but cannot get loose: "The Unicorn / the white one-horned

beast / thrashes about / root toot a toot!" (*P*, 208). And no more
than the unicorn can the whore and the virgin shake off the union
that binds them:

> The whore and the virgin, an identity:
> —through its disguises
>
> thrash about—but will not succeed in breaking free :
>   an identity.

(P, 210)

The poem opens with the worldly equation of "the city / the man,
an identity" (*P*, 3), and now its later pages dwell on the complementary duality of the female who symbolizes the otherworldly
cities. Beneath their many disguises the women find their identity
in doubleness, but what keeps the unicorn captive is the very
integrity of body from which he seeks but cannot separate a chaste
Word accessible to his worldly practice. It may be that "The Unicorn / has no match / or mate" since "the artist / has no peer"
(*P*, 211). But although the peerless, mateless male artist implies
his own superiority to a marriage of equals, the yearning of his
imagination forces him once again to compromise the pure single-
mindedness of his quest by locating his goal in the fallen flesh of
his female dream. The lady of the tapestry who subdues the unicorn has in attracting him offered herself for sale "to the highest bidder! / and who bids higher / than a lover?" (*P*, 238). She
willingly whores herself so that her lover can achieve her.

Yet still the artist sees life "from the two sides" knowing that
"the / imagination must be served" (*P*, 228). Thus in the tapestry
he can see simultaneously beast and Christ, "the hunt of / the Unicorn and / the god of love / of virgin birth" (*P*, 233), and thus in his
account of Brueghel's *Nativity* he can even include Mary, mother of
Jesus, among the ranks of virgin-whores (*P*, 226–28). This blas-
phemous assertion shows the artist's commitment to the idea that
there should truly be "an / interpenetration, both ways" (*P*, 3) of
ideality and reality: if nothing is sacred, then everything is. Instead
of finding whores in heaven, he can delight in earthy, earthly paradox: "no woman is virtuous / who does not give herself to her
lover /—forthwith" (*P*, 229). And instead of explaining how the
ideal is always whored, he can enjoy the process by which the
whore regains her chastity, and a bordello becomes divine:

> The whores grasping for your genitals, faces almost pleading
> ... "two dolla, two dolla" till you almost go in with the sheer

brute desire straining at your loins . . . till a friend grabs you
... "no ... to a real house, this is shit." . . .

   And then the house, ... and see a smooth faced girl against
a door, all white ... snow, the virgin, O bride . . . and she is
smooth-faced and wants four dollars but you make it three
but four she says . . . please and you pay four . . . quatro dollars but twice, I go twice, 'andsome, come on, 'andsome.

(P, 214–15)[66]

Williams excerpted this passage from Gilbert Sorrentino's story
"Bordertown" because it fit so well with the themes he was developing in Book v. True reality, the *casa real*, can be found in a
whorehouse with a virgin bride who understands well her duplicity, and will "go twice" to make her point. The biblical paradigm stands even as it falls:

> The moral
>
>> proclaimed by the whorehouse
>> could not be better proclaimed
> by the virgin, a price on her head,
>> her maidenhead!

(P, 208)

   In the whorehouse of the world, the impossibility of maintaining the virgin ideal becomes so obvious that the poet must
"reflower" fallen women to keep the organic ideal alive. As the
unicorn calls "for its own murder" (P, 208), acknowledging the suffering inherent in sexual and artistic procreation, so it is healed by
the *millefleurs* springtime garden to which it is restored. But the in-
divisibility of the virgin-whore means that to dwell on deathly
Babylon is always to have a virginal New Jerusalem in reserve.
Amid the "babel" of the whorehouse, with its "voices unintelli-
gible" the writer discovers that the prostitute is "white and deep as
birth, deeper than death" (P, 215).

   "Death is a hole / in which we are all buried" (P, 211), Dr. Paterson declares. But Sorrentino's story suggests that sex can empty
out that hole, becoming part of the "marriage" that stared death in
the eye in the earlier books of *Paterson*. That relationship undergoes one further transformation, into a consummatory art that survives its own metaphors:

> The flower dies down
> and rots away   .

But there is a hole
in the bottom of the bag.

It is the imagination
which cannot be fathomed.
It is through this hole
we escape   .   .

So through art alone, male and female, a field of
flowers, a tapestry, spring flowers unequaled
in loveliness.

(P, 212)

Both male and female now enter the poetic "field of flowers," no
longer divided by different metaphors, finding eternal life in the
imagination. Only art holds the sexes in harmony—or distributes
them across a "field" of creative dissonance. Through the poem the
unreality of cities fades, replaced by the reality of art, "the museum became real / *The Cloisters*— / on its rock" (*P*, 209). What *Paterson* v accomplishes is the utter collapse of the polarities of the
opening books: cities forgotten, the poem becomes a flower, as
does a man; the art that could not break through to reality now
founds it on solid rock; and even the regenerated source of *Paterson*'s central metaphors, the drive for sexual knowledge, surrenders a final time to the poet's all-encompassing vision:

—the virgin and the whore, which
most endures? the world
of the imagination most endures.

(P, 213)

Yet ultimately the whole of *Paterson*'s tapestry is woven for another flower-figure in its text. Leaving the Cloisters, Williams returns to the streets of Paterson and to the difficult, unresolved
intricacies of lived experience. Not in a museum but in the form of
a living woman he finds the culminating image of urban life and
poetic aspiration, the *passante*:

There is a woman in our town
walks rapidly, flat bellied
in worn slacks upon the street
where I saw her.
                    neither short
nor tall, nor old nor young
her

face would attract no

adolescent. Grey eyes looked
straight before her.
                    Her
                        hair
was gathered simply behind the
ears under a shapeless hat.

Her
    hips were narrow, her
                            legs
thin and straight. She stopped

me in my tracks—until I saw
her
    disappear in the crowd.

An inconspicuous decoration
made of sombre cloth, meant
I think to be a flower, was
pinned flat to her
                    right

breast—any woman might have
done the same to
say she was a woman and warn
us of her mood. Otherwise

she was dressed in male attire,
as much as to say to hell
with you. Her
                expression was
serious, her
                feet were small.

And she was gone!

        if ever I see you again
as I have sought you
daily without success

I'll speak to you, alas
too late! ask,
What are you doing on the

streets of Paterson? a
thousand questions:
Are you married? Have you any

children? And, most important,
your NAME! which
of course she may not

give me—though
I cannot conceive it
in such a lonely and

intelligent woman

have you read anything that I have written?
It is all for you.

(P, 219–20)

Like the woman in Baudelaire's "A une passante," the feminine
stranger suddenly strides in and out of the poet's life, leaving him
with a "thousand questions."[67] Her height, age, and clothing are
indeterminate, as are her symbolic associations with life or death.
She does not wear an elegant dress revealing a well-sculpted leg, as
Baudelaire's *passante* does, and her vaguely defined face (with its
grey eyes beneath a "shapeless" hat) suggests she may be a "compound ghost," or perhaps an intentionally generalized figure, like
the addressee of Whitman's "To a Stranger." But the androgyny of
her clothing and frame—"male attire" of slacks and hat, slimness
of hips and legs—is lightly counterpointed by the "inconspicuous
decoration" pinned flat to her breast. That it might be a flower implies a sort of vitality immediately contradicted by its "sombre"
cloth. Yet if the rest of her male appearance says "To hell / with
you," then maybe it offers a sign of life in the urban inferno—a gesture towards the springtime tapestry, or a token (an asphodel?) by
which Kore may be distinguished in the Underworld.[68]

The stranger's brief transit returns the poem to "Hell, New
Jersey," rather than the New Jerusalem. Her toughness and infernal associations emphasize that she is not to be confused with virginal brides. Rather, the urban context and her maturity (her face
"would attract no // adolescent"), like her uncertain sexuality, an-
chor her in the doubleness of earthly experience. Her clothing even
allies her with the lover of the lady in the tapestry, a "young
man / sharing the female world / in Hell's despight" (P, 238). For
though her ornament may reiterate the woman-flower metaphor, it
also serves to "warn us of her mood": she may accept "female"
roles only on sufferance. As a fast-moving woman whom the poet
glimpses "too late!" she is, like Baudelaire's stranger, the quintes-
sence of the city rather than of nature, and too elusive to be cate-

gorized. She pins the flower and assigns it an aggressive message; the flower does not pin her. The lineation of the passage, suspending "her" alone on a line four times, and at the end of a line another six times, confirms her independence and isolation.

By ascribing loneliness and intelligence to the stranger, the poet recalls Cress, another wary woman-flower that the poet has used to literary effect. But because the stranger is the exclusive object of *his* daily searches and heartfelt words, the roles are reversed. The aged and weakening Dr. Paterson "has shrunk / to no more than 'a passionate letter' / to a woman, a woman he had neglected / to put to bed in the past" (*P*, 230). He himself has now become a plaintive Cress seeking answers to his own yearning letters, without response. The stranger—or the memory of Cress and other women—represents the still-provocative virgin he wants to whore. Cress, whose fate is alluded to again in Book v in the letter from Denmark about a starving woman writer and her young son (*P*, 229), was unable to write her way to reality, in part because she depended so much on Dr. Paterson's response for her own self-esteem. But here, in the figure of the silent stranger who compels admiration and does not look back, her inner strength has been lifted to full poetic expression. Whether pursued for love or literary effect—Paterson's motives are forever in doubt—the stranger achieves victory over the woman-flower formula.

The poem assails her fleeing form with multiple questions about her occupation, marriage, and children; all reveal that Paterson is still trying to immobilize her with his social conventions. "And, most important, / your NAME!" This last piece of information is the most essential because with it the poet can control her character and fate, as he has already done for Cress, within his poem. In his complacency he "cannot conceive" that she would withhold this vital piece of information, since she is to his mind both lonely and intelligent enough to value his attention. Thus he tosses his poems after her, hoping to define her as the long-sought object toward which his lines converge: "have you read anything that I have written? / It is all for you." The would-be encounter is, fittingly for the displaced and diffused urban world of *Paterson*, a textual one. The meeting of eyes unconsummated on the street will have to be achieved, Whitman-style, from the reader's gaze into the poem.

Longing to be read himself, the poet may be missing the opportunity to read her. For she is perhaps not only the figure of poems past and to come, the self-possessed pretext for his own entry into the arena of words, the crowd into which she will abruptly disappear. She may also be a poet herself, and more sexually ambiguous than Paterson's questions about matrimony would have us think. Her entry is anticipated by Williams' translation from Sappho (*P*, 217), who appears in various incarnations throughout the poem. Paul Mariani argues that the unknown woman is Sappho herself walking the streets of contemporary Paterson. He cites Williams' fascination with her in early manuscripts of Book v: "Sappho was half a man anyhow—and she / could WRITE . . . the virgin turned / whore: an identity."[69] In the final text, she describes herself as being hunted down by the trembling of her love. Sappho thereby becomes a feminine version of the unicorn Paterson likens *him*self to, hunted by "the dog of his thoughts" (*P*, 230). As a lesbian Paterson, both poet and beast, half man and half woman, she is the ultimate figure of male-female interpenetration. Her sexuality turns Paterson's advances back upon himself, and pries the triad of woman/nature/flower free of man/culture/city. To the extent that she will be pursued and "known" by Dr. Paterson's relentless textualizing of experience, she serves as an image of the poet's continual violation of language, his constant search for the always vanishing NAME of poetry. She is a climactic double figure for all that has eluded the poet, as well as all that he has attained.

Such speculations remain, like the passing stranger, an intangible part of the poetic reality of *Paterson*. "A life that is here and now is timeless," wrote Williams. "That is the universal I am seeking: to embody that in a work of art, a new world that is always 'real'" (*SE*, 196). What makes the sexes and the city "real" to one another is the effort to know them beyond the boundaries of accepted convention. "WALK in the world" the poet commands in Book v (*P*, 213), and in exemplary style the unknown woman moves through the "male" sphere of the city as Dr. Paterson had paced the "female" park in Book II. The path of each forms a kind of writing whose subject is the city, and whose conclusion is always just around the next corner. In order to live freely and fully, the poet must keep searching, ever a wanderer in a city that is already language, already a book where "There is no direction" (*P*, 18), where "the serpent / has its tail in its mouth / AGAIN!" (*P*, 233).

But this never-ending search does not represent the failure of the poet's quest; rather, it is a celebration of this world, not the next, the joyful recognition that "The dream / is in pursuit!" (*P*, 222), not capture. Wordsworth prefers the virgin, Baudelaire finally chooses the whore; Whitman desires fulfillment from the body, and Eliot from the text. But the dog-poet Williams chases all of them, alert to the pleasures of looking for the *passante* who is always passing. Since "to measure is all we know" (*P*, 239), the poet can only chart relations, the now intermingled forces of woman-city and man-flower. As Roland Barthes saw so clearly, "The eroticism of the city is the lesson we can draw from the infinitely metaphorical nature of urban discourse. . . . The city, essentially and semantically, is the place of our meeting with the *other*."[70]

With the triumph of the virgin-whore, the woman whose combined innocence and experience make her the ultimate figure for the city that the poet pursues, *Paterson* attempts a decisive break with the tradition it inescapably reinscribes. For the poem argues that the goal of the city poet should not be to dominate the multiplicity of his unwieldy subject, to make order out of confusion and the real out of the unreal. Rather, he should liberate his urban materials from the imposition of conventional form and language, "the finished products" of traditional poetry, and return them to the "rout" of the natural yet artificial locality in which they find their most vivid expression. The neighbors he sought to know "to the whites of their eyes" become fleeting strangers once more. Renouncing the quest of poets over the past two centuries to govern the sprawling vitality of city life, Williams concedes the city's victory over its literature, and celebrates in liberating defeat a more relaxed interpenetration of art and life that would allow city poetry to vanish—and be everywhere:

> The multiple seed,
> packed tight with detail . . .
> is lost in the flux and the mind.
>
> (*P*, 4)

And as the ever-moving image of this dispersal, the passing stranger continues to catch the reader's eye, insuring that the unreal dance of sex, text, and city will never cease.

Notes

The initial epigraph is from Italo Calvino, *Invisible Cities*, trans. William Weaver (New York: Harcourt, Brace, Jovanovich, 1974), 61. The epigraph to the Preface is from Virginia Woolf, "Literary Geography," *The Essays of Virginia Woolf*, vol. 1, ed. Andrew McNeillie (New York: Harcourt, Brace, Jovanovich, 1986), 35.

Chapter One. Unreal Cities: An Introduction

1. According to Mircea Eliade, the first cities sought to imitate the orderly heavenly city of the gods, from which chaos and impermanence could be excluded (*Cosmos and History: The Myth of the Eternal Return*, trans. Willard Trask [New York: Harper, 1959], 12–18).

2. Quotations are from the King James version of the Bible.

3. Text cited from *The Complete Writings of William Blake*, ed. Geoffrey Keynes (London: Oxford University Press, 1966), 216.

4. In his "strong misreading" of "London" in *Poetry and Repression*, Harold Bloom claims that the poem "centers itself upon an opposition between [a lost prophetic] *voice* and [apocalyptic] *writing*" ([New Haven: Yale University Press, 1976], 34–44). I want to stress rather that the voiced cries of Blake's Londoners *become* a form of revelatory writing. The more dynamic opposition lies between what is marked—city, citizens, Harlot—and the absent figures upon which these depend—Jerusalem, the Saved, the Virgin. Although my reading of Blake derives primarily from Genesis and Revelation rather than from Bloom's preferred intertext, Ezekiel (which I also use), I am indebted to him.

5. For overviews of the interpretive strategies applied by critics to this much-read poem, see Jonathan Culler, *The Pursuit of Signs* (Ithaca: Cornell University Press, 1981), 69–79, and Michael Ferber, "'London' and Its Politics," *ELH* 48 (Summer 1981): 310–338. Of the studies not mentioned by Culler and Ferber, I have found the following useful: John D. Rosenberg, "Varieties of Infernal Experience," *Hudson Review* 23 (Autumn 1970): 458–60; Raymond Williams, *The Country and the City* (New York: Oxford University Press, 1973), 148–49; Graham Pechey, "The London Motif in Some Eighteenth-Century Contexts: A Semiotic Study," *Literature and History* 4 (Autumn 1976): 2–29; Max Byrd, *London Transformed* (New Haven: Yale University Press, 1978), 157–61; and Nelson Hilton, "The Heavy Metal of Blake's Language," *New Orleans Review* 13.3 (1986): 37–39. Williams, Pechey, and Ferber all provide compelling historicist readings of the poem. See also David Punter, "Blake and the Shapes of London," *Criticism* 23 (Winter 1981): 1–23 and Kenneth R. Johnston, "Blake's Cities: Romantic Forms of Urban Renewal," *Blake's Visionary Forms Dramatic*. ed. David V. Erdman and John E. Grant (Princeton: Princeton University Press, 1970), 413–42, on the relation of "London" to eighteenth-century city poetry and to Blake's later prophetic works.

6. In his marking of the world (and recreating it in words), the poet is like God.

But he is also like Cain—whose name means "smith" or "artificer"—challenging God's authority with his own authorship (of fictions, texts, cities). In this second sense, the writing of a poem "marks" the poet—as God did Cain—as alienated from the once-unified plenitude of God, Eden, and Logos.

7. Blake had originally written "dirty" street and "dirty" Thames (Keynes, 170); his revision replaces the similarity of physical surface with the deeper bond of metaphoric circumscription. Compare also James Thomson's treatment of the Thames in the "Autumn" section of *The Seasons* (1730), where Commerce

> chok'd up the loaded street
> With foreign plenty; and thy stream, O Thames,
> Large, gentle, deep, majestic, king of floods!
> Chose for his grand resort.
>
> (120–23)

While Blake's streets and river, imprisoned and imprisoning, reveal how the avenues of wealth have become roads to bondage, Thomson's enthusiastic description of the city's prosperity, the product of an earlier era, refuses to take its metaphors seriously: "choking" commerce produces no detrimental effect on river or town.

8. Blake's context, as well as the politics of the 1790s, makes it difficult to read "charter'd" in a positive fashion (see E. P. Thompson, "London," in *Interpreting Blake*, ed. Michael Phillips [Cambridge: Cambridge University Press, 1978], 5–10). Bloom argues that the idea of chartering possesses a Cain-like doubleness ("to be chartered is to be awarded a special privilege or a particular immunity, which is established by a written document" [38]), but it must be remembered that Cain's "privilege" and "particular immunity" ensured continuation of his punishment. Even in the New Jerusalem the granting of written "charters" or marks of salvation to some (Rev. 22:4,14) requires the denying of such "rights" to others (Rev. 22:15).

9. Cf. Revelation 7:2–3, where an angel "with the seal of the living God" commands the angels at the four corners of the earth, "Hurt not the earth, neither the sea, nor the trees, till we have sealed the servants of our God in their foreheads," after which the members of the twelve tribes of Israel to be saved are "sealed" or marked. See also Revelation 14:1: "And I looked, and, lo, a Lamb stood on the mount Sion, and with him an hundred forty and four thousand, having his Father's name written in their foreheads."

10. In his original manuscript Blake first wrote "see," but changed it to the more active and complex "mark" (Keynes, 170). For Bloom, Blake must "mark passively rather than mark actively" (41) because he is a wanderer without direction; he has lost the prophetic voice and authority of Ezekiel. Despite claims to agonistic strength, this could be called a "non-prophet" reading of Blake, for it represses the poetic role of Ezekiel's (and Blake's) marker as prophetic notator for later readers, who have done their best to smite the institutions lacking the sympathetic marks of the first stanza. The full power of these marks and their necessary relation to Cain's wandering will become apparent in my discussion of Babylon.

11. St. Augustine sees their punishment as the result of linguistic pride: "As the tongue is the instrument of domination, in it pride was punished; so that man, who would not understand God when He issued His commands, should be misunderstood when he himself gave orders" (*The City of God*, trans. Marcus Dods [New York: Modern Library, 1950], 528).

12. Informative background to Blake's use of the Harlot can be found in John B. Radner, "The Youthful Harlot's Curse: The Prostitute as Symbol of the City in 18th-Century English Literature," *Eighteenth-Century Life* 2.3 (1976): 59–64.

13. See Culler, 75–76, and Ferber, 328–31.

14. At this point the aptness of the poem's illustration emerges forcefully. A streetwalker like the Harlot, blinded like the Infant, wandering like the poet, the old man London that Blake has drawn "begging thro' the Streets / Of Babylon" embod-

ies his own poem, a reminder from both inside and outside the text of the other worlds through which the poem moves.

15. Augustine, xii.

16. Building upon the polarities of whore and virgin, Revelation sunders a more ancient and complex female symbol for the city's multiplicity. In the Mesopotamian *Gilgamesh Epic* the figure of the harlot represents not only urban corruption but also the city's power to civilize: a prostitute from Uruk subdues the wild, animal-like Enkidu, teaching him first to live among herdsmen and then to seek the companionship that can be found only in the capital. See Rosenberg, 457–58, and David Damrosch, *The Narrative Covenant* (New York: Harper & Row, 1987), 94–99.

17. The woman writer in the city often finds that her very surroundings—in her view a masculine space embodying male power and culture—resist her every attempt at self-realization. But although women have felt many of the sharpest restrictions of a patriarchal society in the city, there they have also found the greatest freedom to express their sense of its limitations. See Susan Merrill Squier, ed., *Women Writers and the City* (Knoxville: University of Tennessee Press, 1984), and Griselda Pollock, "Modernity and the Spaces of Femininity," *Vision and Difference* (New York: Routledge, 1988), 50–90.

18. "In the earthly city," writes Augustine, "we find two things—its own obvious presence, and its symbolic presentation of the heavenly city" (480). Blake strives to remake the earthly city in the image of its heavenly counterpart; as he puts it in the introductory lyric of *Milton:* "I will not cease from Mental Fight / Nor shall my Sword sleep in my hand / Till we have built Jerusalem / In England's green & pleasant Land." For later English writers such as Arnold and Tennyson, London can be judged by the degree to which it successfully imitates the heavenly archetype.

19. See Lewis Mumford, *The City in History* (New York: Harcourt, Brace, World, 1961): "The town itself [is] woman writ large. . . . In Egyptian hieroglyphics, 'house' or 'town' may stand as symbols for 'mother,' as if to confirm the similarity of the individual and the collective nurturing function" (13).

20. If the city can be considered "a folded road," as Philip Fisher suggests ("City Matters: City Minds," *The Worlds of Victorian Fiction,* Harvard English Studies 6, ed. Jerome H. Buckley [Cambridge, Mass.: Harvard University Press, 1975], 389), then exploration of the female city of Revelation would be analogous to exploration of that most mysterious "fold," the vagina, whose paradoxical ability to be both inside and outside prompts Jacques Derrida's concept of "invagination" (see Derrida, "Living On / Border Lines" in *Deconstruction and Criticism,* Harold Bloom et al. [New York: Seabury, 1979], 97, and Jonathan Culler, *On Deconstruction* [Ithaca: Cornell University Press, 1982], 198). The perplexing tendency of internal "centers" of meaning to become external surfaces that confound notions of centrality reinforces the connection between sexual identity and the city. For the New Jerusalem itself is a virginal unviolated "inside" whose hymenal walls stand paradoxically only by virtue of the pressure exerted by those outside—whoremongers, murderers, idolaters, and liars (Rev. 22:15). Thus traces of the corrupt abominations and the freeplay of the harlot, which the crystal city so resolutely shuts out, may be found already inside its own pure identity and truth, its theologically centered self-presence.

21. Sometimes the Other is male, as in the case of Wordsworth's beggar and Whitman's strangers of both sexes. Whatever the situation, the quest for poetic domination of city and Other plays itself out in terms of sexual dynamics (symbolic union, castration, frustration).

22. Both "London" and Wordsworth's encounter with the blind beggar in Book VII of *The Prelude* play upon but defer actual eye contact with the *passant(e),* as a means of accentuating the shock value of this meeting. Thus I explore these repressions of the face-to-face encounter before discussing the actual exhange of gazes in Baudelaire's *Tableaux parisiens.*

23. Fisher, 386.

24. Fisher, 388.

25. See John H. Johnston, *The Poet and the City* (Athens: University of Georgia Press, 1984), 56–87, and Brigitte Peuker, "The Poem as Place: Three Modes of Scenic Rendering in the Lyric," *PMLA* 96 (October 1981): 904–12.

26. One of the main reasons Blake's poem helps turn the poem of place into the poem *as* place is its thematization of urban marking and its intertextual basis in the Bible, which open up the poem to the unreal cities of other texts. For this reason I find Max Byrd's emphasis on the textuality of the city in *London Transformed* (particularly the sections on the textually preoccupied cities of Pope, Gay, and Wordsworth) more suggestive than John H. Johnston's topographical analysis in *The Poet and the City*, not only in understanding eighteenth-century city poetry but also as a basis for following its development into the nineteenth and twentieth centuries. Like Johnston's study, William Thesing's *The London Muse: Victorian Poetic Responses to the City* (Athens: University of Georgia Press, 1982) focuses more on poetic efforts to represent a changed environment than on the literary processes that inform that representation.

27. See Benjamin, *Illuminations*, ed. Hannah Arendt, trans. Harry Zohn (New York: Schocken, 1969), 158–59. For an analysis of Benjamin's remarks on the newspaper, see Jonathan Arac, "Romanticism, the Self, and the City: *The Secret Agent* in Literary History," *Boundary* 2 9 (Fall 1980): 75–90.

28. *The Art of the City* (New York: Oxford University Press, 1985), 306.

29. Conrad, 307.

30. *Reflections*, ed. Peter Demetz, trans. Edmund Jephcott (New York: Harcourt, Brace, Jovanovich, 1978), 30.

Chapter Two. The Other as Text

The epigraph opening the chapter is from Salman Rushdie, *Midnight's Children* (New York: Avon, 1980), 91–92. The epigraph for the second section, "The Shock of the Other," is from Walter Benjamin, "One Way Street," *Reflections*, ed. Peter Demetz, trans. Edmund Jephcott (New York: Harcourt, Brace, Jovanovich, 1978), 92.

1. Max Weber, *The City*, trans. Don Martindale and Gertrude Neuwirth (New York: Free Press, 1958), 39.

2. Walter Benjamin, *Illuminations*, ed. Hannah Arendt, trans. Harry Zohn (New York: Schocken, 1969), 191.

3. In its genuine inability to accommodate the shocks of London's "anarchy and din," Wordsworth's poetry occupies a pivotal point in the history of city literature. On Wordsworth's poetry about the city in general and Book VII of *The Prelude* in particular, see Raymond Williams, *The Country and the City* (New York: Oxford University Press, 1973), 149–52; Max Byrd, *London Transformed* (New Haven: Yale University Press, 1978), 119–56; William Thesing, *The London Muse* (Athens: University of Georgia Press, 1982), 12–24; John H. Johnston, *The Poet and the City* (Athens: University of Georgia Press, 1984), 85–104; François Hugo, "The City and The Country: Books VII and VIII of Wordsworth's 'The Prelude,'" *Theoria* 69 (May 1987): 1–14; and Kristiaan Versluys, *The Poet in the City* (Tübingen: Narr, 1987), 24–42. I share many of the views expressed by Versluys and Byrd, differing from Versluys by emphasizing those passages where Wordsworth does confront the fears of the city that Versluys highlights. Byrd's book describes "the humanizing of London" by eighteenth-century writers, who struggle to control its energies "by imaging it as a human body, as human language, as human art" (7). Beginning with Blake and Wordsworth rather than ending with them, as Byrd does, I maintain that in the nineteenth and twentieth centuries the sense that the city cannot be controlled comes to predominate; organizing metaphors like the body, words, or art seem doomed to failure, or at least insufficiency. But on one vital point we are in accord: "Reality, illusion: Wordsworth's London has been an unreal city from the beginning" (155).

4. Text cited is that of *The Prelude: 1799, 1805, 1850*, ed. Jonathan Wordsworth, M. H. Abrams, and Stephen Gill (New York: Norton, 1979). Unless otherwise noted, I cite the version of 1805. Versluys shows how Wordsworth sharpened his antagonism toward the city in the 1850 revisions (37–40).

5. "The Metropolis and Mental Life," trans. H. H. Gerth, *Classic Essays on the Culture of Cities*, ed. Richard Sennett (Englewood Cliffs, N.J.: Prentice-Hall, 1969), 51.

6. Simmel, 52–53.

7. See Williams, 130–31.

8. In "History in the Background of Wordsworth's 'Blind Beggar,'" (*ELH* 56 [Spring 1989]: 125–48), Geraldine Friedman offers a sophisticated reading of the passage that links it to Wordsworth's life and political context without denying its thematic emphasis on textual and representational instability. Her notes also provide a brief annotated bibliography of other criticism of the passage.

9. On Benjamin's critical method, see Richard Wolin, *Walter Benjamin: An Aesthetic of Redemption* (New York: Columbia University Press, 1982), 213–26. Jonathan Arac skillfully reads Wordsworth through the lens of Benjamin in *Critical Genealogies* (New York: Columbia University Press, 1987), 181–83.

10. Benjamin, *Illuminations*, 162–63.

11. Ibid., 163. For a cogent summary of Benjamin's theory of urban shock experience, see Wolin, 226–30.

12. As Geoffrey Hartman writes, "These natural foci of any observer are shocking because here they are *not* in contrast. Face and label are equally fixed or affixed: we expect the beggar's face and eyes ('his steadfast face and sightless eyes') to be centers of life whereas they are as much a surface as the paper he wears" (*Wordsworth's Poetry, 1787–1814* [New Haven: Yale University Press, 1971], 241–42).

13. In seeing himself attempt to "see" and control the Other, the poet enters what Jacques Lacan defines as a "mirror-stage" of self-definition, one which threatens his belief in the coextensiveness of mind and nature ("Le stade du miroir comme formateur de la fonction du Je," *Ecrits* [Paris: Seuil, 1966], 93–100). In *The Pursuit of Signs* (Ithaca: Cornell University Press, 1981), Jonathan Culler provides a succinct summary of the mirror stage: "the child discovers his 'self' by identifying with the image he perceives in a mirror. The other which he sees in a mirror and which he can grasp as a totality turns out to be himself; thus the constitution of the self is dependent on the perception of the self as other" (156). For a helpful discussion of Lacan's concepts of self and Other, see Leo Bersani, *Baudelaire and Freud* (Berkeley: University of California Press, 1977), 111–17.

14. See the "Prospectus" to *The Recluse*: "For the discerning intellect of Man, / When wedded to this goodly universe / In love and holy passion, shall find [Paradise] / A simple produce of the common day" (52–55). Text is cited from *The Poetical Works of William Wordsworth*, ed. E. de Selincourt and Helen Darbishire, vol. 5 (Oxford: Clarendon Press, 1949), 5. See also M. H. Abrams, *Natural Supernaturalism* (New York: Norton, 1971), 19–70.

15. In *The Pursuit of Signs*, Jonathan Culler notes that "a reading which sought to go beyond the mirror stage" would show that, in *The Prelude*, language itself "disrupts or displaces the self-sufficient visual presence of object to subject in the mirror stage" (166). In other words, the person who has established an image of himself as "unified," through seeing himself reflected as "Other" but entire in a mirror or mirroring world, finds his self-presence challenged by the difficulty of making self and expression coincide.

16. See Hartman, 13, 242. Culler suggests that "many of Wordsworth's most important statements on poetry come in comments on funerary inscriptions, the type of verse furthest removed from the specular relation between subject and object" (167).

17. *The Four Fundamental Concepts of Psycho-Analysis*, ed. Jacques-Alain Miller, trans. Alan Sheridan (New York: Norton, 1979), 118.

18. Wordsworth's face-to-face collision with the beggar and his text thus elicits

what Benjamin calls the "aura" of an object, "the unique phenomenon of a distance, however close it may be" (*Illuminations*, 222). Despite Wordsworth's physical proximity and his efforts to "read" the beggar from his label, the beggar is closer to him—in a more commanding position—than he is to the beggar. As Benjamin comments, "The deeper the remoteness which a glance has to overcome, the stronger will be the spell that is apt to emanate from the gaze" (190). In this case the remoteness and the spell, further indications of his otherworldliness, both belong to the beggar. Although Benjamin felt that the aura's integrity was imperiled by the compression of crowds and cities, here it reasserts itself—so much so that it smites the poet—as the immobile beggar gains all the distance, leaving the poet none. Moreover, as Benjamin notes, words, such as those of the beggar's label, can possess their own aura, such that "the closer the look one takes at a word, the greater the distance from which it looks back" (200). While closeness potentially violates the word, like the object, it also provides the opportunity to discover how distant and Other the word really is.

19. See Heather Glen, "The Poet in Society: Blake and Wordsworth on London," *Literature and History* 3 (March 1976): 2–22. In an astute, socially oriented comparison, Glen argues that both "London" and Book VII of *The Prelude* ultimately move "from a sense of the poet as separate from and in some way superior to what he sees, to the poetic realization that he is inescapably and intimately a part of it" (26).

20. See Jonathan Wordsworth et al. 260, note 7.

21. In "One Way Street" (1928) Walter Benjamin speaks of a "written city" that was already burgeoning in Wordsworth's day: "Before a child of our time finds his way clear to opening a book, his eyes have been exposed to such a blizzard of changing, colorful, conflicting letters that the chances of his penetrating the archaic stillness of the book are slight. Locust swarms of print, which already eclipse the sun of what is taken for intellect for city dwellers, will grow thicker with each succeeding year" (*Reflections*, 78).

22. Théophile Gautier's description of London in the mid-nineteenth century confirms how literal and extensive this urban textuality was: "What a profusion of posters and signboards! Letters of all colors and all dimensions bedeck the buildings from high to low: the capital letters often attain the height of a story. . . . These houses thus checkered, placarded, striped with inscriptions and billboards, seen from the middle of the Thames, present the most bizarre aspect" ("A Day in London" [1842], my translation, *Caprices et Zigzags* [Paris: Victor Lecu, 1852], 109).

23. *The Prose Works of William Wordsworth*, ed. W. J. B. Owen and Jane Worthington Smyser (Oxford: Clarendon Press, 1974), I: 129. Jonathan Arac draws an intriguing parallel between Wordsworth's contrasting "the degraded 'intelligence' of news to the responsive 'feeling' native to our mind's dignity," and Benjamin's theory that the jumbled information of modern newspapers cuts one off from "any lived experience or tradition" ("Romanticism, the Self, and the City: *The Secret Agent* in Literary History," *Boundary* 2 9.1 [1980]: 78).

24. G. K. Chesterton comprehends how the city intermeshes babel-like textuality with Babylonian worldliness when he writes: "while nature is a chaos of unconscious forces, a city is a chaos of conscious ones. . . . There is no stone in the street and no brick in the wall that is not actually a deliberate symbol. . . . Every brick has as human a hieroglyph as if it were a graven brick of Babylon" ("A Defence of Detective Stories," *Defendant* (1901), 158–59; quoted in G. Robert Stange, "The Frightened Poets," *The Victorian City: Images and Realities*, ed. H. J. Dyos and Michael Wolff, 2 vols. (London: Routledge & Kegan Paul, 1973), 2: 489.

25. Wordsworth's language seems to anticipate that of contemporary deconstruction. But whereas Derrideans may emphasize the joyful freeplay of difference and *différance*, Wordsworth is clearly horrified by it. See Jacques Derrida, "Structure, Sign, and Play in the Discourse of the Human Sciences," *The Structuralist Contro-*

versy, ed. Richard Macksey and Eugenio Donato (Baltimore: Johns Hopkins University Press, 1972), 247–65.

26. In *The Politics and Poetics of Transgression* (Ithaca: Cornell University Press, 1986), Peter Stallybrass and Allon White note that Wordsworth here betrays the nature-based, Romantic poetics he had labored to establish. Overwhelmed by the city, he belatedly invokes the "linguistic and generic hierarchies of a classical aesthetic" in order to reassert distinctions that the Fair has frighteningly dissolved (123).

27. Geoffrey Hartman has identified what might seem to be a similar "shock experience" in such poems as "The Solitary Reaper" and "The Daffodils" (*Wordsworth's Poetry*, 15–18, and *Criticism in the Wilderness* [New Haven: Yale University Press, 1980], 28–30). But in these poems Wordsworth manages to accommodate the disturbing power of events by afterwards taming them or turning them to his own uses: "The music in my heart I bore, / Long after it was heard no more," he concludes in "The Solitary Reaper." The poet carries the fruits of his experience with him comfortably, like a cherished photograph—"And then my heart with pleasure fills, / And dances with the daffodils." Comparison of Wordsworth's "I wandered lonely as a cloud" to Blake's "I wander thro' each charter'd street" reveals a crucial difference in sensibility: not only the contrast between rural and urban situation, but that between present and past tenses helps determine the immediacy of poetic effect. Benjamin's citation of Valéry on the poet's effort to master shock could easily be applied to Wordsworth: "Recollection is . . . an elemental phenomenon which aims at giving us time for organizing the reception of stimuli which we initially lacked" (*Illuminations*, 161–62). I discuss this point at greater length in "Urban Theory and Critical Blight: Accommodating the Unreal City," *New Orleans Review* 10 (Spring 1983): 87–88.

28. Thus the opening lines of Book VIII present, in contrast to London's unknowable crowds, a congenial "little family of men— / Twice twenty—with their children and their wives" (7–8) at the rural Grasmere fair set beneath Helvellyn.

29. No doubt Bartholomew Fair is an instance of the "savage torpor" that Wordsworth saw cities promoting. In 1844 Friedrich Engels noted a similar effect: "The inhabitants of modern London have had to sacrifice so much that is best in human nature in order to create those wonders of civilisation with which their city teems. The vast majority of Londoners have had to let so many of their potential creative faculties lie dormant, stunted, and unused" (*The Condition of the Working Class in England*, trans. and ed. W. O. Henderson and W. H. Chaloner [Stanford: Stanford University Press, 1968], 30).

30. Wordsworth's complaint that perception and creation are impossible at too close a distance appears to coincide with Benjamin's theory that the aura decays due to "desire of contemporary masses to bring things 'closer'" (*Illuminations*, 223). But Wordsworth typically distances an object to get a conceptual grip on it, turning it into his own form of *Erlebnis*, "a moment that has been lived," so that he can recall it at his convenience. Such detachment may be said actually to violate both aura and Other. By closing in on the object, threatening its aura with one's proximity, one can see how far from it he really is, as Wordsworth discovers with the blind beggar.

31. Max Byrd comments that in Book VII Wordsworth "verges upon a personification of the city comparable to the one he constructs for the Alps [VI, 561–72], where voice, characters, types, symbols are united into a single, awe-inspiring face," but concludes that the poet is ultimately unsuccessful: in London "no face appears" (139). The apocalyptic effect of the blind beggar, however, along with the use of the words "type" and "emblem," which hark back to the earlier passage, indicate otherwise. In its provocative, suprahuman blankness, the beggar's face becomes the urban counterpart of that great form in Nature which bears "Characters of the great apocalypse, / The types and symbols of eternity" (VI, 570–71).

32. A sense of anticlimax further extends the parallel with the alpine experience. Wordsworth follows this passage with lines originally written to describe his disap-

pointment in the Alps (VIII, 711–27), and immediately after crossing London's threshold, he recalls, "A weight of ages did at once descend / Upon my heart" (VIII, 703–4), words which evoke the earlier dejection (VI, 491–92, 549–50). But a major difference must be borne in mind: the poet's consciousness of the crucial moment in London, his sense of its power and divinity.

33. In *Civilization and Its Discontents* (trans. James Strachey [New York: Norton, 1962], 17–18), Freud compares the palimpsestic quality of the human mind to that of Rome, the Eternal City, where layer upon layer of the town is built and rebuilt, the later levels of culture never fully covering the earlier. Wordsworth too uses the layered complexity of the city to explore the mind, but his reaction to the simultaneous coexistence of so many thoughts, images, and perceptions is one of bafflement and frustration rather than a confident delineation of its laws.

34. Text is cited from de Selincourt and Darbishire, *Poetical Works*, III: 38. The actual day the poem commemorates was July 31, 1802, according to Dorothy Wordsworth's *Grasmere Journal* entry for that date. She records the experience in language (and in an order) much like that of the poem: "It was a beautiful morning. The City, St. Paul's, with the river and a multitude of little boats, made a most beautiful sight as we crossed Westminster Bridge. The houses were not overhung by their cloud of smoke and they were spread out endlessly, yet the sun shone so brightly with such a pure light that there was even something like the purity of one of nature's own grand spectacles" (*The Grasmere Journals*, ed. Pamela Woof [New York: Henry Holt, 1987], 162–63). For an attempt to relate the poem to this journey's effect on Wordsworth's politics and personal life, see Charles Molesworth, "Wordsworth's 'Westminster Bridge' Sonnet: The Republican Structure of Time and Perception," *Clio* 3 (Spring 1977): 261–73.

35. Cleanth Brooks writes that the "most exciting thing that the poet can say about the houses is that they are *asleep*. . . . It is only when the poet sees the city under the semblance of death that he can see it as actually alive—quick with the only life which he can accept, the organic life of 'nature'" (*The Well Wrought Urn* [1947; New York: Harcourt, Brace, Jovanovich, 1975], 6–7). In *The Limits of Mortality: An Essay on Wordsworth's Major Poems* (Middletown, Conn.: Wesleyan University Press, 1959), David Ferry goes a step further, declaring that "the city is not merely sleeping, but dead, its heart stilled. The poet looks at London and sees it as a sort of corpse and admires it as such, welcomes a death which is the death of what the city has come to stand for in his symbolic world" (14). On the history of the London-body motif, see Louis Landa, "London Observed: The Progress of a Simile," *Philological Quarterly* 54 (Winter 1975): 275–88. See also J. Hillis Miller, "The Still Heart: Poetic Form in Wordsworth," *New Literary History* 2 (Winter 1971): 297–310.

36. Michael Riffaterre, for example, remarks that the phrase "smokeless air" is pivotal, because it invokes the very industrial qualities of the city that the poem seeks to repress. Cited in Geoffrey Hartman, "The Unremarkable Wordsworth," *On Signs*, ed. Marshall Blonsky (Baltimore: Johns Hopkins University Press, 1985), 321–22.

37. Thus for John H. Johnston the scene "constitutes [no] challenge to his artistic powers of management . . . because it is already managed in terms of the peaceful cosmic processes and the temporary cessation of human activity" (100).

38. Max Byrd suggests that in its cryptic quality the simile, "like a garment," may function as the beggar's label does, something worn that is radiant and "unutterable" (146–47). I regard it rather as the poet's attempt to clothe in virginal robes the "naked" and promiscuous city of which he has seen too much.

Chapter Three. Poet as Passant

The epigraph is from Italo Calvino, *Invisible Cities*, trans. William Weaver (New York: Harcourt, Brace, Jovanovich, 1974), 51.

1. "Salon de 1846," *Oeuvres complètes*, ed. Claude Pichois, 2 vols. (Paris: Gallimard, Bibliothèque de la Pléiade, 1975–76), II: 495, 496. All texts of Baudelaire are cited from this edition; subsequent references are noted parenthetically. Translations of the poetry and prose are my own. For a stimulating, comprehensive analysis of Baudelaire's treatment of the city, see France Joxe, "Ville et modernité dans *Les Fleurs du mal*," *Europe*, 456–57 (April–May 1967): 139–62.

2. In my discussion of *Tableaux parisiens*, I am greatly indebted to an excellent series of essays by Ross Chambers: "Trois paysages urbains: Les Poèmes liminaires des *Tableaux parisiens*," *Modern Philology* 80 (May 1983): 372–89; "Baudelaire's Street Poetry," *Nineteenth-Century French Studies* 13 (Summer 1985): 244–59; and "Are Baudelaire's 'Tableaux Parisiens' about Paris?" *On Referring in Literature*, ed. Anna Whiteside and Michael Issacharoff (Bloomington: Indiana University Press, 1987), 95–110. Chambers establishes an overall framework in which to read the poems: the first ("Paysage"), tenth ("Le Crépuscule du soir"), and final ("Le Crépuscule du matin") poems are "liminary poems having a mainly intersequential function"; on one side of the pivotal "Le Crépuscule du soir" are poems of daytime encounters in the city streets, from "Le Soleil" to "Le Squelette laboureux," and on the other side, a nocturnal sequence from "Le Jeu" to "Rêve parisien" ("Baudelaire's Street Poetry," 257). In this chapter I deal with the daytime poems because, as Chambers notes, they are conditioned by "the enveloping theme of encounter itself" ("Baudelaire's Street Poetry," 247), and I show how they relate to the larger tradition of sudden confrontations in the unreal city.

3. See Karlheinz Stierle, "Baudelaire and the Tradition of the *Tableau de Paris*," *New Literary History* 11 (Winter 1980): 345–61. Stierle justly argues the need to see Baudelaire's work within the context of the genre of the *tableau de Paris*. For an overview of poetry about Paris, see Pierre Citron, *La Poésie de Paris dans la littérature française de Rousseau à Baudelaire*, 2 vols. (Paris: Minuit, 1961).

4. For further discussion of "Paysage" contrasting Baudelaire's treatment of nature and the city to that of Wordsworth and his Victorian successors, see my "Confronting the Unpoetical City: Arnold, Clough, and Baudelaire," *The Arnoldian* 13.1 (1985-86): 10–22.

5. In "Le Soleil" Baudelaire puns on "vers" as meaning both verses and worms which the sun wakes in the fields. In "Les Petites Vieilles" he urbanizes his word-play by rhyming the two senses of the word "cité"—"city" and "cited"—again calling attention to the city as language.

6. "Practices of Space," *On Signs*, ed. Marshall Blonsky (Baltimore: Johns Hopkins University Press, 1985), 129–30: "On the most elementary level [walking] has in effect a threefold 'uttering' function: it is a process of *appropriation* of the topographic system by the pedestrian (just as the speaker appropriates and assumes language); it is a spatial *realization* of the site (just as the act of speaking is a sonic realization of language): lastly, it implies relationships among distinct positions, i.e. pragmatic '*contracts*' in the form of movements (just as verbal utterance is 'allocution,' 'places the *others*' before the speaker, and sets up contracts between fellow speakers). A first definition of walking thus seems to be a space of uttering."

7. In "Le Peintre de la vie moderne," Baudelaire similarly describes the artist "s'escrimant avec son crayon, sa plume, son pinceau . . . pressé, violent, actif, comme s'il craignait que les images ne lui échappent" ["fencing with his pencil, his pen, his brush . . . hurried, violent, energetic, as if he feared that the images would escape him"]. And when he succeeds, "la fantasmagorie a été extraite de la nature" ["phantasmagoria has been extracted from nature"] (II: 693–94).

8. On Baudelaire's politics, see, among others, J. Mouquet and W. T. Bandy, *Baudelaire en 1848* (Paris: Emile Paul Frères, 1946); Lois Boe Hyslop, *Baudelaire, Man of His Time* (New Haven: Yale University Press, 1980); and T. J. Clark, *The Absolute Bourgeois* (Greenwich, Conn.: New York Graphic Society, 1973). Edward J. Ahearn provides an overview of historically informed approaches to Baudelaire, as well as a

useful bibliography, in "Marx's Relevance for Second Empire Literature: Baude-laire's 'Le Cygne,'" *Nineteenth-Century French Studies* 14 (1986): 269–77. See also Chambers, "Baudelaire's Street Poetry," for a brief account of the revolutionary im-port of Baudelaire's dedicating key poems of *Tableaux parisiens* to Victor Hugo (255–56).

9. I am deferring discussion of "A une mendiante rousse" at this point. While it fits the pattern of ever more unsettling experiences leading up to "Les Sept Vieillards," I believe its function in *Tableaux parisiens* can be better addressed in rela-tion to "A une passante," which I take up below.

10. The quotation comes from a major collection of *tableaux*, the *Diable à Paris*, 1846. See Stierle, 351.

11. The lines invite comparison with the famous conclusion of "Au Lecteur": "—Hypocrite lecteur,—mon semblable,—mon frère!" See also Chambers, "Baude-laire's Street Poetry," 252.

12. *Selected Essays*, new ed. (New York: Harcourt, Brace, World, 1964), 375.

13. "Droit dans les yeux" (1977), *L'Obvie et l'obtus: Essais critiques III* (Paris: Seuil, 1982), 279–80; my translation. I wish to thank Vincent Leitch for bringing the essay to my attention.

14. *Four Fundamental Concepts of Psycho-Analysis*, ed. Jacques-Alain Miller, trans. Alan Sheridan (New York: Norton, 1979), 118.

15. Lacan seems to be unaware that a strong secondary meaning of *fascinum* is already "phallus"; the word contains, for Latin writers, both the blight and the cure, or, to turn it around, both potency and its enemy. Horace combines both senses in the phrase "languet fascinum" (*Epodes*, 8.18). But Lacan insists on seeing as separate the double, reciprocal function of the *fascinum*: "there is no good eye," he finds, "but there are evil eyes all over the place" (119).

16. Lacan, 118. See also Leo Bersani's thoughtful discussion of this topic in *Baude-laire and Freud* (Berkeley: University of California Press, 1977), 57–62. Bersani pro-poses seeing "the castration complex in terms of *an anguished preoccupation with the mobility of meaning*" (59; his emphasis). He then goes on to show how for Baudelaire, as for others, "the floating of desire is a menace to coherent self-definition. Perhaps the principal strategy for stabilizing the self, both for individuals and for entire cul-tures, is to plot the immobilization of desire" (61).

17. Benjamin, "On Some Motifs in Baudelaire," *Illuminations*, ed. Hannah Arendt, trans. Harry Zohn (New York: Schocken, 1969), 165.

18. Ibid., 167.

19. For further discussion of "Les Sept Vieillards," including its relation to "Les Petites Vieilles," see Richard D. E. Burton's detailed reading in *Baudelaire in 1859* (Cambridge: Cambridge University Press, 1988), 105–28.

20. John H. Johnston, *The Poet and the City* (Athens: University of Georgia Press, 1984), 145. See also Edward J. Ahearn, "The Search for Community: The City in Hölderlin, Wordsworth, and Baudelaire," *Texas Studies in Literature and Language* 13 (Spring 1971): 71.

21. Cf. Baudelaire's "Les Fenêtres" in which the poet claims he could have ac-complished the same penetration of hidden life if he had been staring at an old man rather than an old woman. Sima Godfrey speculates that Baudelaire uses a frame or "window" to aestheticize the Otherness that, in the open streets, eludes Poe's nar-rator in "The Man of the Crowd" ("Baudelaire's Windows," *L'Esprit Créateur* 22.4 [1982]: 95–96). Nonetheless, it is a *woman* whom Baudelaire chooses to frame; cap-turing a man of the crowd, even indoors, would be for him a more difficult and less congenial task.

22. Here the speaker's "manifold heart" which embraces both the virtues and the vices of "his family" seems to suggest the multitude-containing gestures of Baude-laire's contemporary, Whitman, as do the catalogues of city life in "Projet d'epi-logue" (see Johnston, 148).

23. This sense of connection accords perfectly with the vocation of the painter of

modern life: "L'amateur de la vie fait du monde sa famille" ["The lover of life makes of the world his family"] (II: 692).

24. The conflicting and incestuous attractions that these relations imply—seeing mothers and daughters as virgins, whores, and wives—may have their source in Baudelaire's complex relationship with his own mother. Baudelaire saw his mother twice widowed, once when he was a little boy, and throughout his life he maintained an emotional and stormy intimacy with her, writing her almost every day, arguing about money, his mistresses, and his stepfather. See Hélène Fredrickson, *Baudelaire, Héros et fils: Dualité et problèmes du travail dans les lettres à sa mère* (Saratoga, Calif.: Anma Libri, 1977).

25. A sustained account of Baudelaire's prose poems about the city would require a separate study. In this chapter I refer to them (and his other prose) only as they bear directly on my concerns with *Tableaux parisiens*. On the relation of the *Petites Poèmes en prose* to the city, see Marshall Berman, *All That Is Solid Melts Into Air* (New York: Simon & Schuster, 1982), 142–64, and Marc Eli Blanchard, *In Search of the City* (Stanford: Stanford French and Italian Studies 37, Anma Libri, 1985), 71–114. On the prose poems in general, see James Hiddleston, *Baudelaire and Le Spleen de Paris* (Oxford: Oxford University Press, 1986); Barbara Johnson, *Défigurations du langage poétique* (Paris: Flammarion, 1979); and Suzanne Bernard, *Le Poème en prose de Baudelaire jusqu'a nos jours* (Paris: Nizet, 1959).

26. Cf. "Ivresse religieuse des grandes villes" ["Religious intoxication of great cities"] (I: 651).

27. Cf. also "Fusées": "*Tout* est nombre. Le nombre est dans *tout*. Le nombre est dans l'individu. L'ivresse est un nombre" ["*Everything* is number. Number is in *everything*. Number is in the individual. Intoxication is a number"] (I: 649).

28. Benjamin, *Illuminations*, 193. Benjamin alludes to the *Journaux intimes*: "Perdu dans ce vilain monde, coudoyé par les foules, je suis comme un homme lassé . . . " (I: 667).

29. See Bersani, 8–12, for an elaboration of this point.

30. In Baudelaire's complex stance toward the crowd, Jerrold Seigel finds that the antinomies of heaven and hell, self and Other so essential to Baudelaire's intellect manifest themselves socially in the form of an alternating attraction toward and repulsion from the poles of dandyism and Bohemianism (*Bohemian Paris* [New York: Penguin, 1987], 97–124).

31. Godfrey points out that the poet defines the feminine Other textually: he writes the "légende" or caption to accompany the picture of her already framed by the window (92–94).

32. As Chambers says, Baudelaire "does not present noise as an impediment to communication so much as he sees noise-traversed communication as the only mode available to modern poetic speech; and the problem for him is not to exclude noise from poetic beauty but to find a means of producing poetry which incorporates noise into its texture, just as modern beauty incorporates death" ("Baudelaire's Street Poetry," 253).

33. In his only direct reference to Babel in the *Tableaux parisiens*, Baudelaire speaks of a "Babel d'escaliers et d'arcades / . . . un palais infini" ["Babel of stairways and arcades . . . an infinite palace"] that fills the dreamworld of "Rêve parisien." The Piranesian image indicates how, outside the daytime poems of encounter, Baudelaire explores the idea of visual rather than auditory confusion—"all for the eye," this vision enjoys the "silence of eternity."

34. Of the six encounter poems, only "Les Sept Vieillards" and "Les Aveugles" are not about women, and these poems too evoke the sexual nature of the poet's relation to the city through words like "raccrocher" and "jouissance." For Baudelaire the city is a place marked by exile and loss, and the quest for the unpossessable female object of desire becomes his deepest image for both the unreality of urban experience and the poetic effort to define it.

35. Benjamin, *Illuminations*, 169.

36. For two insightful readings of "A une passante" that complement my own, see Donald Aynesworth, "A Face in the Crowd: A Baudelairian Vision of the Eternal Feminine," *Stanford French Review* 3 (Winter 1981): 327–39, and Richard Stamelman, "The Shroud of Allegory: Death, Mourning, and Melancholy in Baudelaire's Work," *Texas Studies in Literature and Language* 25 (Fall 1983): 390–409. Other valuable studies include Sima Godfrey, "Foules Rush in . . . Lamartine, Baudelaire and the Crowd," *Romance Notes* 24 (Fall 1983): 33–42; Jean-François Delesalle, "Baudelaire, Jules Viard, et la passante," *Bulletin Baudelairien* 19.3 (1984): 55–67; Per Buvik, "Paris—lieu poétique, lieu érotique: Quelques remarques à propos de Walter Benjamin et de Baudelaire," *Revue Romane* 20.2 (1985): 231–42; and Ross Chambers, "The Storm in the Eye of the Poem: Baudelaire's 'A une passante,'" *Textual Analysis: Some Readers Reading*, ed. Mary Ann Caws (New York: Modern Language Association, 1986), 156–66.

37. There is also an instructive series of oppositions with "Les Sept Vieillards": though both figures are charged with death, the disgusting reproduction of the *vieillard* turns to the joyful rebirth caused by the *passante;* the possibly fatal viewing of an eighth repetition of the *vieillard* gives way to the desperate desire for another, reanimating vision of the *passante;* and the poet who was formerly "exaspéré comme un ivrogne" now becomes "crispé comme un extravagant," shifting his emotion from the tawdry outrage of the drunk to the love-struck spasm of the madman.

38. The fact that the encounter is no longer between two persons, but between a book and a person, between the poet and the image of life-in-death, marks the beginning of another transition: "Le Squelette laboureur" leads into "Le Crépuscule du soir" and the poems of the night world that make up the second half of *Tableaux parisiens.*

39. Cf. "The Painter of Modern Life": "Sa passion et sa profession, c'est d'*épouser la foule.* Pour le parfait flâneur, pour l'observateur passionné, c'est une immense jouissance que d'élire domicile dans le nombre, dans l'ondoyant, dans le mouvement, dans le fugitif et l'infini. Etre hors de chez soi, et pourtant se sentir partout chez soi . . . " ["His passion and his profession are *to embrace the crowd.* For the perfect flâneur, for the impassioned observer, it is an immense ecstasy to elect to live in the multitude, in what flows, in movement, in the fugitive and the infinite. To be outside himself, and yet to feel everywhere at home . . . "] (II: 691–92).

40. The quick shift of the words used for the *passante,* from third person ("a woman passed") to intimate address ("O toi") conveys the rapid evolution of the poet's emotion.

41. These beautiful breasts, "radiant as eyes," complete the eye/*fascinum* association discussed earlier: if the evil eye can dry up milk, these breasts are benificent eyes that will provide the sustenance the poet needs, despite the poverty both he and the beggar girl suffer.

42. For further confrontations with (thought-) provoking beggars, see Baudelaire's prose poem "Assomons Les Pauvres" and Leo Bersani's discussion of it in *Baudelaire and Freud* (137–51).

43. As Jean Rousset remarks in *Leurs Yeux Se Rencontrèrent: La Scène de première vue dans le roman* (Paris: José Corti, 1981), "la première vue [est] un acte de déchiffrage, de lecture instantanée" (29). For an elaboration of Saussure's famous distinction between *langue* and *parole,* see Jonathan Culler, *Ferdinand de Saussure* (New York: Penguin, 1976), 22–48.

44. Wordsworth's meeting with the mysterious Cumberland soldier in Book IV of *The Prelude* makes just this point: the appearance of the stranger reminds members of a community that they *are* a community, and the charity that he receives from them is thus not just a sign of common humanity shared with the beggar, but of their own function as a community defined by his strangeness.

45. Unlike certain other poems of Baudelaire, here there is no return through formal repetition. See Bersani, 51.

46. Benjamin, *Reflections*, ed. Peter Demetz, trans. Edmund Jephcott (New York:

Harcourt, 1979), 335–36. On Benjamin's theory of language see "On Language as Such and on the Language of Man" and "On the Mimetic Faculty," *Reflections*, 314–36, and Irving Wohlfarth, "Walter Benjamin's Image of Interpretation," *New German Critique* 17 (Spring 1979): 70–98.

47. Lacan, 85. Cf. Barthes, 282 ("I see him seeing me . . . I see myself *blind* before him") and Sartre's remarks in "The Other and His Look": "When I am seen, I am seen as an object in a world that is not my world and in which everything is ordered from the viewpoint of the Other. . . . The other as a look is—my transcendence transcended" (*Jean-Paul Sartre: To Freedom Condemned*, ed. Justus Streller, trans. Wade Baskin [New York: Philosophical Library, 1960], 40).

48. Benjamin, *Illuminations*, 188.

49. In a probing essay on Benjamin, Geoffrey Hartman questions why he did not use "A une passante" to show "the decay of the aura" when it so clearly registers the impact of modern urban masses upon poetic consciousness. Hartman argues that "the unreduced notion of the aura, applied directly to this sonnet, would have reintroduced the question of religious or cultic residues" which would have undermined the socioeconomic point Benjamin was making (*Criticism in the Wilderness* [New Haven: Yale University Press, 1980], 69, 70).

50. Benjamin, *Illuminations*, 194.

51. Ibid., 169.

52. In lines that might have been written expressly about "A une passante," Jacques Derrida ponders how the same distance that constitutes and activates the aura also shapes the dynamic of desire: "A distance from distance must be maintained. Not only for protection . . . against the spell of her fascination, but also as a way of succumbing to it" (*Spurs/Nietzsche's Styles*, trans. Barabara Harlow [Chicago: University of Chicago Press, 1978], 49).

53. Benjamin seems to have sensed this, for he says in a note, "Words, too, can have an aura of their own" (*Illuminations*, 200). The move from object to language implicates the critic's own words in the phenomenon he is trying to describe. Thus Richard Schiff brilliantly shows how Benjamin's writing on the decline of the aura has acquired an aura of its own ("Handling Shocks," *New Observations* 47 [April 1987], 16–17).

54. *Walter Benjamin or Towards a Revolutionary Criticism* (London: Verso, 1981), 39.

55. I discuss both this point and the theory of the aura more fully in "J. E. Millais' *Bubbles*: A Work of Art in the Age of Mechanical Reproduction," *Victorian Newsletter* 70 (Fall 1986): 16–18.

56. Benjamin, "Theses on the Philosophy of History," *Illuminations*, 255.

57. Ibid.

58. Benjamin appears to have viewed his personal history in a similar fashion, diagramming his life as an urban labyrinth that he can illuminate only through the agency of the sudden, Baudelairean flash; see *Reflections*, 30.

59. Hartman, 64.

60. Ibid., 70.

61. Ibid., 70.

62. Benjamin, *Illuminations*, 169.

63. De Quincey, *Confessions of an English Opium Eater* (1821; New York: Oxford University Press, 1985), 34. For Baudelaire's translation of the passage, see "Un Mangeur d'opium" in *Les Paradis artificiels* (I: 462).

64. In the "Salon de 1846" Baudelaire points out how mourning dress is a distinctive mark of the era: "N'est-il pas l'habit nécessaire de notre époque, souffrante et portant jusque sur ses épaules noires et maigres le symbole d'un deuil perpétuel? Remarquez bien que l'habit noir . . . [a son] beauté poétique." ["Is it not the requisite dress of our age, suffering and wearing even up to its thin black shoulders the symbol of a perpetual mourning? Note well that black apparel has its own poetic beauty"] (II: 497).

Chapter Four. Walt Whitman's Urban Incarnation

The epigraph is from *Leaves of Grass*, ed. Sculley Bradley and Harold W. Blodgett (1965; New York: Norton, 1973), 153.

1. Wherever possible, Whitman's poems are cited by page number from the above edition, hereafter abbreviated *LG*. This text is based on the final, "death-bed" edition of *Leaves of Grass* (Philadelphia: David McKay, 1891–1892). Dates indicate when poems first appeared in print, even if revised later; but unless noted, the text cited differs only minutely from that originally published. I have also relied on *Leaves of Grass: The First (1855) Edition*, ed. Malcolm Cowley (New York: Viking, 1959) and *Walt Whitman: The Complete Poems*, ed. Francis Murphy (New York: Penguin, 1975) for some early texts, including the original "Song of Myself," and on *Leaves of Grass: Facsimile Edition of the 1860 Text*, ed. Roy Harvey Pearce (Ithaca: Cornell University Press, 1961).

2. Despite the centrality of the city in Whitman's life and work, relatively few critics have focused on its role in his poetry. Among the best essays are those of Kristiaan Versluys ("Walt Whitman's Mannahatta or the Joy of a Romantic," *The Poet in the City* [Tübingen: Narr, 1987], 43–71), James L. Machor ("Pastoralism and the American Urban Ideal: Hawthorne, Whitman, and the Literary Pattern," *American Literature* 54.3 [1982]: 329–53), and M. Wynn Thomas ("Walt Whitman and Mannahatta-New York," *American Quarterly* 34 [Fall 1982]: 362–78). Each explores the tension between Whitman's poetic city of Mannahatta and the actual city of New York. Burton Pike (*The Image of the City in Modern Literature* [Princeton: Princeton University Press, 1981]), John H. Johnston (*The Poet and the City* [Athens: University of Georgia Press, 1984]), and David Weimer (*The City as Metaphor* [New York: Random House, 1966]) discuss Whitman in the context of other urban literature, the last two contending that Whitman fails to unify his city poetry either aesthetically or morally. For other studies see Larzer Ziff, "Whitman and the Crowd," *Critical Inquiry* 10 (June 1984): 579–91; J. Thomas Chaffin, Jr., "Give Me Faces and Streets: Walt Whitman and the City," *Walt Whitman Review* 23 (1977): 109–20; and Stephen Tanner, "Walt Whitman as Urban Transcendentalist," *South Dakota Review* 14.2 (1976): 6–18. An earlier version of my analysis appeared as "City / Body / Text: Walt Whitman's Urban Incarnation," *Cycnos: Politique et Poétique de la Ville* (Nice: University of Nice, 1984), 39–48.

3. Like Wordsworth, Whitman imagines himself as the hero of a new epic extolling the life and thought of the poet, and thus later in "Pictures" he sets himself next to Rousseau and Emerson. The aspiration to achieve this within an urban context ("the young man of Mannahatta . . . him I sing for a thousand years" [*LG*, 647]) did not develop immediately. The early poem "Young Grimes" (1840) concludes by counseling its readers to remain on their farms: "Leave the wide city's noisy din— / The busy haunts of men— / And here enjoy a tranquil life, / Unvexed by guilt or pain" (Murphy, 635).

4. On the importance of the city in Whitman's journalism and prose, see Joseph Jay Rubin, *The Historic Whitman* (University Park: Pennsylvania State University Press, 1973); Joseph Jay Rubin and Charles Brown, eds., *Walt Whitman of the New York Aurora: Editor at Twenty-Two* (n.p.: Bald Eagle Press, 1950); Walt Whitman, *New York Dissected*, ed. Emory Holloway and Ralph Adimari (New York: R. R. Wilson, 1936); and Henry M. Christman, ed., *Walt Whitman's New York* (New York: Macmillan, 1963). The standard biographies also relate Whitman's activities as a journalist in New York to his growth as a poet: Gay Wilson Allen, *The Solitary Singer: A Critical Biography of Walt Whitman*, rev. ed. (1967; Chicago: University of Chicago Press, 1985); Justin Kaplan, *Walt Whitman: A Life* (New York: Simon & Schuster, 1980); and Paul Zweig, *Walt Whitman: The Making of the Poet* (New York: Basic Books, 1984). See Versluys, 43–49 and 65–69, for a consideration of the interplay between Whitman's poetry and his prose.

5. Thomas argues that Whitman's "chronic disappointment" over the materialism

of New York emerges in the poems of 1865, and that in later years he "retreated to the consolations of the ideal" as his poetic Mannahatta "grew increasingly distant from the actual historical New York" (372–77). Similarly, Versluys claims that the intensity of Whitman's joy over New York's preparation for the Civil War can be explained only by his fear that the city had abandoned its democratic ideals (60). But both critics acknowledge that Whitman's declining gusto for urban life is balanced by his unflagging appreciation of its beauty and energy. As Versluys says, "Whitman's doubts about the city are real but intermittent, penetrating yet always adulterated" (70). The present chapter considers the view of the city that emerges in Whitman's early works, rather than how it might have been modified later. For an examination of Whitman's entire *oeuvre* in relation to the larger currents of nineteenth-century politics, see Betsy Erkkila, *Whitman the Political Poet* (New York: Oxford University Press, 1988).

6. On the city in American literature, see Leo Marx, *The Machine in the Garden* (New York: Oxford University Press, 1964) and "Pastoralism in America," *Ideology and Classic American Literature*, ed. Sacvan Bercovitch and Myra Jehlen (New York: Oxford University Press, 1986), 36–69; Blanche Gelfant, *The American City Novel*, 2nd ed. (Norman: University of Oklahoma Press, 1970); and Michael C. Jaye and Ann C. Watts, eds., *Literature and the Urban Experience* (New Brunswick, N.J.: Rutgers University Press, 1981). Conflicting images of the nineteenth-century city are explored in Janis P. Stout, *Sodoms in Eden: The City in American Fiction Before 1860* (Westport, Conn.: Greenwood, 1976), and Adrienne Siegel, *The Image of the American City in Popular Literature 1820–1870* (Port Washington, N.Y.: Kennikat, 1981). Joan Zlotnik in *Portrait of an American City: The Novelist's New York* (Port Washington, N.Y.: Kennikat, 1982) provides useful information on Whitman's city. John H. Johnston, *The Poet and the City*, offers the most extensive consideration to date of American city poetry, including Whitman, Eliot, Hart Crane, Auden, Ginsberg, and Williams.

7. While Whitman's encyclopedic technique argues for the equality of all endeavors and occupations, at the same time it accents the poet's special ability to participate in and record them. See Ziff, 582.

8. Whitman regularly uses ellipsis points, and in quoting passages containing them I have left the four periods unspaced. Where I have omitted material, the points forming the ellipsis have been spaced.

9. By 1860 almost all the major poems of the city were already in place in *Leaves of Grass*, in versions very close to those of the final 1892 edition. While Whitman subtly repressed the sexual content of some poems after 1866, none of the urban poems studied here was significantly altered. M. Jimmie Killingsworth analyzes the effect of the changes in "Whitman's Sexual Themes During a Decade of Revision: 1866–1876," *Walt Whitman Quarterly Review* 4.1 (1986): 7–15; he cites *Leaves of Grass: A Textual Variorum of the Printed Poems*, 3 vols., ed. Sculley Bradley, Harold W. Blodgett, Arthur Golden, and William White (New York: New York University Press, 1980).

10. Of the forty-five poems in the original *Calamus* section of the 1860 *Leaves of Grass*, nine deal explicitly with urban experience, and several others help define the relation between the poet and the physical world. According to Thomas, in *Calamus* Whitman approaches the city in two ways: first, by considering its "uncertain and perhaps unredeemable character," and second, by describing the ideal communities he would like to see in its place (370). But there is a crucial third approach that mediates between the other two: Whitman regards the intimate contact between citizens as the only way to settle qualms about the city's unreality, expressed in the first group of poems, and also as the only way to establish the ideal "city of friends," described in the second group.

11. In 1860 the untitled poem's first line read, "City of my walks and joys!" (Pearce, 363).

12. Whitman was born in 1819, Baudelaire in 1821; *Les Fleurs du mal* appeared just two years after *Leaves of Grass*. Apparently Whitman did not read Baudelaire until 1875, late in his career: "his sole mention of Baudelaire," writes F. O. Matthiessen, "was to quote one of the few beliefs they shared, 'The immoderate taste for beauty and art leads men into monstrous excesses'" (*American Renaissance* [New York: Oxford University Press, 1941], 518). On the source of Whitman's citation of Baudelaire, see W. T. Bandy, "Whitman and Baudelaire," *Walt Whitman Quarterly Review* 1.3 (1983): 53–55.

13. For further comparison of Whitman and Baudelaire, see Johnston, 148, 406; and Versluys, 52–53. The latter examines the two poets' treatment of urban lowlife, concluding that evil in the Baudelairean sense "never touches [Whitman] to the core and he can lay no claim, therefore, to being the poet of the dark side of the city" (53). But Whitman's urban torments, though of a different order from those of Baudelaire, do exist, and stem from his need for poetic self-incarnation through the melding of bodily and textual energies.

14. Whitman took care that in the final order he set for *Leaves of Grass*, his first city lyric should also sound this keynote: "Once I pass'd through a populous city imprinting my brain for future use with its shows, architecture, customs, traditions, / Yet now of all that city I remember only a woman I casually met there who detain'd me for love of me" ("Once I Passed Through a Populous City," 1860; *LG*, 109–10). The manuscript of the poem shows it was originally a man whom the poet met (Murphy, 798).

15. The city is clearly not the only sexual site for Whitman. What are perhaps Whitman's most graphic, "spermatic" evocations of sex and masturbation occur in sections 24, 28, and 29 of "Song of Myself," in pastoral settings. The city is more likely to be the arena of erotic activity with others, but the emphasis falls usually on what is permissible publicly (such as eye contact); what is unseen (all sorts of longings); and what is furtive (i.e., taking place at night or in bed). Often this secret behavior suggests the prolonging of a glance exchanged in the street, and deals in thoughts rather than actions. Thus the sexually charged quality of Whitman's city is due in large part to its sense of *potential* fulfillment—the constant interaction of attractive, attracted strangers who have little time or privacy to pursue physically the desires that their yearning looks signify. For an extended consideration of Whitman's sexual attitudes in their social context, see M. Jimmie Killingsworth, *Whitman's Poetry of the Body: Sexuality, Politics, and the Text* (Chapel Hill: University of North Carolina Press, 1989); see also Harold Aspiz, "Walt Whitman: The Spermatic Imagination," *On Whitman: The Best from "American Literature,"* ed. Edwin H. Cady and Louis J. Budd (Durham: Duke University Press, 1987), 273–89.

16. Usually Whitman does the singling out, even in the most unlikely situations. See Ziff, 590.

17. Edwin H. Miller suggests that Whitman's language of the eyes animates a lonely cityscape through the momentary gratification of "achieving identity among fellow outlaws." Miller quotes J. A. Symonds' *Studies in Sexual Inversion*: "these [homosexual] men know each other at first sight. . . . 'We recognize each other at once,' says the writer of a report. . . . 'A mere glance of the eye suffices'" (*Walt Whitman's Poetry* [Boston: Houghton, Mifflin, 1968], 163).

18. For example, "I Dream'd in a Dream" (1860), "A Noiseless Patient Spider" (1862), "Poem of Joys" (1860), "Mannahatta" (1860), and "Faces" (1855).

19. Other poems that address the reader while making self-conscious reference to their being read in a book include "Now Lift Me Close" (1860), "How Solemn as One by One" (1865), and "Song of Myself."

20. The poem was not a part of the *Calamus* section in 1860 and was later much revised; see *LG*, 176–77.

21. Thomas makes a similar point about Sections 5 and 6 of "Crossing Brooklyn Ferry" (368).

22. Whitman also makes this claim in "Song of the Broad-Axe" (1856), where the

great city ("greatest" in the 1860 version) thrives on the sexual health of its men and women:

> Where the city of the faithfulest friends stands,
> Where the city of the cleanliness of the sexes stands,
> Where the city of the healthiest fathers stands,
> Where the city of the best-bodied mothers stands,
> There the great city stands.
>
> (LG, 190)

For further discussion, see Robin P. Hoople, "Walt Whitman and the City of Friends," in K. W. Cameron, ed. *Scholar's Companion to the American Renaissance*, 1st ser. (Hartford: Transcendental Books, 1977), 45–51.

23. The last two lines did not appear in 1860.

24. See Machor, 333–35; Tanner, 8.

25. See Stout, 21–43, and Robert H. Walker, "The Poet and the Rise of the City," *Mississippi Valley Historical Review* 49 (June 1962–March 1963): 85–99. Whitman's pleasure in the pervasive sexuality of the city also contrasts sharply with the dread felt by his contemporaries in Victorian England. When A. H. Clough's Dipsychus, for example, braves the crowd, he fears violation by it; and in *Maud*, Tennyson "loathe[s] the squares and streets, / And the faces that one meets." But Whitman yearns for precisely that contact. In "The Frightened Poets," G. Robert Stange speculates that Whitman's sexual frankness permits him to deal poetically with the urban environment that his Victorian contemporaries shunned (H. J. Dyos and Michael Wolff, eds., *The Victorian City: Images and Realities*, 2 vols. [London: Routledge & Kegan Paul, 1973], 2: 481).

26. In "The Prairie States" (1880), Whitman imagines

> A newer garden of creation, no primal solitude,
> Dense, joyous, modern, populous millions, cities and farms,
> With iron interlaced, composite, tied, many in one,
> By all the world contributed—freedom's and law's and thrift's society,
> The crown and teeming paradise, so far, of time's accumulations,
> To justify the past.
>
> (LG, 402)

This secularized New Jerusalem is girt with iron instead of gold and precious minerals, and contains modern millions instead of 144,000 ancient saints. Here time is redeemed ("to justify the past") by American virtue and economy. This is Wordsworth's marriage of man and nature, garden and city, on a contemporary social scale.

27. Cf. "Song of Myself": there "will never be any more perfection than there is now, / Nor any more heaven or hell than there is now" (LG, 30).

28. See Thomas, 374–75.

29. In later versions, Whitman made many minor changes in the poem, and dropped two important passages: after the line "A million people . . . young men," the 1860 text reads: "The free city! no slaves! no owners of slaves!" And after the present ending ("my city!") Whitman originally concluded with these two lines: "The city of such women, I am mad to be with them! I will return after death to be with them! / The city of such young men, I swear I cannot live happy, without I often go talk, walk, eat, drink, sleep, with them!" The first excision is likely due to a more sober appraisal of New York's response to the Civil War; and the second due to the poet's recognition that the lines are overly, even desperately enthusiastic. For the complete 1860 text, see Pearce, 404–5.

30. See Clifton J. Furness, ed., *Walt Whitman's Workshop: A Collection of Unpublished Manuscripts* (Cambridge: Harvard University Press, 1928), 61. See also Thomas, 375, and Versluys, 49.

31. In varying degrees, Thomas, Machor, and Versluys all find in Whitman's po-

etry evidence of doubts, expressed explicitly in his prose, about the values of commercial New York and its possible reform. To Thomas, Whitman fails to "knit the visions of poets to the actual growth of cities," and thus is eventually reduced to "blank assertion reinforced by blustering rhetoric" (370, 375). Machor denies that the "pastoral cities" of Whitman's poetry are mimetic, and argues that Whitman's skepticism about social reform made the primary aim of his city poetry the "creation of a separate, subjective, poetic world" (334–35). Taking a position closer to my own, Versluys feels that "Whitman bought his version of perfection at a price" (53), namely the recurrent fear that his unified city was in fact fragmented, a symbol of "universal chaos" (55).

32. According to Webster's Dictionary of 1841, calamus is not only "a sort of reed," a "knotty root, reddish without and white within," but also a "pipe or fistula," a reed, quill, or oaten flute of the type favored by classical pastoral poets (Murphy, 799). The word thus suggests not only a phallic drive for personal and poetic insemination, but the artistic means by which it may be achieved.

33. In 1860 the first two lines of the poem read, "Of the terrible question of appearances, / Of the doubts, the uncertainties after all" (Pearce, 352).

34. Whitman pondered the illusory quality of the material world throughout his career. Thus he assigned an important opening position in his final arrangement of Leaves of Grass to the late poem "Eidólons" (1876), which maintains that "all space, all time," and even the body, "the real I myself," are eidólons or shadows (LG, 7–8).

35. The debate continues in later editions of Leaves of Grass. "Pensive and Faltering" (1868) offers an honest statement of precisely where the problem lies for Whitman: "I the apparition, I the spectre" (LG, 455). But in "The Base of All Metaphysics" (1871), placed after "Of the Terrible Doubt of Appearances" as a response to it, the basis of all things is once more revealed to be the love of friends, "of city for city and land for land" (LG, 121).

36. In the 1855 text the words "and received with wonder or pity or love or dread" are inserted after "look'd upon" in line two (Cowley, 138).

37. "Experience," Essays, Second Series (Boston: Houghton, Mifflin, 1904), 45. Emerson's remarks on skepticism may underlie this whole issue for Whitman, and even suggest its urban context; see "Montaigne; or, the Skeptic," in Representative Men (1850; Boston: Houghton, Mifflin, 1904), 147–86. Speculating on the materiality of the world, Emerson notes that "You that will have all solid, and a world of pig-lead, deceive yourselves grossly. . . . if we uncover the last facts of our knowledge, you are spinning like bubbles in a river . . . and you are bottomed and capped and wrapped in delusions" (155). But he also expresses the Whitmanesque desire, "Let us have to do with real men and women, and not with skipping ghosts" (159). The fit skeptic, says Emerson, would be "a vigorous and original thinker, whom cities cannot overawe, but who uses them" (162); and in keeping with Whitman's peripatetic meditations, Emerson proposes that "the philosophy we want is one of fluxions and mobility" (160).

38. Prose Works 1892, ed. Floyd Stovall, 2 vols. (New York: New York University Press, 1964), II: 371–72.

39. Jonathan Raban, Soft City (Glasgow: Fontana/Collins, 1975), 10–11.

40. In 1860 the line continues with the phrase, "open and above board it goes" (Pearce, 327).

41. The 1860 version read "Mon enfant" for "Camerado" (Pearce, 328). Sometimes Whitman's internal struggle ends in a compromise, as in "Give Me the Splendid Silent Sun" (1865) where the poet attempts to overwhelm his doubts by including them in the catalogue of the joys he celebrates:

> Give me faces and streets—give me these phantoms incessant and endless along the trottoirs!
> Give me interminable eyes—give me women—give me comrades and lovers by the thousand!
>
> (LG, 313)

Here Whitman is true to his inclusive spirit, for the troubling phantoms are as much desired as the faces and eyes that provide his surest path to the essence of city experience. See Versluys, 61–65, for an excellent discussion of how this poem records Whitman's doubts, waverings, and recommitment to the city.

42. The body-text opposition fully reveals itself in "Now Precedent Songs, Farewell" (1888):

From fibre heart of mine—from throat and tongue— (My life's
  hot pulsing blood,
The personal urge and form for me—not merely paper, automatic type
  and ink.)

(*LG*, 534)

43. Emerson, *Representative Men*, 168.

44. See also the Preface to the 1876 edition: "Then, for the enclosing clue of all, it is imperatively and ever to be borne in mind that LEAVES OF GRASS entire is not to be construed as an intellectual or scholastic effort or Poem mainly, but more as a radical utterance out of the abysms of the Soul, the Emotions and the Physique" (*LG*, 753).

45. For "touch'd you" the 1860 version read "been near you," and after "the dead" inserted "I think" (Pearce, 317).

46. The text cited here, from the 1892 *Leaves of Grass*, differs only slightly in phrasing and punctuation from the text of the 1860 edition, with the exception that a few lines, which Whitman rightly saw as redundant, are dropped. For the full 1860 text, see Pearce, 379–88. A major difference from the original 1856 text, the changed ending, is noted below.

47. See I Corinthians 13:12 and Susan Strom, "'Face to Face': Whitman's Biblical Reference in 'Crossing Brooklyn Ferry,'" *Walt Whitman Review* 24 (1978): 7–16. In *The Prelude*, Wordsworth too speaks of "The comers and the goers face to face— / Face after face" (1805; VII, 172–73). This is not a moment of lasting insight for Wordsworth, but rather its fleeting, ironic opposite.

48. As Ziff notes, "Whitman translates himself into his audience, joining it finally to view the 'I' of the poem as apart. . . . The 'we' at the close of the poem is the poet among the readers, and the 'you' . . . becomes the objects of their shared world, among which the poem now takes its place" (587–88).

49. Of Whitman's refusal to distinguish between city and self, Quentin Anderson writes, "bodies and images are simply correlative with 'soul.' They exist only in that they are apprehended; we exist only in the measure that we apprehend them. . . . It is an assertion that what is seen is correlative with a seer or seers. . . . In sum, there is no evidence that in the Whitman of 1856 there is a separate realm in which 'soul' enjoys an existence independent of a presented scene" (*The Imperial Self* [New York: Vintage, 1971], 127). I am indebted to Professor Anderson's reading of Whitman (119–65) throughout this section.

50. Cf. "To You" (1856): "I paint myriads of heads, but paint no head without its nimbus of gold-color'd light" (*LG*, 234). Ziff's comment on the passage is applicable to the disintegrated yet inviolable identities of "Crossing Brooklyn Ferry" as well: "What we must gaze upon is the wonder of the similarity of the halos for all the difference in the faces beneath them, the wonder of the difference in the faces for all the sameness of the halos that crown them. The one is not the salvation of the many; the many is the salvation of the one" (590).

51. "Song of Myself" anticipates this moment, the poet appearing to be a pilgrim whose progress has been guaranteed, one who already possesses a key to the Celestial City: "Our rendezvous is fitly appointed....God will be there and wait till we come." Whitman even echoes St. John in Revelation as he beholds a city in the sky: "This day before dawn I ascended a hill and looked at the crowded heaven" (1855; Murphy, 731, 732).

52. See Machor, 339.

53. The original 1856 conclusion of the poem placed even more emphasis on the

substantiality of the scene, and the capacity of its objects to shape the poet's own body and soul:

> We descend upon you and all things, we arrest you all,
> We realize the soul only by you faithful solids and fluids
> Through you color, form, location, sublimity, ideality,
> Through you every proof, comparison, and all the suggestions
>   and determinations of ourselves.
>
>   (Murphy, 806)

"Creator and receiver both"—in Wordsworth's phrase—of the world the mind intuits, Whitman cannot imagine himself without the objects of nature that lend him being. Similarly, Wordsworth recalls that "I was often unable to think of external things as having external existence, and I communed with all that I saw as something not apart from, but inherent in, my own immaterial nature" (*The Poetical Works of William Wordsworth*, ed. E. de Selincourt and Helen Darbishire [Oxford: Clarendon Press, 1947], IV: 463). But whereas for Wordsworth soul seems to both underlie and undermine substance, for Whitman "solids and fluids" are what make the soul possible.

54. Edwin Haviland Miller, ed., *The Correspondence*, 5 vols. (New York: New York University Press, 1969), IV: 299 (5 March 1889).

Chapter Five. The Waste Land *and Urban Renewal*

The epigraph is from *The Waste Land: A Facsimile and Transcript of the Original Drafts Including the Annotations of Ezra Pound*, ed. Valerie Eliot (New York: Harcourt, Brace, Jovanovich, 1971), 31.

1. Hereafter, the above edition will be cited parenthetically as *WLFT*. Other references to Eliot's writing will be cited according to the following abbreviations:

ILP—"The Influence of Landscape upon the Poet," *Daedalus* 89 (1960): 420–22.

NWL—Notes to *The Waste Land*, cited by line numbers, from T. S. Eliot, *The Complete Poems and Plays* (New York: Harcourt, Brace, 1952), 50–55. All quotations of Eliot's poetry are cited by line number from this edition.

OPP—*On Poetry and Poets* (New York: Noonday, 1961).

SE—*Selected Essays* (New York: Harcourt, Brace, World, 1964).

SP—*Selected Prose of T. S. Eliot*, ed. Frank Kermode (New York: Harcourt, Brace, Jovanovich / Farrar, Straus & Giroux, 1965).

TCTC—*To Criticize the Critic* (New York: Farrar, Straus & Giroux, 1965).

UPUC—*The Use of Poetry and the Use of Criticism: Studies in the Relation of Criticism to Poetry in England*, 2nd ed. (London: Faber & Faber, 1964).

The standard bibliography of Eliot's works is Donald Gallup, *T. S. Eliot: A Bibliography*, rev. ed. (New York: Harcourt, Brace, Jovanovich, 1969).

2. "We lived on in a neighbourhood which had become shabby to a degree approaching slumminess. . . . So it was, that for nine months of the year my scenery was almost exclusively urban, and a good deal of it seedily, drably urban at that. My urban imagery was that of St. Louis, upon which that of Paris and London have been superimposed" (ILP, 422). Here Eliot omits mention of Boston, where his backstreet wanderings provided material for "Prufrock" and "Preludes"—the latter poem originally entitled "Preludes in Roxbury." According to Lyndall Gordon, "Prufrock" and sections I, II, and IV of "Preludes" were composed in Boston; section III of "Preludes" and "Rhapsody on a Windy Night" in Paris; and "Morning at the Window" and "A Cooking Egg" in London. See *Eliot's Early Years* (New York: Oxford University Press, 1977), 18–19, 40–45. Other commentary on the city in Eliot's early poetry can be found in John H. Johnston, *The Poet and the City* (Athens: University of Georgia Press, 1984), 164–68, and Kristiaan Versluys, *The Poet in the City* (Tübingen: Narr, 1987), 172–78.

3. "Not only the title, but the plan and a good deal of the incidental symbolism of

the poem were suggested by Miss Jessie L. Weston's book on the Grail legend. . . . Indeed so deeply am I indebted, Miss Weston's book will elucidate the difficulties of the poem much better than my notes can do" (NWL, introductory note).

4. *From Ritual to Romance* (1920; Garden City, N.Y.: Doubleday, 1957), 23.

5. See lines 139–67 and 279–89, respectively. The blight Eliot describes ranges comprehensively from townhouse to pub, riverbank to bedsitter, and ancient Thebes to modern London. Among the other examples of sexual dysfunction and misery in the poem are, in a modern urban context, the neurotic upper-class couple (111–38), the typist and clerk (215–56), and the three "Thames-daughters" (290–305); and in the past, Tristan and Isolde (31–42), Philomel and Tereus (98–103), and Hamlet and Ophelia (128, 172).

6. The breadth of Eliot's vision accords with his belief that the individual artist must concern himself with "the whole of the literature of Europe from Homer," which "has a simultaneous existence" for him (*SE*, 4). For explorations of the view that Virgilian Rome too ought to be considered one of the central cities whose meaning informs the poem, see Bernard F. Dick, "*The Waste Land* and the *Descensus ad Infernos*," and Eleanor Cook, "T. S. Eliot and the Carthaginian Peace," both in Harold Bloom, ed., *T. S. Eliot's "The Waste Land"* (New York: Chelsea House, 1986), 67–79 and 81–97, respectively. See also Hugh Kenner, "The Urban Apocalypse," *Eliot in His Time*, ed. A. Walton Litz (Princeton: Princeton University Press, 1973), 23–49; Kenner argues that the London of Dryden and the English Augustans played a vital role in the poem's genesis.

7. Eliot did not like Lawrence, and in his undergraduate lectures on "English Literature from 1890 to the Present Day" at Harvard in spring 1933, he criticized Lawrence for his individualism and lack of moral sense (Houghton Library MS, English 26; cited and discussed in Maud Ellmann, *The Poetics of Impersonality: T. S. Eliot and Ezra Pound* [Brighton: Harvester Press, 1987], 47–48).

8. See, for example, Versluys, 179, and Calvin Bedient's full-scale effort to see through the blind seer, *He Do the Police in Different Voices: "The Waste Land" and Its Protagonist* (Chicago: University of Chicago Press, 1986).

9. Sophocles' *Oedipus Rex*, ed. R. D. Dawe (Cambridge: Cambridge University Press, 1982), line 629. Like the Grail legend, the Oedipus story serves Eliot's purpose as a "mythical method" that can make the "futility and anarchy" of the modern world "possible for art" (*SP*, 177–78). J. G. Keogh analyzes the Eliot-Sophocles conjunction in "O City, City: Oedipus in *The Waste Land*," *Antigonish Review*, 69–70 (1987): 89–112.

10. *Metamorphoses* III, 322–40.

11. Weston, 63.

12. Tiresias is the chief but far from only "reader" in the poem. Before he announces himself in Section III, several others appear, led by the clairvoyante Madame Sosostris, whose Tarot reading is frustrated and incomplete. While her scrutiny does forecast the return of the Phoenician Sailor, the Merchant, and "crowds of people" (NWL, 46), she is still "forbidden to see" the merchant's goods, and she cannot locate the Hanged Man, the sign of fertility that would redeem the land. In Section II the tongueless Philomel weaves a tapestry to relate the past to her sister; Procne interprets the textile to discover how her husband Tereus has raped and mutilated Philomel, a reading of violence that prompts a violent revenge. Then in Section III Mr. Eugenides' propositions link the separate commercial and sexual aspects of Madame Sosostris's and Philomel's readings. Looking over the shoulder of all these readers, Tiresias enters in the very next lines.

13. Eliot describes similar self-protective combinations of foresight and personal detachment in other early poems of the city: amid his "visions and revisions" Prufrock prepares "a face to meet the faces that you meet," and the disillusioned personae of poems such as "Preludes" and "Morning at the Window" speak in a tone of Tiresian inevitability. As the narrator of "Portrait of a Lady" remarks, "I remain self-possessed."

14. But perhaps it could be prolonged into a homosexual weekend at Brighton's Metropole Hotel. Eliot claimed to be unaware that the proposal could be interpreted this way (see Robert A. Day, "The 'City Man' in *The Waste Land*: The Geography of Reminiscence," *PMLA* 80 [1965]: 288). But in his notes to the poem, Eliot links Mr. Eugenides to the one-eyed merchant of the Tarot deck, further suggesting both his phallic properties and his disturbing physical presence (NWL, 218).

15. J. Hillis Miller, *Poets of Reality* (Cambridge: Belknap Press of Harvard University Press, 1965), 178. Eliot's effort to define the poet's relation to his material as "impersonal" fails, then, to provide that "escape from personality" (*SE*, 10) he had envisioned. Eliot confessed as much when he later remarked that *The Waste Land* was not "social criticism" but rather "a personal . . . grouse against life" (*WLFT*, 1).

16. We search in vain for the "organic whole" of literature that Eliot himself proposes (*SE*, 12). As Roy Harvey Pearce remarks, since the unity of the poem depends on the informing strength of Tiresias's vision, it "cannot be self-contained. . . . That enormous range of allusiveness which has set so many exegetes to work is accordingly the central technique of the poem, as it is the means of preventing [its] self-containment" (*The Continuity of American Poetry* [Princeton: Princeton University Press, 1961; new format, 1977], 307).

17. "Decentering the Image," *Textual Strategies*, ed. Josué V. Harari (Ithaca: Cornell University Press, 1979), 345–46. If, as Riddel argues, the institutional effort to make *The Waste Land* "readable" results from New Critical formalism and from Eliot's own advocacy of a "mythical method" to order the chaos of the modern world, then perhaps Eliot's claim for the centrality of Tiresias confirms the poet's status as an *hypocrite lecteur*, a would-be "closer" of his own ever-opening poem.

18. Nonetheless, Marjorie Perloff has forcefully argued, the poem possesses "a perfectly coherent symbolic structure" in comparison to the "indeterminacy" of non-symbolists texts by Rimbaud, Williams, and others (*The Poetics of Indeterminacy* [Princeton: Princeton University Press, 1981], 13).

19. See "Of the Gaze as *Objet Petit a*," *The Four Fundamental Concepts of Psycho-Analysis*, trans. Alan Sheridan (New York: Norton, 1979), 65–119.

20. See Daniel O'Hara, "'The Unsummoned Image': T. S. Eliot's Unclassic Criticism," *Boundary* 2 9.1 (1980): 104: "A poem is thus not only about itself alone in the narrow sense of the phrase, but it is also about itself amidst the various weaves of tradition . . . [providing] its self-conscious commentary on its own belated and desperate generation as a text."

21. *Golden Codgers: Biographical Speculations* (New York: Oxford University Press, 1973), 155.

22. With his commitment to shock and surrender, Eliot thus applies to himself the same criteria for fruitful poetic experience as Walter Benjamin applies to Baudelaire. The value of both encounters, with the *passante* or literary text, depends upon one's openness to experience, what Benjamin calls *Erfahrung*, which the poet must allow to "survive," unmastered, as part of the continuity of mental and emotional life, if he is to represent his urban experience successfully. Benjamin's description of the urban defense mechanism, or *Erlebnis*, that turns disturbing experiences into "a moment that has been lived," also finds its parallels in Eliot's work, in the emotional numbness of the Wastelanders whose self-containment keeps them from the "intenser experience" of reading both themselves and their city. See "On Some Motifs in Baudelaire," *Illuminations*, trans. Harry Zohn (New York: Schocken, 1969), 163, 193. As I indicate in chapter three, for Benjamin the "flash" of comprehension in the act of reading is also imaged by the force and brevity of urban encounters.

23. Trans. Mark Musa (Bloomington: Indiana University Press, 1973), 5. As in "A une passante," where the poet is "crispé comme un extravagant" by the lady's look, the words of Beatrice make Dante "ecstatic . . . like a drunken man" (5).

24. Stephen Spender, "Remembering Eliot," *T. S. Eliot: The Man and His Work*, ed. Allen Tate (New York: Dell, 1966), 55–56. Frank Kermode points out that the phrase "bewildering minute" is from *The Revenger's Tragedy*, and that Eliot had quoted it

earlier in "Tradition and the Individual Talent" (1919), another essay concerned with "surrender." The letter to Spender reveals, Kermode comments, "an aspect not only of Eliot's critical, but of his poetic genius" (Introduction to *Selected Prose of T. S. Eliot*, 13). In part, the present chapter seeks to expand this insight, and apply it to *The Waste Land*, which Kermode does not explore in detail.

25. "The existing monuments form an ideal order among themselves, which is modified by the introduction of the new (the really new) work of art among them" (*SE*, 5).

26. As Eliot argued in "Tradition and the Individual Talent," the poet can make use of his literary tradition only by "a continual surrender of himself as he is at the moment to something which is more valuable" (*SE*, 6–7). The surrender of the reader to the text that Eliot later described to Spender closely parallels this process of poetic composition. Thus Eliot was beginning to elaborate in the 1919 essay a means whereby future readers of *The Waste Land* might approach it, and at a time when the poem was already in progress. See Richard Ellmann, 165.

27. The tripartite structure of the experience of reading a single text is also analogous to the three stages that, in *The Use of Poetry and the Use of Criticism*, Eliot suggests are undergone by the young poet or critic in developing a taste for poetry. First there is the moment of discovery, "at puberty," figured in sexual and religious terms—"possessed," "craving," "conversion" (32–33). The second stage, only slightly less intense, awakens in the reader the desire to respond in kind, by writing: "much as in our youthful experiences of love" this new interest results in "an outburst of scribbling which we may call imitation" (34). The last stage implies authentic creation, "having something to say," although Eliot prefers to stress the poet-reader's recovery of critical self-possession as he accepts the independence of the tradition from him. The mature self, much changed by its intense, evolving relationship to texts, is now ready to respond to them intelligently, but always personally, for taste in poetry "cannot be isolated from one's other interests and passions" (36).

28. While Eliot acknowledges "the capital importance of criticism in the work of creation itself" as the poet composes and edits his own work, he hesitates to say that critical reading can be creative: "You cannot fuse creation with criticism as you can fuse criticism with creation. The critical activity finds its highest, its true fulfillment in a kind of union with creation in the labour of the artist" (*SE*, 18–19). Yet as this remark seems directed at those, like Arnold or Wilde, who suggest the creativity of the critic, it leaves open the question of what happens creatively when the poet reads his fellow poets critically. I am maintaining that criticism's "true fulfillment" covers the poet's reading activity as well as his compositional one.

29. Eliot thus seeks to establish his own originality, the ability to deal in English with the "intractably unpoetic," by claiming that his largest debt was to a foreign poet. He later admitted that the late Victorian poets of London's darker side, such as John Davidson, Arthur Symons, and James Thomson, had also influenced his writing. See Eliot's Preface to *John Davidson, A Selection of His Poems*, ed. Maurice Lindsay (London: Hutchinson, 1961), n.p., and Lindsay's introduction to the same book (8). In *The Savage and the City in the Work of T. S. Eliot* (Oxford: Clarendon Press, 1987), Robert Crawford explores Eliot's debt to Thomson's *The City of Dreadful Night* (36–53) as well as the influence of Davidson (54–60) and Baudelaire (44 ff.). On Thomson's relation to the city and Eliot, see also my essay, "Learning to Read *The City*," *Victorian Poetry* 22.1 (1984): 65–84. G. Robert Stange traces the tradition of Victorian city poetry behind Eliot in "The Frightened Poets," *The Victorian City: Images and Realities*, ed. H. J. Dyos and Michael Wolff (London: Routledge & Kegan Paul, 1973), II: 475–94. On Eliot's larger debt to the Victorians, see David Ned Tobin, *The Presence of the Past: T. S. Eliot's Victorian Inheritance* (Ann Arbor: UMI Research Press, 1983).

30. On Eliot's debt to Baudelaire, see Nicole Ward, " 'Fourmillante Cité': Baudelaire and *The Waste Land*," in *"The Waste Land" in Different Voices*, ed. A. D. Moody

(London: Edward Arnold, 1974), 87–104; Nancy D. Hargrove, *Landscape as Symbol in the Poetry of T. S. Eliot* (Jackson: University of Mississippi Press, 1978), 27–35; and K. Weinberg, *T. S. Eliot and Charles Baudelaire*, Studies in General and Comparative Literature 5 (The Hague: Mouton, 1969).

31. As Crawford notes, Eliot mistakenly capitalizes "cité" in quoting Baudelaire's lines (82). Reading himself back into his master, Eliot seems to wish to make Baudelaire the source for his London reference in the line "O City city."

32. See Ross Chambers, "Are Baudelaire's 'Tableaux Parisiens' About Paris?" *On Referring in Literature*, ed. Anna Whiteside and Michael Issacharoff (Bloomington: Indiana University Press, 1987), 95–110. As Chambers says, "Paris is less the place he writes about than *the place out of which he speaks*"; it is "an imaginary Paris which figures as a cultural item in the encyclopedia of speakers of French, the 'Paris' invented by Baudelaire and his contemporaries as a symbol of modern life" (99–100).

33. Here Eliot seems to be fashioning his own version of Baudelaire's twofold definition of art as being composed of both contingent and eternal elements. For Eliot, Baudelaire captures something that is "new" or specific to his time and place, but it will become "universal" to life in the modern world.

34. The poem's original title, "He Do the Police in Different Voices," further emphasizes the literariness of Eliot's London. The quotation from *Our Mutual Friend* not only implies that *The Waste Land* is in some sense an extension of the Dickensian metropolis of dirty rivers and rubbish heaps central to the novel, but it also suggests that Eliot's representation of the city will be filtered through the additional textual layers of Sloppy's ventriloquistic readings from the *Police Gazette*.

35. "True civilization," Baudelaire wrote, resides "not in gas or steam or Ouija boards," but "in the diminution of traces of original sin." See Ward, 104, and Claude Pichois, ed. *Baudelaire: Oeuvres complètes*, 2 vols. (Paris: Gallimard, 1975–76), I: 697, my translation.

36. A dictatorial commercial clock makes even church bells greedy ("kept the hours"), and the "dead sound on the final stroke of nine" represents the halt of the regenerative cycle of the seasons, just at the moment when office workers are due at their desks. For further analysis of how Eliot makes his city unreal, see Johnston, 170–72, and Versluys, 180–88.

37. Plato, *The Republic*, trans. Desmond Lee (Harmondsworth: Penguin, 1955), 420.

38. As Eliot wrote in his dissertation, the concept of unreality depends upon a notion of reality maintained in opposition to it: "We only say that an object is unreal with respect to something else which we declare to have been affirmed at the same time and which continues to be real, while the other does not" (*Knowledge and Experience in the Philosophy of F. H. Bradley* [New York: Farrar, Straus, 1964], 117). In the final draft of *The Waste Land*, the "real" heavenly city of Plato and St. John tacitly continues to ground the notion that the earthly city of London-Babylon is "unreal." For more on Eliot's city as an unreal Babylon set against "the timeless pattern of the eternal city," see Frank Kermode, "A Babylonish Dialect," in C. B. Cox and Arnold Hinchliffe, eds., *T. S. Eliot: "The Waste Land": A Casebook* (London: Macmillan, 1968), 229–31.

39. The decision to excise such urban visionaries as St. John and Plato while retaining their jaundiced counterparts, Madame Sosostris and Tiresias, indicates Eliot's desire to stress the burden of the earthly city rather than the existence of a heavenly alternative. He and Pound may also have considered that the irony produced by allusions to an ideal city would be too heavy-handed.

40. Eliot himself is something of a Tiresias ("I had lived it before") in regard to Baudelaire, his urban "foresuffering" not only opening his eyes to the methods of his precursor, but compelling him to repeat them. Influenced by the phrase "fourmillante cité," Eliot included a long passage on "swarming" London in the original typescript of *The Waste Land*. It begins:

> London, the swarming life you kill and breed
> Huddled between the concrete and the sky;
> Responsive to the momentary need,
> Vibrates unconscious to its formal destiny.

Unimpressed by this translation of Baudelaire's idiom, Pound wrote "B-ll-S" in the margin next to the passage (*WLFT*, 31).

41. Kenner offers an intriguing guess as to what the initial formal intention was (23–40). For an attempt to recover the social and political context of the poem, see John Xiros Cooper, *T. S. Eliot and the Politics of Voice: The Argument of "The Waste Land"* (Ann Arbor: UMI Research Press, 1987); for a highly speculative psychosexual account of the poem's origins, see James E. Miller, Jr., *T. S. Eliot's Personal Waste Land* (London: Pennsylvania State University Press, 1977).

42. Ward contends that in comparison to Baudelaire, Eliot's "distinctly 'poetic' voice" cannot "maintain its pitch in its encounter with the actual" (92–93); "the cultural reminiscences, instead of magnifying the contemporary they are brought into touch with, reductively contrast with it or are sucked into its quicksands" (96).

43. Miller, 77.

44. *Axel's Castle* (New York: Scribner's, 1931), 110.

45. "Gareth and Lynette," in *Idylls of the King* (1859–1885; New York: New American Library, 1961), 33.

46. In Eliot's own terms, the present text needs those past to "complete" it, but in fact the present work supplements or "completes" that "whole" tradition which was supposed to complete it (*SE*, 5). The new poem thus rewrites that whole, pointing to an ever-incomplete state that no number of footnotes can heal: "The past text is never the present text. And the present text, insofar as it alludes to a past text, is never fully present" (Riddel, 347).

47. Through surrender to the moment, the "presence" of what is read or experienced can become possible for Eliot. But as a poem, *The Waste Land* does not become fully "present" to itself, and thus readable in an original, creative way, until the Thunder speaks. As Eliot himself says, "When you have the words for it, the 'thing' for which the words had to be found has disappeared, replaced by a poem," a new, admittedly further displaced "presence," the expression of a "demon" that has haunted the poet (*OPP*, 106–07).

48. I am indebted to Harold Bloom's theories of poetic creation throughout this chapter, particularly *The Anxiety of Influence* (New York: Oxford University Press, 1973). For a powerful Bloomian reading of *The Waste Land* that shows how Eliot himself anticipates Bloom's theory, see Gregory S. Jay, *T. S. Eliot and the Poetics of Literary History* (Baton Rouge: Lousiana State University Press, 1983), 67–198.

49. Pearce, 308.

50. In a provocative reading that stresses this aspect of the poem, Maud Ellmann views it as "a sphinx without a secret" (91–113).

51. Eliot himself draws attention to the links between these passages, and the role that Dante plays in them. Of "Little Gidding" he writes: "The intention, of course, was the same as with my allusions to Dante in *The Waste Land*: to present to the mind of the reader a parallel, by means of contrast, between the Inferno and the Purgatorio, which Dante visited and a hallucinated scene after an air-raid" (*TCTC*, 128).

52. See Helen Gardner, *The Composition of Four Quartets* (London: Faber, 1978), 195. For Maud Ellmann, the passage exemplifies how "the *Quartets* picture figuration in the form of phantoms" (126), and she notes that in the manuscripts "Eliot systematically defaced the ghost to render him 'Both intimate and unidentifiable'" (125).

53. On Eliot's debts to Whitman, see Sydney Musgrove, *T. S. Eliot and Walt Whitman* (Wellington: New Zealand University Press, 1952); Jay, 168–71 and 180–86; and Cleo McNelley Kearns, "Eliot, Russell, and Whitman: Realism, Politics, and Liter-

ary Persona in *The Waste Land*" in Harold Bloom, ed., *T. S. Eliot's "The Waste Land*," 137–52. Both Jay and Kearns demonstrate the extent to which elements of Whitman's "When Lilacs Last in the Dooryard Bloom'd" underlie Eliot's poem, in particular Section v, where verbal echoes are especially strong. See also Philip Hobsbaum, "Eliot, Whitman, and the American Tradition," *Journal of American Studies* 3 (1969): 239–64.

54. Eliot's struggle with his greatest American predecessor is hinted at in a late essay: "The writers of the past, especially of the immediate past, in one's own place and language may be valuable to the young [American] writer simply as something definite to rebel against. He will recognize the common ancestry: but he needn't necessarily *like* his relatives" (*TCTC*, 56). The poor quality of American city poetry between Whitman and Eliot may also have encouraged Eliot to distance himself from his countrymen. See Robert H. Walker, "The Poet and the Rise of the City," *Mississippi Valley Historical Review* 49 (June 1962–March 1963): 85–99, and Johnston, 155–64.

55. See Day, 285–91.

56. The continuation of the passage ("where the walls / Of Magnus Martyr hold / Inexplicable splendour of Ionian white and gold") also supports the contention of many commentators that Eliot's "fishmen" are apostolic, and intimate the true rewards of Christian fellowship, a radiantly "inexplicable" gift amid the gloom of commercial London. And like pubs, the churches, especially those as beautiful as Magnus Martyr, are a lunchtime haven for City office workers. Here the poet finds human and worldly, as well as spiritual, refreshment.

57. "Whitman and Tennyson," *The Nation and Athenaeum* 40 (December 18, 1926), 426.

58. *The Mysteries of Identity* (New York: Oxford University Press, 1977), 113.

59. *Leaves of Grass*, ed. Sculley Bradley and Harold W. Blodgett (1965; New York: Norton, 1973), 334. See Jay, 184–85, and Kearns, 149–50. Jay offers a rich and detailed reading of Whitman's presence in "What the Thunder Said" (180–88).

60. See Jay, 182–85.

61. Matthew Little suggests that this passage may be read as a mirage; see "A Source for 'The City Over the Mountains' in *The Waste Land*," *ELN* 17.4 (1980): 279–81.

62. Eliot refers the reader to "the fable of the meaning of the Thunder" (NWL, 401) in the *Upanishads*: when the gods, men, and demons ask their one father Prajapati to tell them their duty, he responds with the single syllable "DA," to which each group gives a different interpretation, the men taking it as *da*tta, give alms; the demons as *da*yadhvam, have compassion; and the gods as *da*myata, practice self-control. The demons of Eliot's *dayadhvam* passage, "each in his prison," suggest the "demon" or impulse behind a poem that struggles for liberation by being finally put into words (*OPP*, 107). Men must give or surrender, as the entire poem has been trying to show, and the gods, by their control, act almost as muses in shaping the resultant emotion into art.

63. "The Waste Land" in *T. S. Eliot: A Collection of Critical Essays*, ed. Hugh Kenner (Englewood Cliffs, N.J.: Prentice-Hall, 1962), 103.

Chapter Six. One Woman Like a City

The epigraph is from *The Selected Letters of William Carlos Williams* (1957; New York: New Directions, 1984), 236–37.

1. Hereafter, the above edition will be cited as *SL*. References for subsequent quotations from Williams will be cited in the text as follows:

A—*The Autobiography of William Carlos Williams* (New York: New Directions, 1967).

CP,1—*The Collected Poems of William Carlos Williams*, vol. 1, 1909–1939, ed. A. Walton Litz and Christopher MacGowan (New York: New Directions, 1986).

CP,II—*The Collected Poems of William Carlos Williams*, vol. 2, 1939–1962, ed. Christopher MacGowan (New York: New Directions, 1988).

IAG—*In the American Grain* (New York: New Directions, 1956).

Imag.—*Imaginations* (New York: New Directions, 1970).

P—*Paterson* (New York: New Directions, 1963).

SE—*The Selected Essays of William Carlos Williams* (New York: Random House, 1954).

IWWP—*I Wanted to Write a Poem* (New York: New Directions, 1977).

2. "Author's Note" to *Paterson*, n.p.

3. Williams, quoted. in John C. Thirwall, "William Carlos Williams' *Paterson*," *New Directions in Prose and Poetry 17* (Norfolk, Conn.: New Directions, 1961), 254.

4. A number of critics have treated the man/city identification as one of the major themes in the poem. See Joel Conarroe, *William Carlos Williams' Paterson: Language and Landscape* (Philadelphia: University of Pennsylvania Press, 1970), 63–80; Sister M. Bernetta Quinn, *The Metamorphic Tradition in Modern Poetry* (New Brunswick, N.J.: Rutgers University Press, 1966), 89–129; and Margaret Glynne Lloyd, *William Carlos Williams' Paterson: A Critical Reappraisal* (Cranbury, N.J.: Associated University Presses, 1980), 18, 52–109. Lloyd provides a fairly comprehensive review of criticism on the city in *Paterson* (38–54), but does not mention Joseph Riddel's *The Inverted Bell* (Baton Rouge: Louisiana State University Press, 1974), which contains a stimulating chapter on the relation of the city metaphor to *Paterson*'s structure (155–204). See also John H. Johnston's *The Poet and the City* (Athens: University of Georgia Press, 1984), 212–25; and William Sharpe, "'That Complex Atom': The City and Form in William Carlos Williams's *Paterson*," *Poesis* 6.2 (1985): 65–93.

5. See Stephen J. Tapscott, *American Beauty: William Carlos Williams and the Modernist Whitman* (New York: Columbia University Press, 1984), 166–67. In the best short survey of the poem I have read, Tapscott also mentions other unifying themes: the motion of the river toward the sea; the progress of the poem through the seasons—"spring, summer, fall and the sea"; and the four elements (167–69).

6. See Tapscott, 178–191.

7. On Whitman's importance for Williams, see James Breslin, *William Carlos Williams: An American Artist* (New York: Oxford University Press, 1970), 4, 19–20, 26–30; and Tapscott, especially his chapter "Whitman in *Paterson*," 178–91. See also Benjamin Sankey, *A Companion to William Carlos Williams' "Paterson"* (Berkeley: University of California Press, 1971), 201, 210–11.

8. Quoted in Thirwall, 263. For local sources of the poem's structure and major motifs, see Mike Weaver, *William Carlos Williams: The American Background* (Cambridge: Cambridge University Press, 1971), 7–16, 116–64.

9. For further discussion of Williams' poetic relationship to Eliot and Pound, and his responses to them in *Paterson*, see Lloyd, 23–51.

10. William Carlos Williams, "The Fatal Blunder," *Quarterly Review of Literature* 2.2 (1944): 126.

11. *Finnegans Wake* also played an important part in Williams' plans for *Paterson*: Lloyd compares the man/city metaphor and the sleeping giants to Joyce's Finnegan and HCE (96–101).

12. Quoted in Thirwall, 282.

13. The tension between the small city and the larger world, and the need to believe that travel is not betrayal, comes through in Allen Ginsberg's letter in Book v. Claiming that "I have NOT absconded from Paterson," Ginsberg implies that nothing can escape Paterson's grasp, as either poem or place: "When I've seen enough I'll be back to splash in the Passaic again" (*P*, 212–13).

14. Quoted in Thirwall, 308. On the relation of Williams' earlier poetry to the city and New York, see Jacqueline Saunier-Ollier, *William Carlos Williams: L'Homme et L'Oeuvre Poétique* (Nice: Faculté des lettres et sciences humaines, 1979), 405–15.

15. See Thirwall, 263, 308; *A*, 391.

16. In the climate of tradition-minded intellectualism and technical rigor that

Eliot fostered through *The Waste Land* and *The Criterion*, the poet who espoused the open, spontaneous expression of present-day New Jersey was indeed "most defeated." As Williams was well aware, he would be the last of the major modernist poets to receive critical recognition. On the New York-centered revolution in the arts that inspired Williams and rivaled Pound's "second Renaissance" in London, see Bram Dijkstra, *Cubism, Steiglitz, and the Early Poetry of William Carlos Williams: The Hieroglyphics of a New Speech* (Princeton: Princeton University Press, 1969); Hugh Kenner, *A Homemade World* (New York: Morrow, 1975); and Dickran Tashjian, *William Carlos Williams and the American Scene, 1920–1940* (Berkeley: University of California Press, 1979).

17. "Eliot had turned his back on the possibility of reviving my world. . . . I needed him: he might have become our adviser, even our hero. By his walking out on us we were stopped, for the moment, cold" (*A*, 174).

18. "An Essay on *Leaves of Grass*," in *"Leaves of Grass" One Hundred Years After*, ed. Milton Hindus (Stanford: Stanford University Press, 1955; reprinted in *Leaves of Grass*, ed. Sculley Bradley and Harold W. Blodgett (New York: Norton, 1973), 905; 907–8. In the same essay Williams noted that Whitman was an unwanted ghost not just for Eliot, but for Eliot's audience, and he scathingly recalled this fear: "The dreams of right-thinking students of English verse had long been disturbed by the appearance among them of the horrid specter of Whitman's free verse. Now it was as if a liberator, a Saint George, had come just in the nick of time to save them. The instructors in all the secondary schools were grateful" (905).

19. "An Essay on *Leaves of Grass*," 905.

20. The intensity of Williams' attack on Eliot, and its sexually charged rhetoric ("In a discussion of local and general culture Eliot is a maimed man" [*SL*, 224]) prompts complex Oedipal speculations: as son of his many fathers (Dr. Pater-son), Williams must avenge the apparent silencing of Whitman, his favored poetic father, on Eliot, a paternal literary disciplinarian—who, as a royalist expatriate, also stands in for Williams' actual father, an Englishman. Williams said as much in an interview with Walter Sutton in 1960, bringing Pound into the picture as a fourth father-figure, whom he wanted to please: "I went along with Pound. Later on he switched to Eliot and his *Waste Land*, which I admired too, but I was intensely jealous of this man, who was much more cultured than I was. . . . But when I recognized what he was doing I didn't like it at all. He was giving up America. And maybe my attachment to my father, who was English and who had never become an American citizen influenced me because I was—You know, the Oedipus complex between father and son—I resented him being English and not being American. And that was when Eliot was living in England and had given up America" ("A Visit with William Carlos Williams," *Speaking Straight Ahead: Interviews with William Carlos Williams*, ed. Linda W. Wagner [New York: New Directions, 1976], 47). See also Kerry Driscoll, *William Carlos Williams and the Maternal Muse* (Ann Arbor: UMI Research Press, 1987), a book which deftly explores Williams' intricate poetic genealogy, examining the contest with fathers in the context of the perhaps even more abiding influence of his mother.

21. The geological table detailing the composition of Paterson's rock and soil that Williams uses in Book III to mock modernist literary archeology while valorizing his native ground can be read in two ways: while it serves to establish the "depth" of American culture, it also suggests its permeation by foreign substances: "The fact that the rock salt of England, and of some of the other salt mines of Europe, is found in rocks of the same age as this, raises the question whether it may not also be found here" (*P*, 139).

22. For a discussion of Williams and newspaper techniques, see Lloyd, 196–207. As Williams himself wrote, "The epic poem would be our 'newspaper'" (University of Buffalo MS., cited in Weaver, 120).

23. In *The Visual Text of William Carlos Williams* (Urbana: University of Illinois

Press, 1983), Henry Sayre offers valuable insights into the nature of "*Paterson* as Collage" (93–117).

24. See Ralph Nash, "The Use of Prose in *Paterson*," *Perspective* 6 (Autumn 1953): 191–99; Sankey, 16–18; Lloyd, 177–228; and Brian A. Bremen, "'The Radiant Gist': 'The Poetry Hidden in the Prose' of Williams' *Paterson*," *Twentieth-Century Literature* 32.2 (1986): 221–41.

25. For contemporary reviews of the sections of *Paterson* as they appeared, see Charles Doyle, ed., *William Carlos Williams: The Critical Heritage* (Boston: Routledge & Kegan Paul, 1980), 173–98, 210–21, 232–45, 316–22.

26. Charles Olson, *Mayan Letters*, ed. Robert Creeley (London: Cape Editions, 1968), 30. Similarly, finding a "political, historical, and economic" gap in the presentation of Paterson, Michael André Bernstein argues that the city is "curiously missing, a virtual blank at the poem's core" (*The Tale of the Tribe: Ezra Pound and the Modern Verse Epic* [Princeton: Princeton University Press, 1980], 209).

27. Raymond Williams, *The Country and the City* (New York: Oxford University Press, 1973), 243. Roland Barthes' definition of the city might equally be applied to *Paterson*: "The city is a discourse and this discourse is truly a language: the city speaks to its inhabitants, we speak our city, the city where we are, simply by living in it, by wandering through it, by looking at it" ("Semiology and the Urban," trans. Karin Boklund-Lagopoulou et al., in M. Gottdiener and Alexandros Ph. Lagopoulos, eds., *The City and the Sign: An Introduction to Urban Semiotics* [New York: Columbia University Press, 1986], 92).

28. Quoted in Thirwall, 263.

29. Dr. Paterson himself is a multiplex figure, incorporating in his oneness aspects and actions of the mythic giant, the composite figure of Dr. Noah Faitoute Paterson, the leaper of the Falls Sam Patch, and, of course, Williams himself.

30. In one way or another, most accounts of the city's birth describe it as a mode of compensation, an attempted recovery from what Georg Lukács calls a "transcendental homelessness" (*The Theory of the Novel*, trans. Anna Bostock [Cambridge, Mass.: MIT Press, 1971], 61). Williams' contribution to the subject is his notion of "ground," that which anchors a city or man, giving him value and substance: "Unless everything that is, proclaim a ground on which it stand, it has no worth" (*IAG*, 109).

31. For Williams, all value in American art and life depends on deep native roots: "There is a source in AMERICA for everything we think or do . . . what has been morally, aesthetically worth while in America has rested upon our own peculiar and discoverable ground" (*IAG*, 109). Or as he says in *Paterson*: "Roots? // Everybody has roots" (*P*, 32).

32. See *P*, 74, and Weaver, 84.

33. Quoted in Thirwall, 277.

34. In addition to topical references ("You also, I am sure, have read / Frazer's Golden Bough" [*P*, 74]) and the central idea of sexual estrangement, *Paterson* parallels *The Waste Land* in other important ways: in Book I the giants suggest that Williams too has a "mythical method" to deal with his alienated city and its filthy river; a Tiresias-like Dr. Paterson passes through the city observing, particularly in Book II, the sordid world of working-class leisure; in Book III raging fires in the library purge an atmosphere stale with deathly texts; and in Book IV Dr. Paterson enters a "female phase" in the person of Corydon, whose thoughts dwell on floating corpses and pastoral fishing expeditions. Like *The Waste Land*, *Paterson* is a babelish collage-text, but it speaks out of local sources from the Paterson library rather than the larger Western tradition. In comparison to Eliot's benumbed city Paterson may be already (partly) redeemed as a result of the energies he continually finds in the Falls, fire, and even the vulgar poor people in the poem.

35. Some critics have felt that the poetry-prose format of *Paterson* successfully simulates "blockage" to the detriment of its overall design; see Jerome Mazzaro,

William.Carlos Williams: The Later Poems [Ithaca: Cornell University Press, 1973], 72).

36. "Essay on *Leaves of Grass*," 904. Paul Valéry also links poetry to the dance and prose to walking, in "Poetry and Abstract Thought" (1938), *The Art of Poetry*, trans. Denise Folliot (Princeton: Princeton University Press, 1958), 70. In "Valéry and the Poetics of Language" (in *Textual Strategies*, ed. Josué V. Harari [Ithaca: Cornell University Press, 1979], 359–73, Gérard Genette points out how, for Valéry, the "dance" of poetry can overcome the arbitrariness of linguistic signs by creating at least the illusion of a harmony between word and thing, signifier and signified. In *Paterson*, Williams utilizes the romantic, nostalgic power of this vision of harmony, but he also does not hesitate to show that the relation between the object and the sign is itself a dance, an arbitrary relation or "measure" (*P,* 239).

37. According to Williams, Corydon, "the charming old Lesbian," is "an image to typefy the impact of 'Paterson' in his young female phase with a world beyond his own, limited in the primitive, provincial, environment. . . . I didn't want him to 'disappear' before this fulfillment" (*SL,* 301, 305).

38. Barthes, 92.

39. Ibid. For a consideration of how metaphor conditions urban perception, see William Sharpe and Leonard Wallock, "From 'Great Town' to 'Nonplace Urban Realm': Reading the Modern City," *Visions of the Modern City*, ed. Sharpe and Wallock (Baltimore: Johns Hopkins University Press, 1987), 1–50.

40. On the larger anthropological issue of the perception of gender and nature, see Sherry B. Ortner, "Is Female to Male as Nature Is to Culture?" in *Woman, Culture, and Society*, ed. Michelle Zimbalist Rosaldo and Louise Lamphere (Stanford: Stanford University Press, 1974), 67–87. Here I wish to thank Kimball Fenn for her insights into Williams' use of feminine symbolism.

41. See, for example, "The Flower" (*CP,*I: 322). Sayre notes that the flower-city in Williams' early work is part of his organic theory of poetic form, and that later, as he rejects that organic ideal, the city becomes a more "artificial" part of nature, a man—even as women are turned into flowers (60 ff.).

42. Weaver, 153.

43. See Tapscott, 172.

44. Williams apparently took the words of Cress to heart late in life. In "Asphodel, That Greeny Flower" (1955), presented to his wife in commemoration of their marriage, he says, "You were like those [violets] / though I quickly / correct myself / for you were a woman / and no flower / and had to face / the problems which confront a woman" (*CP,*II: 332).

45. For a detailed account of the circumstances surrounding Marcia Nardi's composition of the letters and Williams' response to them, see Theodora R. Graham, "'Her Heigh Compleynte': The Cress Letters of William Carlos Williams' *Paterson*," in Daniel Hoffman, ed., *Ezra Pound and William Carlos Williams: The University of Pennsylvania Conference Papers* (Philadelphia: University of Pennsylvania Press, 1983), 164–93. Graham also reviews important positions in the criticism on "Cress." Other studies include Sandra Gilbert, "Purloined Letters: William Carlos Williams and 'Cress,'" *William Carlos Williams Review* 11.2 (1985): 5–10; and Cale C. Schricker, "The Case of Cress: Implications of Allusion in *Paterson*," *William Carlos Williams Review* 11.2 (1985): 10–20.

46. Graham, 188.

47. Randall Jarrell raised the issue that nothing has been done to Cress's letters "to make it possible for us to respond to them as art and not as raw reality. . . . *It takes a lot of context to make somebody else's eight-page letter the conclusion to a book of a poem* ("A View of Three Poets," *Partisan Review* 18 [November-December 1951]: 699). Williams actually altered the letters slightly but significantly: Graham argues that "these changes weaken Cress's character, making her vacillation between protest and lament, independence and dependency, more marked" (181).

48. Of course in the poem Williams has stacked the deck against her—the Chau-

cerian and vegetative resonances of the name "Cress," like her residence on Pine St. (changed from Grove St.), consign her to a languishing, plaintive fate.

49. Letter to Robert D. Pepper, 21 August 1951, quoted in Weaver, 208–09.

50. The passage continues: "It does not belong in the poem any more than a note on—Dante would" (SL, 265). Just as Dante was indeed crucial for Eliot's formation as a "shocked" reader and productive writer, so Williams' long prose "notes" act in the same way, not only calling attention to the poem's dependence on other texts, but also using such texts boldly in order to generate new life.

51. "I rather like my old gal who appears in the first pages of Paterson iv. . . . She has a hard part to play, and to my mind plays it rather well.

"As far as the story goes, she represents the 'great world' against the more or less primitive world of the provincial city. She is informed, no sluggard, uses her talents as she can. There has to be that world against which the other tests itself" (SL, 304).

52. Buffalo MS, quoted in Sankey, 75.

53. Graham, 188.

54. A concerted androgyny becomes part of the poem's method, in order to cover the limitations of the poet's own masculinity. As Williams says in his note to Book iii: "Paterson is a man (since I am a man) who dives from cliffs and the edges of waterfalls to his death—finally. But for all that he is a woman (since I am not a woman) who is the cliff and the waterfall" (quoted in Thirwall, 254).

55. Tapscott puts this complex matter clearly: Williams "writes a magnificent poem about the thwarted modern possibilities for poetry. The thematic hope for marriage or androgyny within the poem is an ambition to realize the poem: it is the poem Paterson. And Paterson works in structure as in theme; Williams tries to make his structures in the poem both 'male' (patterned and ordered) and 'female' (improvisational and diverse)" (161–62).

56. Her treatment thus contrasts with another poet whom Williams aided, Allen Ginsberg. Like Cress a product of Paterson, he too has had his traumas, but he has nonetheless managed to transmute the dross of the city into poetry, learning his lesson from this very poem: "I know you will be pleased to realize that at least one actual citizen of your community has inherited your experience in his struggle to love and know his own world-city, through your work" (P, 174). Designating himself the inheriting son of a still—despite Cress—very patriarchal pater, Ginsberg reappears buoyantly in later pages (P, 194–5, 212–13). On the Cress and Ginsberg letters, see Bernard Duffey, A Poetry of Presence: The Writing of William Carlos Williams (Madison: University of Wisconsin Press, 1986), 73, 80, 88–89; and Gay Sibley, "Documents of Presumption: The Satiric Use of the Ginsberg Letters in William Carlos Williams' Paterson," American Literature 55 (March 1983): 1–23.

57. Yale MS, quoted in Graham, 187.

58. Since it was concern for the mental health of her illegitimate son that first caused Marcia Nardi to contact Williams (Graham, 168), "Cress" can be regarded as an important stimulus to Williams' thinking about the virgin/whore dichotomy.

59. Audrey T. Rodgers, Virgin and Whore: The Image of Women in the Poetry of William Carlos Williams (Jefferson, N.C.: McFarland, 1987), 107. Rodgers traces the evolution of the virgin/whore motif throughout Williams' career, and provides a fuller consideration of the "beautiful thing" and virgin/whore images in Book iii (106–9).

60. Williams consistently associates urban violence with love, creation, and beauty: in "Perpetuum Mobile: The City," for example, he describes bank robbery, murder, and mutilation all done "for love, for love!" (CP,i: 433).

61. Letter from Williams to John Riordan, 13 October 1926, quoted in Weaver, 164.

62. I agree with Tapscott that "even in its radical discontinuity of style Paterson v in effect asserts the coherence of the first four books and the continuity of the poem's entire quest" (173).

63. Rodgers gives an informative reading of Williams' use of the tapestries (112–21) as does Paul Mariani, "The Whore/Virgin and the Wounded One-Horned Beast, 1956–1958," *William Carlos Williams: A New World Naked* (New York: McGraw-Hill, 1981), 695–721. Joseph N. Riddel provides an extensive discussion of Williams' play on the doubleness of sexuality and language in "'Keep Your Pecker Up'—*Paterson Five* and the Question of Metapoetry," *Glyph* 8, ed. Walter Benn Michaels (Baltimore: Johns Hopkins University Press, 1981), 202–31.

64. Paul Mariani writes that in the 1950s Williams "could survey with a newly earned leisure Paterson as the redeemed city located along the River of Heaven, that river which also ran through the Unicorn tapestries" (701). The image was also related to Allen Ginsberg's remarks about River Street in Paterson (*P*, 196). The phrase "river of heaven" dates from Williams' manuscript of *Paterson* IV, but in 1952 what would become the opening lines of "Asphodel" appeared as "Paterson, Book V: The River of Heaven" (704).

65. Mariani, 701.

66. In this passage my ellipses are spaced, those of Williams are unspaced.

67. The passage may be based on an actual incident that more closely paralleled the situation in Baudelaire's poem. On the morning of August 9, 1955, Williams sighted an attractive woman at a distance on a downtown Rutherford street, and the account he wrote later indicates that she was tall, dark-haired, dressed in black, with long shapely legs. He was unable to catch up with her, and he lost her (Mariani, 712). Yet in *Paterson* Williams changes the encounter (or gives us another one) to despecify the female death image into an androgynous force tenuously associated with natural life.

68. See Tapscott, 171–72, and Mariani, 712.

69. Mariani, 711.

70. Barthes, 96.

Bibliography

Abrams, M. H. *Natural Supernaturalism: Tradition and Revolution in Romantic Literature*. New York: Norton, 1971.

Ahearn, Edward J. "Confrontation with the City: Social Criticism, Apocalypse, and the Reader's Responsibility in City Poems by Blake, Hugo, and Baudelaire." *Hebrew University Studies in Literature* 10 (Spring 1982): 1–22.

———. "Marx's Relevance for Second Empire Literature: Baudelaire's 'Le Cygne.'" *Nineteenth-Century French Studies* 14 (1986): 269–77.

———. "The Search for Community: The City in Hölderlin, Wordsworth, and Baudelaire." *Texas Studies in Literature and Language* 13 (Spring 1971): 71–89.

Allen, Gay Wilson. *The Solitary Singer: A Critical Biography of Walt Whitman*. Rev. ed., 1967. Chicago: University of Chicago Press, 1985.

Anderson, Quentin. *The Imperial Self: An Essay in American Literary and Cultural History*. New York: Vintage, 1971.

Arac, Jonathan. *Critical Genealogies: Historical Situations for Postmodern Literary Studies*. New York: Columbia University Press, 1987.

———. "Romanticism, the Self, and the City: *The Secret Agent* in Literary History." *Boundary 2* 9 (Fall 1980): 75–90.

Aspiz, Harold. "Walt Whitman: The Spermatic Imagination." *On Whitman: The Best from "American Literature."* Ed. Edwin H. Cady and Louis J. Budd. Durham: Duke University Press, 1987. 273–89.

Augustine, Saint. *The City of God*. Trans. Marcus Dods. New York: Modern Library, 1950.

Aynesworth, Donald. "A Face in the Crowd: A Baudelairian Vision of the Eternal Feminine." *Stanford French Review* 3 (Winter 1981): 327–39.

Bandy, W. T. "Whitman and Baudelaire." *Walt Whitman Quarterly Review* 1.3 (December 1983): 53–55.

Barthes, Roland. "Droit dans les yeux." *L'Obvie et l'obtus: Essais critiques III*. Paris: Seuil, 1982. 279–83.

———. "Semiology and the Urban." Trans. Karin Boklund-Lagopoulou et al. *The City and the Sign: An Introduction to Urban Semiotics*. Ed. M. Gottdiener and Alexandros Ph. Lagopoulos. New York: Columbia University Press, 1986. 87–98.

Baudelaire, Charles. *Oeuvres complètes*. Ed. Claude Pichois. 2 vols. Paris: Gallimard, Bibliothèque de la Pléiade, 1975–76.

Bedient, Calvin. *He Do the Police in Different Voices: "The Waste Land" and Its Protagonist*. Chicago: University of Chicago Press, 1986.

Benjamin, Walter. *Illuminations*. Ed. Hannah Arendt. Trans. Harry Zohn. New York: Schocken, 1969.

———. *Reflections*. Ed. Peter Demetz. Trans. Edmund Jephcott. New York: Harcourt, Brace, Jovanovich, 1978.

Berman, Marshall. *All That Is Solid Melts into Air: The Experience of Modernity*. New York: Simon & Schuster, 1982.

Bernard, Suzanne. *Le Poème en prose de Baudelaire jusqu'à nos jours*. Paris: Nizet, 1959.

Bernstein, Michael André. *The Tale of the Tribe: Ezra Pound and the Modern Verse Epic*. Princeton: Princeton University Press, 1980.

Bersani, Leo. *Baudelaire and Freud*. Berkeley: University of California Press, 1977.

Blake, William. *The Complete Writings of William Blake, with Variant Readings*. Ed. Geoffrey Keynes. London: Oxford University Press, 1966.

Blanchard, Marc Eli. *In Search of the City: Engels, Baudelaire, Rimbaud*. Stanford French and Italian Studies 37. Stanford: Anma Libri, 1985.

Bloom, Harold. *The Anxiety of Influence: A Theory of Poetry*. New York: Oxford University Press, 1973.

———. *Poetry and Repression: Revisionism from Blake to Stevens*. New Haven: Yale University Press, 1976.

———, ed. *T. S. Eliot's "The Waste Land."* New York: Chelsea House, 1986.

Bremen, Brian A. "'The Radiant Gist': 'The Poetry Hidden in the Prose' of Williams' *Paterson*." *Twentieth-Century Literature* 32.2 (Summer 1986): 221–41.

Breslin, James. *William Carlos Williams: An American Artist*. New York: Oxford University Press, 1970.

Brooks, Cleanth. *The Well Wrought Urn: Studies in the Structure of Poetry*. 1947. New York: Harcourt, Brace, Jovanovich, 1975.

Burton, Richard D. E. *Baudelaire in 1859: A Study in the Sources of Poetic Creativity*. Cambridge: Cambridge University Press, 1988.

Buvik, Per. "Paris—lieu poétique, lieu érotique: Quelques remarques à propos de Walter Benjamin et de Baudelaire." *Revue Romane* 20.2 (1985): 231–42.

Byrd, Max. *London Transformed: Images of the City in the Eighteenth Century*. New Haven: Yale University Press, 1978.

Calvino, Italo. *Invisible Cities*. Trans. William Weaver. New York: Harcourt, Brace, Jovanovich, 1974.

Certeau, Michel de. "Practices of Space." *On Signs*. Ed. Marshall Blonsky. Baltimore: Johns Hopkins University Press, 1985. 122–45.

Chaffin, J. Thomas, Jr. "Give Me Faces and Streets: Walt Whitman and the City." *Walt Whitman Review* 23 (1977): 109–20.

Chambers, Ross. "Are Baudelaire's 'Tableaux Parisiens' about Paris?" *On Referring in Literature*. Ed. Anna Whiteside and Michael Issacharoff. Bloomington: Indiana University Press, 1987. 95–110.

———. "Baudelaire's Street Poetry." *Nineteenth-Century French Studies* 13 (Summer 1985): 244–59.

———. "Trois paysages urbains: Les Poèmes liminaires des *Tableaux parisiens*." *Modern Philology* 80 (May 1983): 372–89.

———. "The Storm in the Eye of the Poem: Baudelaire's 'A une passante.'" *Textual Analysis: Some Readers Reading*. Ed. Mary Ann Caws. New York: Modern Language Association, 1986. 156–66.

Christman, Henry M., ed. *Walt Whitman's New York*. New York: Macmillan, 1963.

Citron, Pierre. *La Poésie de Paris dans la littérature française de Rousseau à Baudelaire*. 2 vols. Paris: Minuit, 1961.

Clark, T. J. *The Absolute Bourgeois: Artists and Politics in France, 1841–1851*. Greenwich, Conn.: New York Graphic Society, 1973.

Conarroe, Joel. *William Carlos Williams' "Paterson": Language and Landscape*. Philadelphia: University of Pennsylvania Press, 1970.

Conrad, Peter. *The Art of the City: Views and Versions of New York*. New York: Oxford University Press, 1985.

Cook, Eleanor. "T. S. Eliot and the Carthaginian Peace." Bloom, *T. S. Eliot's "The Waste Land."* 81–97.

Cooper, John Xiros. *T. S. Eliot and the Politics of Voice: The Argument of "The Waste Land."* Ann Arbor: UMI Research Press, 1987.

Crawford, Robert. *The Savage and the City in the Work of T. S. Eliot.* Oxford: Clarendon Press, 1987.

Culler, Jonathan. *Ferdinand de Saussure.* New York: Penguin, 1976.

———. *On Deconstruction: Theory and Criticism after Structuralism.* Ithaca: Cornell University Press, 1982.

———. *The Pursuit of Signs: Semiotics, Literature, Deconstruction.* Ithaca: Cornell University Press, 1981.

Damrosch, David. *The Narrative Covenant: Transformations of Genre in Biblical Literature.* New York: Harper & Row, 1987.

Dante. *La Vita Nuova.* Trans. Mark Musa. Bloomington: Indiana University Press, 1973.

Day, Robert A. "The 'City Man' in *The Waste Land*: The Geography of Reminiscence." *PMLA* 80 (1965): 285–91.

Delesalle, Jean-François. "Baudelaire, Jules Viard, et la passante." *Bulletin Baudelairien* 19.3 (December 1984): 55–67.

De Quincey, Thomas. *Confessions of an English Opium Eater.* 1821. New York: Oxford University Press, 1985.

Derrida, Jacques. "Living On / Border Lines." Trans. James Hulbert. *Deconstruction and Criticism.* Harold Bloom et al. New York: Seabury, 1979. 75–176.

———. *Spurs/Nietzsche's Styles.* Trans. Barbara Harlow. Chicago: University of Chicago Press, 1978.

———. "Structure, Sign, and Play in the Discourse of the Human Sciences." *The Structuralist Controversy.* Ed. Richard Macksey and Eugenio Donato. Baltimore: Johns Hopkins University Press, 1972. 247–65.

Dick, Bernard F. "*The Waste Land* and the *Descensus ad Infernos.*" Bloom, *T. S. Eliot's "The Waste Land."* 67–79.

Dijkstra, Bram. *Cubism, Steiglitz, and the Early Poetry of William Carlos Williams: The Hieroglyphics of a New Speech.* Princeton: Princeton University Press, 1969.

Doyle, Charles, ed. *William Carlos Williams: The Critical Heritage.* Boston: Routledge & Kegan Paul, 1980.

Driscoll, Kerry. *William Carlos Williams and the Maternal Muse.* Ann Arbor: UMI Research Press, 1987.

Duffey, Bernard. *A Poetry of Presence: The Writing of William Carlos Williams.* Madison: University of Wisconsin Press, 1986.

Eagleton, Terry. *Walter Benjamin or, Towards a Revolutionary Criticism.* London: Verso, 1981.

Eliade, Mircea. *Cosmos and History: The Myth of the Eternal Return.* Trans. Willard Trask. New York: Harper, 1959.

Eliot, T. S. *The Complete Poems and Plays.* New York: Harcourt, Brace, 1952.

———. "The Influence of Landscape upon the Poet." *Daedalus* 89 (Spring 1960): 420–22.

———. *Knowledge and Experience in the Philosophy of F. H. Bradley.* New York: Farrar, Straus, 1964.

———. *On Poetry and Poets.* New York: Noonday, 1961.

———. Preface. *John Davidson: A Selection of His Poems.* Ed. Maurice Lindsay. London: Hutchinson, 1961. N.p.

———. *Selected Essays.* New ed. New York: Harcourt, Brace, World, 1964.

———. *Selected Prose of T. S. Eliot.* Ed. Frank Kermode. New York: Harcourt, Brace, Jovanovich / Farrar, Straus & Giroux, 1965.

———. *To Criticize the Critic.* New York: Farrar, Straus & Giroux, 1965.

———. *The Use of Poetry and the Use of Criticism: Studies in the Relation of Criticism to Poetry in England.* 2nd ed. London: Faber & Faber, 1964.

———. "Whitman and Tennyson." *The Nation and Athenaeum* 40 (December 18, 1926): 426.

Eliot, Valerie, ed. *"The Waste Land": A Facsimile and Transcript of the Original Drafts including the Annotations of Ezra Pound.* New York: Harcourt, Brace, Jovanovich, 1971.

Ellmann, Maud. *The Poetics of Impersonality: T. S. Eliot and Ezra Pound.* Brighton: Harvester Press, 1987.

Ellmann, Richard. *Golden Codgers: Biographical Speculations.* New York: Oxford University Press, 1973.

Emerson, Ralph Waldo. "Experience." *Essays, Second Series.* 1844. Boston: Houghton Mifflin, 1904. 43–86.

———. "Montaigne; or, the Skeptic." *Representative Men.* 1850. Boston: Houghton Mifflin, 1904. 147–86.

Engels, Friedrich. *The Condition of the Working Class in England.* Trans. and ed. W. O. Henderson and W. H. Chaloner. Stanford: Stanford University Press, 1968.

Erkkila, Betsy. *Whitman the Political Poet.* New York: Oxford University Press, 1988.

Ferber, Michael. "'London' and Its Politics." *ELH* 48 (Summer 1981): 310–38.

Ferry, David. *The Limits of Mortality: An Essay on Wordsworth's Major Poems.* Middletown, Conn.: Wesleyan University Press, 1959.

Fisher, Philip. "City Matters: City Minds." *The Worlds of Victorian*

Fiction. Ed. Jerome H. Buckley. Harvard English Studies 6. Cambridge, Mass.: Harvard University Press, 1975. 371–89.

Fredrickson, Hélène. *Baudelaire, Héros et fils: Dualité et problèmes du travail dans les lettres à sa mère*. Stanford French and Italian Studies 8. Saratoga, Calif.: Anma Libri, 1977.

Freud, Sigmund. *Civilization and Its Discontents*. Trans. James Strachey. New York: Norton, 1962.

Friedman, Geraldine. "History in the Background of Wordsworth's 'Blind Beggar.'" *ELH* 56 (Spring 1989): 125–48.

Gallup, Donald. *T. S. Eliot: A Bibliography*. Rev. ed. New York: Harcourt, Brace, Jovanovich, 1969.

Gardner, Helen. *The Composition of Four Quartets*. London: Faber, 1978.

Gautier, Théophile. "Une Journée à Londres." *Caprices et Zigzags*. Paris: Victor Lecu, 1852. 101–40.

Gelfant, Blanche. *The American City Novel*. 2nd ed. Norman: University of Oklahoma Press, 1970.

Genette, Gérard. "Valéry and the Poetics of Language." *Textual Strategies*. Ed. Josué V. Harari. Ithaca: Cornell University Press, 1979. 359–73.

Gilbert, Sandra. "Purloined Letters: William Carlos Williams and 'Cress.'" *William Carlos Williams Review* 11.2 (1985): 5–10.

Glen, Heather. "The Poet in Society: Blake and Wordsworth on London." *Literature and History* 3 (March 1976): 2–22.

Godfrey, Sima. "Baudelaire's Windows." *L'Esprit Créateur* 22.4 (1982): 83–100.

———. "Foules Rush in . . . Lamartine, Baudelaire and the Crowd." *Romance Notes* 24 (Fall 1983): 33–42.

Gordon, Lyndall. *Eliot's Early Years*. New York: Oxford University Press, 1977.

Graham, Theodora R. "'Her Heigh Compleynte': The Cress Letters of William Carlos Williams' *Paterson*." *Ezra Pound and William Carlos Williams: The University of Pennsylvania Conference Papers*. Ed. Daniel Hoffman. Philadelphia: University of Pennsylvania Press, 1983. 164–93.

Hargrove, Nancy D. *Landscape as Symbol in the Poetry of T. S. Eliot*. Jackson: University of Mississippi Press, 1978.

Hartman, Geoffrey. *Criticism in the Wilderness: The Study of Literature Today*. New Haven: Yale University Press, 1980.

———. "The Unremarkable Wordsworth." *On Signs*. Ed. Marshall Blonsky. Baltimore: Johns Hopkins University Press, 1985. 321–33.

———. *Wordsworth's Poetry 1787–1814*. New Haven: Yale University Press, 1971.

Hiddleston, James. *Baudelaire and Le Spleen de Paris*. Oxford: Oxford University Press, 1986.

Hilton, Nelson. "The Heavy Metal of Blake's Language." *New Orleans Review* 13.3 (1986): 34–39.

Hobsbaum, Philip. "Eliot, Whitman, and the American Tradition." *Journal of American Studies* 3 (1969): 239–64.

Hoople, Robin B. "Walt Whitman and the City of Friends." *Scholar's Companion to the American Renaissance*. Ed. K. W. Cameron. first series. Hartford: Transcendental Books, 1977. 45–51.

Hugo, François. "The City and the Country: Books VII and VIII of Wordsworth's 'The Prelude,'" *Theoria* 69 (May 1987): 1–14.

Hyslop, Lois Boe. *Baudelaire, Man of His Time*. New Haven: Yale University Press, 1980.

Jarrell, Randall. "A View of Three Poets." *Partisan Review* 18 (November–December 1951): 691–700.

Jay, Gregory S. *T. S. Eliot and the Poetics of Literary History*. Baton Rouge: Louisiana State University Press, 1983. 67–198.

Jaye, Michael C., and Ann C. Watts, eds. *Literature and the Urban Experience: Essays on the City in Literature*. New Brunswick, N.J.: Rutgers University Press, 1981.

Johnson, Barbara. *Défigurations du langage poétique*. Paris: Flammarion, 1979.

Johnston, John H. *The Poet and the City: A Study in Urban Perspectives*. Athens: University of Georgia Press, 1984.

Johnston, Kenneth R. "Blake's Cities: Romantic Forms of Urban Renewal." *Blake's Visionary Forms Dramatic*. Ed. David V. Erdman and John E. Grant. Princeton: Princeton University Press, 1970. 413–42.

Joxe, France. "Ville et modernité dans *Les Fleurs du mal*." *Europe*. Nos. 456–57 (April–May 1967): 139–62.

Kaplan, Justin. *Walt Whitman: A Life*. New York: Simon & Schuster, 1980.

Kearns, Cleo McNelley. "Eliot, Russell, and Whitman: Realism, Politics, and Literary Persona in *The Waste Land*." Bloom, *T. S. Eliot's "The Waste Land."* 137–52.

Kenner, Hugh. *A Homemade World: The American Modernist Writers*. New York: Morrow, 1975.

———. "The Urban Apocalypse." *Eliot in His Time*. Ed. A. Walton Litz. Princeton: Princeton University Press, 1973. 23–49.

Keogh, J. G. "O City, City: Oedipus in *The Waste Land.*" *Antigonish Review* 69–70 (1987): 89–112.

Kermode, Frank. Introduction. *Selected Prose of T. S. Eliot.* 11–27.

———. "A Babylonish Dialect." *T. S. Eliot: "The Waste Land": A Casebook.* Ed. C. B. Cox and Arnold Hinchliffe. London: Macmillan, 1968. 224–35.

Killingsworth, M. Jimmie. *Whitman's Poetry of the Body: Sexuality, Politics, and the Text.* Chapel Hill: University of North Carolina Press, 1989.

———. "Whitman's Sexual Themes during a Decade of Revision: 1866–1876." *Walt Whitman Quarterly Review* 4.1 (1986): 7–15.

Klink, William R. "William Carlos Williams's *Paterson*: Literature and Urban History." *Urban Affairs Quarterly* 23 (December 1987): 171–85.

Lacan, Jacques. *The Four Fundamental Concepts of Psycho-Analysis.* Ed. Jacques-Alain Miller. Trans. Alan Sheridan. New York: Norton, 1979.

———. "Le stade du miroir comme formateur de la fonction du Je." *Ecrits.* Paris: Seuil, 1966. 93–100.

Landa, Louis. "London Observed: The Progress of a Simile." *Philological Quarterly* 54 (Winter 1975): 275–88.

Langbaum, Robert. *The Mysteries of Identity: A Theme in Modern Literature.* New York: Oxford University Press, 1977.

Leavis, F. R. "The Waste Land." *T. S. Eliot: A Collection of Critical Essays.* Ed. Hugh Kenner. Englewood Cliffs, N.J.: Prentice-Hall, 1962. 89–103.

Little, Matthew. "A Source for 'The City Over the Mountains' in *The Waste Land.*" *ELN* 17.4 (June 1980): 279–81.

Lloyd, Margaret Glynne. *William Carlos Williams' "Paterson": A Critical Reappraisal.* Cranbury, N.J.: Associated University Presses, 1980.

Lukács, Georg. *The Theory of the Novel.* Trans. Anna Bostock. Cambridge, Mass.: MIT Press, 1971.

Machor, James L. *Pastoral Cities: Urban Ideals and the Symbolic Landscape of America.* Madison: University of Wisconsin Press, 1987.

———. "Pastoralism and the American Urban Ideal: Hawthorne, Whitman, and the Literary Pattern." *American Literature* 54.3 (October 1982): 329–53.

Mariani, Paul. "The Whore/Virgin and the Wounded One-Horned Beast, 1956–1958." *William Carlos Williams: A New World Naked.* New York: McGraw-Hill, 1981. 695–721.

Marx, Leo. *The Machine in the Garden: Technology and the Pastoral Ideal in America*. New York: Oxford University Press, 1964.

————. "Pastoralism in America." *Ideology and Classic American Literature*. Ed. Sacvan Bercovitch and Myra Jehlen. New York: Oxford University Press, 1986. 36–69.

Matthiessen, F. O. *American Renaissance: Art and Expression in the Age of Emerson and Whitman*. New York: Oxford University Press, 1941.

Mazzaro, Jerome. *William Carlos Williams: The Later Poems*. Ithaca: Cornell University Press, 1973.

Miller, Edwin H. *Walt Whitman's Poetry: A Psychological Journey*. Boston: Houghton Mifflin, 1968.

Miller, James E., Jr. *T. S. Eliot's Personal Waste Land*. University Park: Pennsylvania State University Press, 1977.

Miller, J. Hillis. *Poets of Reality: Six Twentieth-Century Writers*. Cambridge: Belknap Press of Harvard University Press, 1965.

————. "The Still Heart: Poetic Form in Wordsworth." *New Literary History* 2 (Winter 1971): 297–310.

Molesworth, Charles. "Wordsworth's 'Westminster Bridge' Sonnet: The Republican Structure of Time and Perception." *Clio* 3 (Spring 1977): 261–73.

Moquet, J., and W. T. Bandy. *Baudelaire en 1848*. Paris: Emile Paul Frères, 1946.

Mumford, Lewis. *The City in History: Its Origins, Its Transformations, and Its Prospects*. New York: Harcourt, Brace, World, 1961.

Musgrove, Sydney. *T. S. Eliot and Walt Whitman*. Wellington: New Zealand University Press, 1952.

Nash, Ralph. "The Use of Prose in *Paterson*." *Perspective* 6 (Autumn 1953): 191–99.

O'Hara, Daniel. "'The Unsummoned Image': T. S. Eliot's Unclassic Criticism." *Boundary 2* 9 (Fall 1980): 91–124.

Olson, Charles. *Mayan Letters*. Ed. Robert Creeley. London: Cape Editions, 1968.

Ortner, Sherry B. "Is Female to Male as Nature Is to Culture?" *Woman, Culture, and Society*. Ed. Michelle Zimbalist Rosaldo and Louise Lamphere. Stanford: Stanford University Press, 1974. 67–87.

Pearce, Roy Harvey. *The Continuity of American Poetry*. 1961. Princeton: Princeton University Press, 1977.

Pechey, Graham. "The London Motif in Some Eighteenth-Century Contexts: A Semiotic Study." *Literature and History* 4 (Autumn 1976): 2–29.

Perloff, Marjorie. *The Poetics of Indeterminacy: Rimbaud to Cage*. Princeton: Princeton University Press, 1981.

Peuker, Brigitte. "The Poem as Place: Three Modes of Scenic Rendering in the Lyric." *PMLA* 96 (October 1981): 904–12.

Pike, Burton. *The Image of the City in Modern Literature*. Princeton: Princeton University Press, 1981.

Pollock, Griselda. *Vision and Difference: Femininity, Feminism, and the Histories of Art*. New York: Routledge, 1988.

Punter, David. "Blake and the Shapes of London." *Criticism* 23 (Winter 1981): 1–23.

Quinn, Sister M. Bernetta. *The Metamorphic Tradition in Modern Poetry*. New Brunswick, N.J.: Rutgers University Press, 1966.

Raban, Jonathan. *Soft City: The Art of Cosmopolitan Living*. Glasgow: Fontana/Collins, 1975.

Radner, John B. "The Youthful Harlot's Curse: The Prostitute as Symbol of the City in Eighteenth-Century English Literature." *Eighteenth-Century Life* 2.3 (1976): 59–64.

Riddel, Joseph. "Decentering the Image." *Textual Strategies: Perspectives in Post-Structuralist Criticism*. Ed. Josué V. Harari. Ithaca: Cornell University Press, 1979. 322–58.

———. *The Inverted Bell: Modernism and the Counterpoetics of William Carlos Williams*. Baton Rouge: Louisiana State University Press, 1974.

———. "'Keep Your Pecker Up'—*Paterson Five* and the Question of Metapoetry." *Glyph* 8. Ed. Walter Benn Michaels. Baltimore: Johns Hopkins University Press, 1981. 202–31.

Rodgers, Audrey T. *Virgin and Whore: The Image of Women in the Poetry of William Carlos Williams*. Jefferson, N.C.: McFarland, 1987.

Rosenberg, John D. "Varieties of Infernal Experience." *Hudson Review* 23 (Autumn 1970): 454–80.

Rousset, Jean. *Leurs Yeux Se Rencontrèrent: La Scène de première vue dans le roman*. Paris: José Corti, 1981.

Rubin, Joseph Jay. *The Historic Whitman*. University Park: Pennsylvania State University Press, 1973.

Rubin, Joseph Jay, and Charles Brown, eds. *Walt Whitman of the New York Aurora: Editor at Twenty-Two*. N.p.: Bald Eagle Press, 1950.

Rushdie, Salman. *Midnight's Children*. New York: Avon, 1980.

Sankey, Benjamin. *A Companion to William Carlos Williams' "Paterson."* Berkeley: University of California Press, 1971.

Sartre, Jean-Paul. "The Other and His Look." *Jean-Paul Sartre: To*

Freedom Condemned. Ed. Justus Streller. Trans. Wade Baskin. New York: Philosophical Library, 1960. 37–45.

Saunier-Ollier, Jacqueline. *William Carlos Williams: L'Homme et L'Oeuvre Poétique*. Nice: Faculté des lettres et sciences humaines de Nice, 1979.

Sayre, Henry. *The Visual Text of William Carlos Williams*. Urbana: University of Illinois Press, 1983.

Schiff, Richard. "Handling Shocks." *New Observations* 47 (April 1987): 14–19.

Schricker, Cale C. "The Case of Cress: Implications of Allusion in *Paterson.*" *William Carlos Williams Review* 11.2 (1985): 10–20.

Seigel, Jerrold. *Bohemian Paris: Culture, Politics, and the Boundaries of Bourgeois Life, 1830–1930*. New York: Penguin, 1987.

Sharpe, William. "City / Body / Text: Walt Whitman's Urban Incarnation." *Cycnos: Politique et Poétique de la Ville*. Nice, France: University of Nice, 1984. 39–48.

———. "Confronting the Unpoetical City: Arnold, Clough, and Baudelaire." *Arnoldian* 13.1 (1985/86): 10–22.

———. "J. E. Millais' *Bubbles*: A Work of Art in the Age of Mechanical Reproduction." *Victorian Newsletter* 70 (Fall 1986): 16–18.

———. "Learning to Read *The City.*" *Victorian Poetry* 22.1 (1984): 65–84.

———. "'That Complex Atom': The City and Form in William Carlos Williams's *Paterson.*" *Poesis* 6.2 (1985): 65–93.

———. "Urban Theory and Critical Blight: Accommodating the Unreal City." *New Orleans Review* 10 (Spring 1983): 79–88.

Sharpe, William, and Leonard Wallock. "From 'Great Town' to 'Nonplace Urban Realm': Reading the Modern City." *Visions of the Modern City*. Ed. Sharpe and Wallock. Baltimore: Johns Hopkins University Press, 1987. 1–50.

Sibley, Gay. "Documents of Presumption: The Satiric Use of the Ginsberg Letters in William Carlos Williams' *Paterson.*" *American Literature* 55 (March 1983): 1–23.

Siegel, Adrienne. *The Image of the American City in Popular Literature 1820–1870*. Port Washington, N.Y.: Kennikat, 1981.

Simmel, Georg. "The Metropolis and Mental Life." Trans. H. H. Gerth. *Classic Essays on the Culture of Cities*. Ed. Richard Sennett. Englewood Cliffs, N. J.: Prentice-Hall, 1969. 47–60.

Sophocles. *Oedipus Rex*. Ed. R. D. Dawe. Cambridge: Cambridge University Press, 1982.

Spender, Stephen. "Remembering Eliot." *T. S. Eliot: The Man and His Work*. Ed. Allen Tate. New York: Dell, 1966. 38–64.

Squier, Susan Merrill, ed. *Women Writers and the City: Essays in Feminist Literary Criticism*. Knoxville: University of Tennessee Press, 1984.

Stallybrass, Peter, and Allon White. *The Politics and Poetics of Transgression*. Ithaca: Cornell University Press, 1986.

Stamelman, Richard. "The Shroud of Allegory: Death, Mourning, and Melancholy in Baudelaire's Work." *Texas Studies in Literature and Language* 25 (Fall 1983): 390–409.

Stange, G. Robert. "The Frightened Poets." *The Victorian City: Images and Realities*. Ed. H. J. Dyos and Michael Wolff. 2 vols. London: Routledge & Kegan Paul, 1973. 2: 475–94.

Stierle, Karlheinz. "Baudelaire and the Tradition of the *Tableau de Paris*." *New Literary History* 11 (Winter 1980): 345–61.

Stout, Janis P. *Sodoms in Eden: The City in American Fiction Before 1860*. Westport, Conn.: Greenwood, 1976.

Strom, Susan. "'Face to Face': Whitman's Biblical Reference in 'Crossing Brooklyn Ferry.'" *Walt Whitman Review* 24 (1978): 7–16.

Sutton, Walter. "A Visit with William Carlos Williams." *Speaking Straight Ahead: Interviews with William Carlos Williams*. Ed. Linda W. Wagner. New York: New Directions, 1976.

Tanner, Stephen. "Walt Whitman as Urban Transcendentalist." *South Dakota Review* 14.2 (1976): 6–18.

Tapscott, Stephen J. *American Beauty: William Carlos Williams and the Modernist Whitman*. New York: Columbia University Press, 1984.

Tashjian, Dickran. *William Carlos Williams and the American Scene, 1920–1940*. Berkeley: University of California Press, 1979.

Tennyson, Alfred. *Idylls of the King*. 1859–1885. New York: New American Library, 1961.

Thesing, William. *The London Muse: Victorian Poetic Responses to the City*. Athens: University of Georgia Press, 1982.

Thirwall, John C. "William Carlos Williams' *Paterson*." *New Directions in Prose and Poetry 17*. Norfolk, Conn.: New Directions, 1961. 252–310.

Thomas, M. Wynn. "Walt Whitman and Mannahatta-New York." *American Quarterly* 34 (Fall 1982): 362–78.

Thompson, E. P. "London." *Interpreting Blake*. Ed. Michael Phillips. Cambridge: Cambridge University Press, 1978. 5–31.

Thomson, James. *The Seasons*. 1730. London: Murray, 1794.

Tobin, David Ned. *The Presence of the Past: T. S. Eliot's Victorian Inheritance*. Ann Arbor: UMI Research Press, 1983.

Tobin, Patricia. "The City in Post-Romantic Figuration." *Comparative Literature Studies* 18 (March 1981): 33–48.

Valéry, Paul. "Poetry and Abstract Thought." *The Art of Poetry.* Trans. Denise Folliot. Princeton: Princeton University Press, 1958. 52–81.

Versluys, Kristiaan. *The Poet in the City: Chapters in the Development of Urban Poetry in Europe and the United States (1800–1930).* Tübingen: Narr, 1987.

Walker, Robert H. "The Poet and the Rise of the City." *Mississippi Valley Historical Review* 49 (June 1962-March 1963): 85–99.

Ward, Nicole. "'Fourmillante Cité': Baudelaire and 'The Waste Land.'" *"The Waste Land" in Different Voices.* Ed. A. D. Moody. London: Edward Arnold, 1974. 87–104.

Weaver, Mike. *William Carlos Williams: The American Background.* Cambridge: Cambridge University Press, 1971.

Weber, Max. *The City.* Trans. Don Martindale and Gertrude Neuwirth. New York: Free Press, 1958.

Weimer, David. *The City as Metaphor.* New York: Random House, 1966.

Weinberg, K. *T. S. Eliot and Charles Baudelaire.* Studies in General and Comparative Literature 5. The Hague: Mouton, 1969.

Weston, Jessie. *From Ritual to Romance.* 1920. Garden City, N.Y.: Doubleday, 1957.

Whitman, Walt. *The Correspondence.* 5 vols. Ed. Edwin H. Miller. New York: New York University Press, 1969.

———. *Leaves of Grass.* Ed. Sculley Bradley and Harold W. Blodgett. 1965; New York: Norton, 1973.

———. *Leaves of Grass: Facsimile Edition of the 1860 Text.* Ed. Roy Harvey Pearce. Ithaca: Cornell University Press, 1961.

———. *Leaves of Grass: The First (1855) Edition.* Ed. Malcolm Cowley. New York: Viking, 1959.

———. *Leaves of Grass: A Textual Variorum of the Printed Poems.* 3 vols. Ed. Sculley Bradley, Harold W. Blodgett, Arthur Golden, and William White. New York: New York University Press, 1980.

———. *New York Dissected: A Sheaf of Recently Discovered Newspaper Articles by the Author of Leaves of Grass.* Ed. Emory Holloway and Ralph Adimari. New York: R. R. Wilson, 1936.

———. *Prose Works 1892.* 2 vols. Ed. Floyd Stovall. New York: New York University Press, 1963–64.

———. *Walt Whitman: The Complete Poems.* Ed. Francis Murphy. New York: Penguin, 1975.

———. *Walt Whitman's Workshop: A Collection of Unpublished Manuscripts.* Ed. Clifton J. Furness. Cambridge, Mass.: Harvard University Press, 1928.

Williams, Raymond. *The Country and the City*. New York: Oxford University Press, 1973.

Williams, William Carlos. *The Autobiography of William Carlos Williams*. New York: New Directions, 1967.

——. *The Collected Poems of William Carlos Williams*. Vol. 1. 1909–1939. Ed. A. Walton Litz and Christopher MacGowan. New York: New Directions, 1986.

——. *The Collected Poems of William Carlos Williams*. Vol. 2. 1939–1962. Ed. Christopher MacGowan. New York: New Directions, 1988.

——. "An Essay on *Leaves of Grass*." *"Leaves of Grass" One Hundred Years After*. Ed. Milton Hindus. Stanford: Stanford University Press, 1955. 22–31. Rpt. Bradley and Blodgett, eds., *Leaves of Grass*. 903–12.

——. "The Fatal Blunder." *Quarterly Review of Literature* 2.2 (1944): 125–26.

——. *I Wanted to Write a Poem*. New York: New Directions, 1977.

——. *Imaginations*. New York: New Directions, 1970.

——. *In the American Grain*. New York: New Directions, 1956.

—— *Paterson*. New York: New Directions, 1963.

——. *The Selected Essays of William Carlos Williams*. New York: Random House, 1954.

——. *The Selected Letters of William Carlos Williams*. 1957. New York: New Directions, 1984.

Wilson, Edmund. *Axel's Castle: A Study in the Imaginative Literature of 1870–1930*. New York: Scribner's, 1931.

Wohlfarth, Irving. "Walter Benjamin's Image of Interpretation." *New German Critique* 17 (Spring 1979): 70–98.

Wolin, Richard. *Walter Benjamin: An Aesthetic of Redemption*. New York: Columbia University Press, 1982.

Woolf, Virginia. "Literary Geography." *The Essays of Virginia Woolf*. Vol. 1. 1904–1912. Ed. Andrew McNeillie. New York: Harcourt, Brace, Jovanovich, 1986. 32–36.

Wordsworth, Dorothy. *The Grasmere Journals*. Ed. Pamela Woof, with an Introduction by Jonathan Wordsworth. New York: Henry Holt, 1987.

Wordsworth, William. *The Poetical Works of William Wordsworth*. Ed. E. de Selincourt and Helen Darbishire. 5 vols. Oxford: Clarendon Press, 1940–49.

——. *The Prelude: 1799, 1805, 1850*. Ed. Jonathan Wordsworth, M. H. Abrams, and Stephen Gill. New York: Norton, 1979.

——. *The Prose Works of William Wordsworth*. Ed. W. J. B. Owen and Jane Worthington Smyser. 2 vols. Oxford: Clarendon Press, 1974.

Ziff, Larzer. "Whitman and the Crowd." *Critical Inquiry* 10 (June 1984): 579–91.

Zlotnik, Joan. *Portrait of an American City: The Novelist's New York.* Port Washington, N.Y.: Kennikat, 1982.

Zweig, Paul. *Walt Whitman: The Making of the Poet.* New York: Basic Books, 1984.

Index

Designed by Kachergis Book Design

Composed by G&S Typesetters, Inc., in Palatino
Printed by Thomson Shore, Inc., on 50-lb. Glatfelter and
bound in Holliston Roxite B